READING AMERICAN HORIZONS

READING AMERICAN HORIZONS

PRIMARY SOURCES FOR U.S. HISTORY IN A GLOBAL CONTEXT, VOLUME I: TO 1877

EDITED BY

Michael Schaller
UNIVERSITY OF ARIZONA

Robert D. Schulzinger
UNIVERSITY OF COLORADO, BOULDER

John Bezís-Selfa
WHEATON COLLEGE

Janette Thomas Greenwood
CLARK UNIVERSITY

Andrew Kirk
UNIVERSITY OF NEVADA, LAS VEGAS

Sarah J. Purcell
GRINNELL COLLEGE

Aaron Sheehan-Dean
WEST VIRGINIA UNIVERSITY

NEW YORK   OXFORD
OXFORD UNIVERSITY PRESS

Oxford University Press is a department of the University of Oxford. It furthers the University's objective of excellence in research, scholarship, and education by publishing worldwide.

Oxford New York
Auckland Cape Town Dar es Salaam Hong Kong Karachi
Kuala Lumpur Madrid Melbourne Mexico City Nairobi
New Delhi Shanghai Taipei Toronto

With offices in
Argentina Austria Brazil Chile Czech Republic France Greece
Guatemala Hungary Italy Japan Poland Portugal Singapore
South Korea Switzerland Thailand Turkey Ukraine Vietnam

Oxford is a registered trade mark of Oxford University Press in the UK and certain other countries.

Published in the United States of America by
Oxford University Press
198 Madison Avenue, New York, NY 10016

© Oxford University Press 2013

For titles covered by Section 112 of the US Higher Education Opportunity Act,
please visit www.oup.com/us/he for the latest information about
pricing and alternate formats.

Library of Congress Cataloging-in-Publication Data

Reading American horizons: primary sources for U.S. history in a global context / Michael Schaller ... [et al.].
p. cm.
Primary source documents. Complements the survey textbook: American horizons.
    ISBN 978-0-19-976849-3 (volume 1)   1. United States—History—Sources.   I. Schaller, Michael, 1947-
II. American horizons.
    E178.R375 2012
    973—dc23   2012023302

Printing number: 9 8 7 6 5 4 3 2 1

Printed in the United States of America
on acid-free paper

CONTENTS

PREFACE

Reading American Horizons is a Primary Sources Reader for the survey course in American history, designed to accompany the textbook *American Horizons.*

For more than four hundred years, North America has been part of a global network centered upon the exchange of peoples, goods, and ideas. Human migrations—sometimes freely, sometimes forced—have continued over the centuries, along with the evolution of commerce in commodities as varied as tobacco, sugar, and computer chips. Europeans and Africans came or were brought to the continent, where they met, traded with, fought among, and intermarried with native peoples. Some of these migrants stayed, while others returned to their home countries. Still others came and went periodically. This initial circulation of people across the oceans foreshadowed the continuous movement of people, goods, and ideas that forged the United States. These forces shaped American history, both dividing and unifying the nation. American "horizons" truly stretch beyond our nation's borders, embracing the trading networks established during and after the colonial era to the digital social networks connecting people globally today.

Reading American Horizons uses primary source materials to help tell the story of the United States, by exploring this exchange on a global scale and placing it at the center of that story. By doing so, we provide a different perspective on the history of the United States, one that we hope broadens the horizons of those who read our work and are ever mindful of the global forces that increasingly and profoundly shape our lives. At the same time, *Reading American Horizons* considers those ways in which U.S. influence reshaped the lives and experiences of people of other nations.

Understanding documents and visual artifacts from the past is vital to the study of history. *Reading American Horizons* presents a selection of these materials, all carefully selected to complement the narrative and themes presented in the accompanying *American Horizons.* It is our intention that students more deeply understand the historical narrative in the textbook by examining the original sources in this reader, and that the contextual introductions and review questions enrich the interpretations we offer in the textbook.

What qualities make the United States unique? What experiences did it share with other people around the globe? What accounts for the diversity of dialect and lifestyle across this country? How did the United States become a major player on the world stage of nations? History includes many storylines that contribute to this narrative. *Reading American Horizons* provides insight into the story of where this nation came from and how it has been shaped by its own set of shared values as well as its interaction with the rest of the world. *Reading American Horizons* depicts the intersection of storylines from many nations that influenced, and were influenced by, the United States of America.

As readers engage these materials, we encourage them to think explicitly about what makes history. What matters? What forces or events shaped how people lived their lives? What types of sources do historians rely on to explain the past? With all the sources in this book, readers should consider both what the creators hoped to accomplish and how people at the time might have read or viewed them. We encourage you to become your own historian, to read, analyze, and imagine the connections among the different voices that helped make the United States.

THE DEVELOPMENT STORY

The seven co-editors of this book specialize in a variety of time periods and methodologies. Based on our research and teaching, we all share the idea that the nation's history can best be understood by examining how, from the colonial era forward, the American experience reflected the interaction of many nations, peoples, and events. We present this idea in a format that integrates traditional narrative history with the enhanced perspective of five centuries of global interaction.

READING AMERICAN HORIZONS

1. who The author is?
2. who is The intended Reader?!
3. when or where?!
4. whaT is The historical context!?
5. why is This ImportanT enough To be in an anthology!?
6. whaT is he source's value in our course?!
7. whaT else would you like To know!?

CHAPTER 1

NORTH AMERICA ENCOUNTERS THE ATLANTIC WORLD, PREHISTORY–1565

1.1. ACOMA, EXCERPTS FROM "THE EMERGENCE OF THE ACOMA INTO THE UPPER WORLD" (1930 AND UNDATED ORAL TRADITIONS)

Acoma, a Keresan-speaking town in New Mexico, is one of the oldest continuously settled areas of what is today the United States. What follows are excerpts from a modern version of an Acoma creation story by Richard Erdoes and Alonso Ortiz, based on a legend that C. Daryll Forde reported in 1930 and a number of oral accounts. The work focuses on two sisters, Ia'tik ("bringing to life") and Nao'tsiti ("more of everything in the basket"), who were born and raised underground before ascending to the surface bearing baskets that contained images of the plants and animals that they were to bring to life.

EMERGENCE INTO THE UPPER WORLD

...They prayed and sang the creation song, and for the first time they asked Tsitctinako why they had been created. The spirit replied, "It was not I but your father, Utc'tsiti, who made you. He made the world, the sun, the sky, and many other things, but he is not yet satisfied. For this reason he has made you in his image. You will rule over the world and create the things he has given you in the baskets."

...When it became dark at the end of the first day, the sisters were frightened. They thought that Tsitctinako had betrayed them, but she explained, "This is the way it will always be. The sun will go down and a new sun will come up in the east tomorrow. Rest and sleep while it is dark." So the sisters slept, and the next day the sun rose. Happy to feel its warmth, they prayed to it as they had been taught....

The sun was too bright for Ia'tik; it hurt her eyes. She tilted her head sideways so that her hair hung as a sunscreen, producing a reddish shade on her face. "The sun has not appeared for you," Tsitctinako observed.

Source: Carla Mumford, ed., *Early American Writings* (New York: Oxford University Press, 2002), 18–22.

"See how it shines on Nao'tsiti, and how white she looks." Hastily Ia'tik also bared her face to the sun. But it did not make her as white as Nao'tsiti, and Ia'tik's mind was slowed down, while Nao'tsiti's was made quick. Even so, both always remembered to do everything Tsitctinako taught them.

"From now on," Tsitctinako told the sisters, "you will rule in every direction, north, west, south, and east. Bring everything in your baskets to life for Utc'tsiti has created you to help him complete the world. Now is the time to plant the seeds."

So far the sisters had not eaten food, and they did not understand what the seeds in their baskets were for. "First plant the corn, and when it grows, it will produce a part that you can eat," Tsitctinako said. Highly interested, the two women watched the growing corn every day. The spirit showed them where the pollen formed so that they could continue to offer pollen and cornmeal every morning to the sun. And they always did, though sometimes Nao'tsiti was a little lazy.

After a while the corn turned hard and ripe. Ia'tik carefully picked two ears without hurting the plant; Nao'tsiti yanked two off, and Ia'tik told her to handle it more gently. Tsitctinako had said that the corn must be cooked, but the sisters did not understand what "cooked" meant until a red light dropped from the sky that evening. Explaining that it was fire, the spirit taught them to scoop some of the flames up on a flat rock and feed them with branches from the pine tree.

Following Tsitctinako's directions, they roasted the corn and seasoned it with salt from their baskets. Nao'tsiti grabbed some and ate it, exclaiming how good it was. Then she gave a piece to Ia'tik, and so it was that the two women had their first meal. "You have been fasting for a long time, and your father has nourished you," the spirit told them. "Now you will eat in order to live."

The sisters learned to give life to their salt by praying to the earth, whereupon salt appeared in each of the four directions. Then Tsitctinako taught them their first song for creating an animal—a mouse. When they had sung it, they said, "Come to life, mouse," and their mouse image breathed. "Go and increase," they told it, and it ran away and soon bred many offspring. Tsitctinako showed them how to take one back, kill it, and roast it with the corn and salt. They prayed to their father and offered him little pieces of the meal before they ate. There was not much food on the mouse, but they thought it was good.

Looking into their baskets for larger animals to eat, the women found images of a rat, a mole, and a prairie dog. "Before you give life to them," Tsitctinako said, "you must plant grass for their food." The sisters took grass seed and scattered it north, west, south, and east—and grass immediately covered the ground. Then they gave life to the animals, telling each its name as it began to breathe. Before commanding them to run away and increase, they told the three creatures to live in the ground, because there was no shade on earth.

"Now we are going to make the mountains," Tsitctinako said, and showed them how to throw a certain stone from the basket toward the north while speaking certain words. There a large mountain arose. They did the same in the other directions, and mountains appeared all around them. "Now that you have the mountains," the spirit said, "you must clothe them with growing things." From the trees they had planted underground the sisters took seeds, which they scattered in all the directions. "These will be tall trees," Tsitctinako said, "and large enough to form the logs you will use to build houses."

There were many seeds left in their baskets. The women planted the food-yielding trees—piñon, cedar, oak, and walnut—with the prayer, "Grow on this mountain and yield fruit for food. Your places are in the mountains. You will grow and be useful." They planted other seeds, such as pumpkin, squash, and beans, that Tsitctinako said would be important to them. As these crops ripened, she showed them which parts to eat.

The sisters too were growing, and they needed more food. They began to bring the larger animals to life: first rabbits, jackrabbits, antelope, and water deer; then deer, elk, mountain sheep, and buffalo. They told the buffalo to live in the plains, the elk and deer in the mountains, and the sheep on the very high mountain slopes. They ate their meat and enjoyed the new tastes, and always they prayed to their father before they began a meal.

The sisters made mountain lions, wolves, wildcats, and bears—strong beasts that hunted the same game the humans used. They made birds—eagles and hawks, which hunted small game, and little birds whose bright colors beautified the country. They made the wild turkey and told it not to fly. They told the smaller birds to eat various seeds on the mountains and plains.

Tsitctinako pointed out that there were still fish, snakes, and turtles to be created, and the sisters gave life to all these and tried them for food. They found that some were good to eat and others were not, but whenever they ate they prayed first to their father. So it happened that many animals came alive in the world.

...Both sisters were now having selfish thoughts. Nao'tsiti was full of plans to outwit Ia'tik, but Ia'tik watched her and anticipated everything. Nao'tsiti saw that Ia'tik was not happy; Ia'tik noticed that Nao'tsiti wandered off alone.

Tsitctinako had told them that their father forbade them to think about having children. She promised that other humans would be born to them at the appropriate time. But now Nao'tsiti met a snake who said, "Why are you sad? If you bore a child in your likeness, you wouldn't have to be lonely just because you and your sister don't get along."

"What can I do?" Nao'tsiti asked.

"Go to the rainbow; he will show you."

Soon afterward Nao'tsiti was sitting alone on a rock when it rained. It was so hot that the rain cracked on the ground, and she lay on her back to receive the drops. As the water dripped into her, the rainbow did his work and she conceived without knowing it. Ia'tik noticed that her sister was growing very fat, and after a time Nao'tsiti bore two children, both boys.

Very angry, Tsitctinako came to them. "Why have you disobeyed your father?" she said. "For your sin, he is taking me away. You are alone now."

Tsitctinako left them, but instead of feeling sorry, the two sisters found that they were happier. It turned out that Nao'tsiti disliked one of her children, so Ia'tik

took him and brought him up. The two women still did not get along, but they were so busy with the children that it hardly mattered.

When the children were almost grown, Nao'tsiti said to her sister, "We aren't really happy together. Let's divide what remains in our baskets and separate. I still have many things, though they require a lot of work." Nao'tsiti pulled out sheep and cows, seeds for wheat and vegetables, and many metals. But Ia'tik refused them, saying they would be too difficult to take care of. Nao'tsiti looked again in her basket and found something written. She offered it, but Ia'tik did not want the gift of writing either. "You should have taken some of the things I offered," Nao'tsiti said. "In a long time we will meet again, and then you will desire my possessions. We'll still be sisters, but I'll have the better of you again."

Taking the boy she had brought up, Nao'tsiti disappeared into the east. Ia'tik said to the other boy, "We will continue to live here with everything our father has given us." The years passed, and Tia'muni, as she called him, grew up to become her husband. Ia'tik bore him a girl, who was entered into the clan of her sister, the Sun clan. After the fourth day of the baby's birth, Ia'tik put some pollen and sacred cornmeal into its hands and took it to pray to the sun. And with the many children that Ia'tik bore afterwards, she followed this same ritual that she herself had been taught when she came up into the light....

QUESTIONS

1. Acoma's extended kinship system is matrilineal, meaning that one inherits one's status from one's mother. In what ways does this story demonstrate Acoman society's matrilineal nature?

2. In what ways does this creation story reflect and explain the Acomans' encounter with Europeans and the goods and ideas that they brought?

1.2. GOMES EANNES DE AZURARA, EXCERPTS FROM *THE CHRONICLE OF THE DISCOVERY AND CONQUEST OF GUINEA* (1453)

In the early 1440s, Portuguese mariners launched what would become the transatlantic slave trade. In 1453, Gomes Eannes de Azurara, an official chronicler and aide to Prince Henry (identified by Azurara in the following excerpt as "the Infant"), principal sponsor of Portuguese expansion into Africa, completed a history that celebrated the Portuguese "discovery and conquest of Guinea." In the following excerpt, Azurara narrates the arrival of a Portuguese slaving expedition led by Lançarote de Freitas in 1444 and the subsequent division of the people whom de Freitas enslaved.

The caravels arrived at Lagos, whence they had set out, having excellent weather for their voyage, for fortune was not less gracious to them in the serenity of the weather than it had been to them before in the capture of their booty.

And from Lagos the news reached the Infant, who happened to have arrived there a few hours before, from other parts where he had been for some days. And as you see that people are desirous of knowledge, some endeavoured to get near the shore; and others put themselves into the boats they found moored along the beach, and went to welcome their relations and friends; so that in a short time the news of their good fortune was well known, and all were much rejoiced at it. And for that day it sufficed for those who had led the enterprize to kiss the hand of the Infant their Lord, and to give him a short account of their exploits: after which they took their rest, as men who had come to their fatherland and their own homes; and you may guess what would be their joy among their wives and children.

And next day Lançarote, as he who had taken the main charge of the expedition, said to the Infant: "My Lord, your grace well knoweth that you have to receive the fifth of these Moors, and of all that we have gained in that land, whither you sent us for the service of God and of yourself.

"And now these Moors, because of the long time we have been at sea; as well as for the great sorrow that you must consider they have at heart, at seeing themselves away from the land of their birth, and placed in captivity, without having any understanding of what their end is to be;—and moreover because they have not been accustomed to a life on shipboard—for all these reasons are poorly and out of condition; wherefore it seemeth to me that it would be well to order them to be taken out of the caravels at dawn, and to be placed in that field which lies outside the city gate, and there to be divided into five parts, according to custom; and that your Grace should come there and choose one of these parts, whichever you prefer."

The Infant said that he was well pleased, and on the next day very early, Lançarote bade the masters of the caravels that they should put out the captives, and take them to that field, where they were to make the divisions, as he had said already....And the Moors of that capture were in number 235.

...O, Thou heavenly Father—...—I pray Thee that my tears may not wrong my conscience; for it is not their religion but their humanity that maketh mine to weep in pity for their sufferings. And if the brute animals, with their bestial feelings, by a natural instinct understand the sufferings of their own kind, what wouldst

---

Source: Gomes Eannes de Azurara, *The Chronicle of the Discovery and Conquest of Guinea*, vol. 1, trans. Charles Raymond Beazley and Edgar Prestage (New York: Burt Franklin, 1963), 79–86.

Thou have my human nature to do on seeing before my eyes that miserable company, and remembering that they too are of the generation of the sons of Adam?

On the next day, ... the seamen began to make ready their boats, and to take out those captives, and carry them on shore, as they were commanded. And these, placed all together in that field, were a marvellous sight; for amongst them were some white enough, fair to look upon, and well proportioned; others were less white like mulattoes; others again were as black as Ethiops[1], and so ugly, both in features and in body, as almost to appear (to those who saw them) the images of a lower hemisphere. But what heart could be so hard as not to be pierced with piteous feeling to see that company? For some kept their heads low and their faces bathed in tears, looking one upon another; others stood groaning very dolorously, looking up to the height of heaven, fixing their eyes upon it, crying out loudly, as if asking help of the Father of Nature; others struck their faces with the palms of their hands, throwing themselves at full length upon the ground; others made their lamentations in the manner of a dirge, after the custom of their country. And though we could not understand the words of their language, the sound of it right well accorded with the measure of their sadness. But to increase their sufferings still more, there now arrived those who had charge of the division of the captives, and who began to separate one from another, in order to make an equal partition of the fifths; and then was it needful to part fathers from sons, husbands from wives, brothers from brothers. No respect was shewn either to friends or relations, but each fell where his lot took him.

O powerful fortune, that with thy wheels doest and undoest, compassing the matters of this world as pleaseth thee, do thou at least put before the eyes of that miserable race some understanding of matters to come; that they may receive some consolation in the midst of their great sorrow. And you who are so busy in making that division of the captives, look with pity upon so much misery; and see how they cling one to the other, so that you can hardly separate them.

And who could finish that partition without very great toil? For as often as they had placed them in one part the sons, seeing their fathers in another, rose with great energy and rushed over to them; the mothers clasped their other children in their arms, and threw themselves flat on the ground with them; receiving blows with little pity for their own flesh, if only they might not be torn from them.

And so troublously they finished the partition; for besides the toil they had with the captives, the field was quite full of people, both from the town and from the surrounding villages and districts, who for that day gave rest to their hands (in which lay their power to get their living) for the sole purpose of beholding this novelty. And with what they saw, while some were weeping and others separating the captives, they caused such a tumult as greatly to confuse those who directed the partition.

The Infant was there, mounted upon a powerful steed, and accompanied by his retinue, making distribution of his favours, as a man who sought to gain but small treasure from his share; for of the forty-six souls that fell to him as his fifth, he made a very speedy partition of these; for his chief riches lay in his purpose; for he reflected with great pleasure upon the salvation of those souls that before were lost.

And certainly his expectation was not in vain; for, as we said before, as soon as they understood our language they turned Christians with very little ado; and I who put together this history into this volume, saw in the town of Lagos boys and girls (the children and grandchildren of those first captives, born in this land) as good and true Christians as if they had directly descended, from the beginning of the dispensation of Christ, from those who were first baptised. ...

QUESTIONS

1. What terms do Azurara and the Portuguese use to refer to the enslaved captives? In what ways did their use of such terms reflect centuries of Islamic influence in Iberia?

2. Why did a crowd gather to witness the separation of the captives? In what ways, according to Azurara, did the crowd react to what they witnessed?

3. What explanation or justification does Azurara provide for the enslavement of the African captives and the sundering of their families?

---

1. Ethiopians.

1.3. LETTERS FROM AFONSO, KING OF KONGO, TO JOÃO III, KING OF PORTUGAL (1526)

author.

The Catholic convert Afonso I assumed the throne of Kongo with Portuguese support in 1506 and ruled until 1543. Unfortunately, by the 1520s Kongo had little to pay for the imports that flooded the kingdom or provide for the Portuguese craftsmen, missionaries, arms specialists, and teachers whom Afonso invited—except enslaved captives, most of whom were shipped to Portuguese sugar plantations on the island of São Tomé, located off the coast of Africa. The excerpted letters that follow, originally written in Portuguese in 1526, are among the few surviving documents written by an African during the 16th century. Basil Davidson translated them from transcripts of the original letters printed in *História do Congo: Obra Posthuma do Visconde de Paiva Manso* (Lisbon, 1877).

[1526] Sir, Your Highness [of Portugal] should know how our Kingdom is being lost in so many ways that it is convenient to provide for the necessary remedy, since this is caused by the excessive freedom given by your factors and officials to the men and merchants who are allowed to come to this Kingdom to set up shops with goods and many things which have been prohibited by us, and which they spread throughout our Kingdoms and Domains in such an abundance that many of our vassals, whom we had in obedience, do not comply because they have the things in greater abundance than we ourselves; and it was with these things that we had them content and subjected under our vassalage and jurisdiction, so it is doing a great harm not only to the service of God, but the security and peace of our Kingdoms and State as well.

And we cannot reckon how great the damage is, since the mentioned merchants are taking every day our natives, sons of the land and the sons of our noblemen and vassals and our relatives, because the thieves and men of bad conscience grab them wishing to have the things and wares of this Kingdom which they are ambitious of; they grab them and get them to be sold; and so great, Sir, is the corruption and licentiousness that our country is being completely depopulated, and Your Highness should not agree with this nor accept it as in your service. And to avoid it we need from those [your] Kingdoms no more than some priests and a few people to teach in schools, and no other goods except wine and flour for the holy sacrament. That is why we beg of Your Highness to help and assist us in this matter, commanding your factors that they should not send here either merchants or wares, because it is *our will that in these Kingdoms there should not be any trade of slaves nor outlet for them.*[2] Concerning what is referred above, again we beg of Your Highness to agree with it, since otherwise we cannot remedy such an obvious damage. Pray Our Lord in His mercy to have Your Highness under His guard and let you do for ever the things of His service. I kiss your hands many times.

Source: Basil Davidson, *The African Past: Chronicles from Antiquity to Modern Times* (Boston: Little, Brown, 1964), 191–93. Davidson translated the letters from *História do Congo: Obra Posthuma do Visconde de Paiva Manso* (Lisbon, 1877).

2. Emphasis in the original.

At our town of Congo, written on the sixth day of July.
João Teixeira[3] did it in 1526.
The King. Dom Afonso

[*On the back of this letter the following can be read:* To the most powerful and excellent prince Dom João, King our Brother.]

THE ORIGINS OF SLAVING

[1526] Moreover, Sir, in our Kingdoms there is another great inconvenience which is of little service to God, and this is that many of our people [*naturaes*], keenly desirous as they are of the wares and things of your Kingdoms, which are brought here by your people, and in order to satisfy their voracious appetite, seize many of our people, freed and exempt men; and very often it happens that they kidnap even noblemen and the sons of noblemen, and our relatives, and take them to be sold to the white men who are in our Kingdoms; and for this purpose they have concealed them; and others are brought during the night so that they might not be recognized.

And as soon as they are taken by the white men they are immediately ironed and branded with fire, and when they are carried to be embarked, if they are caught by our guards' men the whites allege that they have bought them but they cannot say from whom, so that it is our duty to do justice and to restore to the freemen their freedom, but it cannot be done if your subjects feel offended, as they claim to be.

And to avoid such a great evil we passed a law so that any white man living in our Kingdoms and wanting to purchase goods in any way should first inform three of our noblemen and officials of our court whom we rely upon in this matter, and these are Dom Pedro Manipanza and Dom Manuel Manissaba, our chief usher, and Gonçalo Pires our chief freighter, who should investigate if the mentioned goods are captives or free men, and if cleared by them there will be no further doubt nor embargo for them to be taken and embarked. But if the white men do not comply with it they will lose the aforementioned goods. And if we do them this favor and concession it is for the part Your Highness has in it, since we know that it is in your service too that these goods are taken from our Kingdom, otherwise we should not consent to this....

QUESTIONS

1. In what terms does Afonso characterize the influence of imported goods on his subjects? What does he propose that João do to regulate trade with Kongo? What actions does Afonso take to restrict the impact of the slave trade on Kongo?
2. In what ways did Afonso's Christian beliefs shape the message that he sent to João and what he asked of the Portuguese king?

· 1520 The Kongo is getting Imports. bering school guns.....
King of Kongo is not happy with The effect of
King of portuguese. There are african Readers.

---

3.   Probably, from the evidence, a Congolese secretary educated by Portuguese missionaries at Mbanza Congo (S. Salvador). See J. Cuvelier, *L'Ancien Royaume de Congo* (Brussels: Desclée de Brouwer, 1946), 294.

1.4. FERNANDO AND JUANA, MONARCHS OF CASTILE AND ARAGON (SPAIN), EXCERPTS FROM "INSTRUCTIONS GIVEN BY THE MONARCHS TO RODRIGO DE ALBURQUERQUE AND TO LICENTIATE IBARRA TO BE CARRIED OUT DURING THE GENERAL DISTRIBUTION OF THE INDIANS IN THE ISLAND OF HISPANIOLA" (1513)

By 1512, outcries from missionaries and other reports from Española had alerted royal officials in Spain that conquest and colonization had decimated the island's Taíno peoples. Although imperial officials enacted some reforms intended to protect Taínos, they also knew and had to acknowledge that Española's economy and royal revenues from the island depended on compulsory Taíno labor. The following document contains excerpts from royal orders issued in 1513 to two officials conducting a *repartimiento*, an allocation of Taínos on the island amongst towns and individual colonists, a task that in effect required that they compile a census of Española's Indians. Officials hoped that the *repartimiento* and other reforms would help to stem the decline of the Taínos.

Valladolid, October 4, 1513

This copy was faithfully transcribed from a decree given by the King.

The King: What you, Licentiate Ibarra and Rodrigo de Alburquerque, must do, in your position of *encomendador*[4] of the Indians, so that, according to the lettered men's[5] resolution, they would be treated and indoctrinated in Our Holy Catholic Faith is to abide by the following:...

2. Second, by the virtue of the decree you carry, you shall revoke and annul, through a public announcement, the current Allocations of the Indians, this is, as determined by our erudite men, in order to cleanse our conscience. And you should order that everyone, including our officials, anyone under our name, the Admiral[6] and his wife, the appellate judges, as well as our officers and all the people, of every class and condition, report each of the Indians they possess, and the name of the *caciques*[7] under whose command they are, and the name of each Indian, be it men or women, boys or girls, to the Indian Visitor and a delegate, who will be elected in every town for such, and other, purposes....

4. And then, you should order each of the town mayors to visit, within a twenty-day period, the Indians

Source: Ernesto Sagás and Orlando Inoa, eds., *The Dominican People: A Documentary History* (Princeton: Markus Wiener Publishers, 2003), 17–23. The editors translated this document from Luis Arranz Márquez, *Repartimientos y encomiendas en la Isla Española: El Repartimiento de Alburquerque de 1514* (Santo Domingo: Fundación García Arévalo, 1991), 263–73.

4.   A good rough translation would be "caretaker."
5.   Theologians of the Spanish royal court, charged with advising monarchs on the morality of proposed laws and policies.
6.   Diego Columbus, Christopher's son.
7.   Taíno chiefs.

in the neighboring farms and ask their *caciques* for a list of names and allocation of each of their Indians. The lists should be sent to you by the mayors within a reasonable period of time.

5. And then, you should order that a record of all the people that live in each town should be created under the supervision of the mayor and the secretary of each town. And these records should be signed by the mayor and the secretary and brought to you by the delegate, as well as the list of the declared Indians, and a report of the visit that the mayors paid to each of the *caciques*....

7. Completed this first part of the task, what you shall do next is to see that the general distribution of the Indians is just, according to its population, so that no town is affected by having fewer Indians. At the same time, you should consider if a town has been allocated too many Indians in respect to its population. This is so that no one feels the need to present a protest as in the village of Puerto Real where people were affected. They say they have very few, and extremely necessary Indians, who are very useful in the trade with Cuba. Make sure that no other town, but the one already mentioned, is affected.... The Indians should stay in their original places to avoid the inconveniences of moving them around. But if a general redistribution of Indians is necessary, make sure you privilege those communities that have mines in them, because they will be more useful to us....

9. [Having] completed the general Allocation, and if changes must be made in order to meet the needs of each town, and if nothing else needs to be done, then you should proceed to make the individual distributions.

10. In this matter, the first thing to be considered...is that no Indian shall be allocated in two places at the same time. This is because by their [the Indians] being in several places, the control as to their instruction and doctrine in our sacred Catholic faith and in the communication with Christians as to their good treatment, in the hands of the people who have them, cannot be clearly maintained....

12. And because it has been called to our attention that the number of Indians in the island has been declining, and at the same time, some people have too many of them and cannot, therefore, indoctrinate them and teach them the tenets of Our Holy Faith nor can they all be well treated, as reasonable, and because more can now communicate in Christian, and in order to expedite their individual allocations, we mandate that you adhere to the instructions, following the number of Indians allocated without exceeding them.

13. In our Haciendas you may leave the number of Indians that are now there, as long as that number does not exceed one thousand. The Admiral shall keep three hundred and his wife, María de Toledo, two hundred Indians. To the people who serve me but are not in the island, who are: the First Chaplain of my Council, the Reverend in Christ Father Don Juan Fonseca, Bishop of Palencia, shall receive two hundred Indians; Fernando Vega, Comendador Mayor of Castile, two hundred; Chamberlain Juan Cabrero, two hundred; Secretary Lope Conchillos, two hundred; to the judges, officers, mayors, I order each shall receive two hundred; and to the descendants of the Admiral and their uncles two hundred Indians each.

14. The rest of the people who live in the island to whom you shall allocate Indians, should be divided within four groups as follows: The most honorable and respectful people, among which you will surely find my servants Villoria and Porros amongst others, should receive the largest possible number of Indians which will be of one hundred and fifty.

15. The second group will be of one hundred Indians and those would be allocated to the next following honorable people you hear of.

16. The third group shall receive seventy-five Indians.

17. The last group shall receive forty Indians, and the rest of the people shall receive none because I understand that less than forty are of no use, and of no profit because those who have them would not bring the one-third profit that was established in the ordinance.

18. And also, because we have been informed that many people have ten or fewer Indians and for this small number we receive no profit. So we order that you collect those Indians from the people that only have three, four, or six and up to ten, so that they may be relocated, especially the Indian men. But the Indian women can stay because many of them are used as house servants and maids, and they shall be indoctrinated and taught in the house. This is so long as they

are not married, because according to the Lettered Men, the married women and the children under thirteen years of age must do as the Indian man orders, for they are subjected to his will. If any of these Indians hold vital positions in the mines such as blacksmith or similar occupations, they should be left there....

20. And also, make sure that the Indians are not overworked as they have been until now, a matter that has caused a lot of harm and a decrease in the number of Indians. Those who have Indians, as it has been determined, shall have them use oxen to plough their land, to the extent that this could be possible, so that the Indians can preserve energy. You shall order anyone who has more than fifty Indians to obtain a pair of oxen as well to help work the land; and those people who have more than a hundred Indians shall have two pairs of oxen, and those with over two hundred should have three pairs. That is so that the more

oxen they have the less overworked the Indians shall be, therefore they could serve us better, and they could have more time to be indoctrinated and to celebrate their festivities and holidays....

Given in Valladolid, on the fourth day of October 1513.
I, the King. The Bishop of Palencia, Earl.

QUESTIONS

1. In what ways did these instructions to redistribute Indian laborers reflect and reinforce the distribution of power and wealth among colonists on Española?
2. What measures did the Spanish Crown seek to implement in order to protect Taíno lives? Which of the Crown's instructions threatened to disrupt and endanger Taíno lives, and how might those instructions have disrupted and endangered Taíno lives?

1.5. PEDRO MENÉNDEZ DE ÁVILES, MEMORANDUM TO PHILIP II, KING OF SPAIN (1565)

In early 1565, Philip II requested that Pedro Menéndez de Áviles report on his knowledge of French designs on eastern North America, the threat that such designs posed to the Spanish Empire, and what the Spanish might do to safeguard their claims to North America. Menéndez, a naval commander who had explored the Atlantic coast of North America and sailed with the royal fleet that protected Spanish shipping from French privateers, responded with the following message. Shortly after receipt of this memorandum, Philip authorized Menéndez to organize an invasion of Florida to oust the French and colonize "La Florida," the term that the Spanish then used to refer to areas along the Atlantic and Gulf coasts north of the Rio Grande.

To His Catholic Royal Majesty Pedro Menendez says: That what he sends your Majesty is what he declares to know of the coast and lands of Florida, and of the corsairs whom it is said have gone to populate

it and seize the vessels coming from the Indias[8]—and the damage they may do, and the remedy to be used in cases where they should have settled. Give them no quarter, and appropriate the coast and lands so that

---

Source: A. M. Brooks, ed., *The Unwritten History of Old St. Augustine*, trans. Annie Averette (St. Augustine: The Record Co., 1909[?]), 5–10.

8. The term that the Spanish used to refer to their overseas colonies, including those in the Americas.

they can be the more easily turned out—that your Majesty can send to spread the Gospel, prevent the damages that can be done the vessels coming from the Indias is as follows: If…the English, French or any other nation should feel disposed to go and settle any part of Florida, it would be very damaging to these kingdoms, because on said coast of Florida and in said strait of the Bahamas, they could settle and fortify themselves in such a way, that they could have galleons and vessels of war to capture the fleets and other private vessels that came from the Indias, and pass through there, as they would run great risk of being captured.

Also, that if last summer the French and English went to Florida as we are certain they did, and should have settled and built a fort in any port, and summered there, giving notice to their home government as to how they are situated, and should they be supplied this summer before we can raid upon them, and turn them out, it would be very difficult to do so on account of the friendship formed by them with the natives who would help them in such a way as to cause serious difficulty, and even should we finally succeed the natives would remain our enemies, and this would be extremely disadvantageous. Should they be supplied this summer the merchantmen which we expect from the Indias would also run great risk of being captured. Also, that it would be very annoying to have the above mentioned or others settle in Florida. Considering the proximity of the Islands of Santo Domingo, Puerto Rico and Cuba, where there are such vast numbers of negroes and mulattoes of bad disposition, there being in each of these islands more than thirty negroes to each Christian. And it is a land in which this generation multiplies with great rapidity. In the power of the French and English, all these slaves would be freed, and to enjoy their freedom would help them even against their own masters and lords and there would be an uprising in the land, and with the help of the negroes it would be easy to capture us. As an example of this, take Jaques de Soria, France, which in the year fifty-three[9], with one boat of a hundred tons and eighty men, by simply freeing the negroes, took and plundered the Islands of Margarite and Saint Martha,

and burned Carthagena, plundered Santiago de Cuba and Havana, although at the time there were two hundred Spaniards there. They took the Fort with all it contained, and twelve pieces of bronze artillery and carried them all off. I consider these negroes a great obstacle to having the French or English settle in Florida or to have them so near, even though they should not be in favor with these two nations, there is danger of an uprising as there are so many cunning and sagacious ones who desire this liberty that I feel sure the design of those who should settle in Florida is to domineer over those islands, and stop the navigation with the Indias, which they can easily do by settling in said Florida. Also he says: That on account of these dangers and many others, it seems to him it would be to the service of God Our Lord, and your Majesty for the general good of your Kingdoms the Indies it would be well for your Majesty to try and domineer over these lands and coasts, which on account of their position, if other nations should go on settling and making friends with the Indians, it would be difficult to conquer them, especially if settled by French and English Lutherans[10], as they and the Indians having about the same laws, they would be friendly, and being near could rule and each year send out a thousand vessels to easily treat and contract with these lands which are said to be fertile and prolific for sugar plantations, which they so much need and are supplied from these Kingdoms. There might also be many cattle good for their tallow and wool and other necessities. What seems to him that your Majesty should do in the service of God and your Majesty's and for the salvation of so many souls, and the aggrandizement of your kingdoms and your royal estates, is as follows:

As there are neither French nor English nor any other nation to disturb them, that your Majesty should send five hundred persons, sailors, laborers, etc., and that among them should be one hundred master carpenters, blacksmiths, plasterers and builders of mud walls, all with their implements and appurtenances for every thing, with their arms of defense, such as arquebuses, cross-bows, etc. That among this number of five hundred people should be four Friars, four teachers and twelve Christian children, so that the principal Indians

---

9. 1553.
10. Spaniards of the era often referred to Protestants as "Lutherans."

would send their children to school to learn to read and learn the doctrine of Christianity. There should be three surgeons who would go about in small boats, canoes or row boats with supplies for one year—go straight to Santa Elena and from there find all the paths, rivers and ports most suited and best, by land and water. See the condition of the land for planting and settle two or three towns in the best vicinity, build their fort, to be able to defend themselves against the Indians, that each of these forts should have artillery and ammunition. All this supply with the cost of the voyage will amount to eighty thousand ducats or more. There will be left vessels enough to carry a number of cattle. These must be sent from Spain, because in the Indias we could not find suitable vessels nor head workmen of the necessary qualifications and it could not give the desired results, besides the delay would cause much damage. It would be difficult to find the proper kind of people, and even if found the cost would be very much greater, as head workmen gain very large wages in those parts, as do

also laborers and sailors. From Havana it would be still more impossible to bring them, as there are none to be obtained, and if they have to settle they must go a long way 'round, as they cannot enter the mouth of the Bahama Channel, it being as easy and quick to come from Spain as from Havana....

Pedro Menendez

QUESTIONS

1. On what grounds does Menéndez advocate that the Spanish conquer and colonize Florida? In what ways does Menéndez use the knowledge of North America and the Caribbean that he acquired through his travels around the Atlantic world to make his case?

2. What kind of relationship does Menéndez envision existing between Spanish colonists and Florida's Indians? In what ways does his memorial acknowledge Indian power in Florida?

1.6. VISUAL DOCUMENT: TEXAS FRAGMENT, "ARRIVAL OF CORTÉS AND MALINTZÍN IN ATLIHUETZYAN" (1530s OR 1540s)

Long before the Spanish arrived in Mexico, Nahuas (Nahuatl-speaking Indians) recorded or commemorated events and agreements by painting them in stylized ways. Shortly after central Mexico came under Spanish rule, Nahuas continued and modified this tradition to provide their own perspective on their histories, including their memories of the Spanish conquest. Artists of Tlaxcala, one of Cortés's principal allies against the Mexica, created the painting featured below. It was probably completed in the 1530s or 1540s and depicts the arrival of Cortés, Malintzín (with her hand raised to indicate that she is speaking), and a party of Spanish soldiers on horseback to Atlihuetzyan in Tlaxcala. Tepolouatecatl, a noble member of Tlaxcalan leader Xicotencatl's family, greets the visitors and offers them birds, bread, and corn, all of which are intended as tribute.

Source: Courtesy of the Nettie Lee Benson Collection of the University of Texas Library.

QUESTIONS

1. The road with footprints proceeding in one direction traditionally signified travel in such paintings. In what way did Tlaxcalan artists modify this sign to reflect the arrival of the Spanish?

2. Malintzín occupies a central place in this scene. Why?

3. The scene depicted here clashes with non-Tlaxcalan accounts, which indicate that many Tlaxcalan leaders decided to fight the invaders. Among the last holdouts against the Spanish was Xicotencatl's son. For what reasons did the Tlaxcalan artist(s) choose to portray the initial reception of the Spanish as peaceful?

CHAPTER 2

COLONISTS ON THE MARGINS, 1565–1640

2.1. FRAY ALONSO DE BENAVIDES, EXCERPTS FROM "PETITION TO RESTRICT INDIAN TRIBUTE AND PERSONAL SERVICE" (c. 1630)

One of the principal sources of friction between friars and governors in Florida and New Mexico concerned the amount of tribute and personal service that Indians owed and to whom, friars or colonists, they owed that tribute and service. The friar Alonso de Benavides, who oversaw New Mexico's missions from 1626 to 1629, likely wrote the petition excerpted below. Benavides composed his petition shortly after he returned to Spain in 1630 and addressed it to the King of Spain. It appears that Benavides's efforts succeeded. In 1635, a royal decree exempted Indians in New Mexico who converted to Christianity from paying tribute or rendering personal service for ten years.

Through royal decrees it is ordered that no tributes or personal services be imposed on the Indians of New Mexico until after they have been baptized. Before any can be levied against them, the governor of the province and the custodian must notify the viceroy and the royal *audiencia*[1] of Mexico stating the reasons why they should be imposed, this to be done by the viceroy himself and the royal *audiencia*, and in no other way. At present everything is done in just the opposite manner; even before the pueblos are converted, the governor himself gives them out in *encomienda*[2] without notifying the custodian or the viceroy. Even before they are converted and baptized, when they are only pacified, they [Spaniards] constrain them to pay tribute and to do personal service, taking them far from their pueblos and treating them badly. As a result, the heathen Indians who have not yet been converted or even pacified say that they do not want to become converted, or even pacified, that they do not want to become Christians, in order not to pay tribute or serve. They have even

Source: Frederick W. Hodge, George P. Hammond, and Agapito Rey, eds., *Fray Alonso de Benavides: Revised Memorial of 1634 with Numerous Supplementary Documents Elaborately Annotated* (Albuquerque: University of New Mexico Press, 1945), 168–77.

1. A group of judges headquartered in Mexico City who had jurisdiction over cases from New Mexico.
2. A grant to a prominent colonist of control over the services of Indians.

been sent to be sold as slaves in New Spain[3], as was the practice. They escape these and other abuses as long as they remain free and do not become Christians.

Wherefore your Majesty is entreated to order, under severe penalties, that the Indians of New Mexico be not given in *encomienda* by the governors of New Mexico until five years after the whole pueblo has been baptized, and in order to be given in *encomienda*, the said governor and the custodian there must notify the viceroy and the *audiencia*, reporting that the five years have passed, so that they may be authorized to do it; that the *encomenderos*[4] of the said pueblos should have no other power or rights over the pueblos and Indians than the tribute owed them; that the Indians must remain always as tributary vassals of your Majesty, in whose name they pay the tribute to their *encomenderos*, without owing them any more obligations than to those who are not *encomenderos*; that neither the *encomenderos* nor any other Spaniards be allowed to live in their pueblos without the consent of the Indians themselves; that they may not have houses in the pueblos for their employment or other gain, by which they cause much harm to the pueblos and the Indians.

Likewise, it has been established by the first governors of New Mexico, and is being continued by order of the viceroy that each house pay a tribute consisting of a cotton blanket, the best of which are about a yard and a half square, and a *fanega*[5] of corn. This is understood to be for each house and not for each Indian, even though many Indian families live in such houses. It often happens that the pueblos increase or decrease in houses, or, if one tumbles down, its dwellers move to that of their relatives, and none of these pay tribute, except for the house in which they live. This works against the increase in houses, as tribute is collected as soon as the owners occupy them.

The *encomenderos* compel the Indians whose houses may have fallen down, or which they may have lost for other reasons, to pay tribute, even though they live in someone else's house. It is requested of your Majesty that the Indians of New Mexico do not pay tribute by the person, but by the house, as has always been done; that, as the *encomendero* is ready to receive the tribute of houses added to their pueblos, he should also be ready to lose and cease taking tribute from abandoned houses, even though the owners live in someone else's house.

It is requested that the Indians who, of their own will, move to live in other pueblos, being free, as they are, must not be hindered by their *encomenderos*, the governors, or other persons; that they may live freely in whatever pueblo they wish, and that, after they have established residence there for one year and a day, they become taxpayers at the place like the others of the same pueblo to the *encomendero* with whom they live. For the Indians suffer much harm when, if they do not get along with the *encomendero* in a pueblo where they do not find as good facilities for their work and farming as in some other one, they are forced to live there for the accommodation of the *encomendero*, whether they like it or not. If they have this freedom, the *encomenderos* will help and accord good treatment to their tributary Indians so that they will not leave their pueblos and their tributes diminish.

It is requested that all the *caciques*[6], chief captains, governors, *alcaldes*[7], and *fiscales*[8] of the churches, on account of the big tasks they perform for the republic and the service of your Majesty, be exempt from tribute and personal service while they hold these offices. They are so busy in their offices that even their planted fields are cared for by others, as they are unable to do it themselves. The native lords and chieftains resent very much that they are compelled to pay tribute. Likewise,

---

3. In this case, Benavides probably means what we today would call Mexico.
4. Individuals to whom a grant of *encomienda* had been given.
5. Approximately 2 cubic feet, or just over a bushel and a half.
6. What Taíno peoples in the Caribbean called their chiefs, a term that the Spanish subsequently used to refer to Indian chiefs in North America, Mexico, Central America, and parts of South America.
7. Indian magistrates who often oversaw the apprehension of criminals, among other duties.
8. *Fiscales* acted as assistants to priests, helping with the management of parishes and the discipline of those who violated church teachings.

all the Indians who are choir singers and assistants in the churches are free only from personal service, but not from tribute, because of their regular attendance in church and in the schools.

It is requested that the Spanish governors be forbidden to issue warrants or permits to take Indian boys or girls from the pueblos on the pretext that they are orphans, and take them to serve permanently in the houses of the Spaniards where they remain as slaves. As a matter of fact, the orphans are well cared for at the homes of their grandparents or other relatives where they are brought up as if they were their own children. In case there should be any one without a home, the governor should not issue warrants without the consent of the ecclesiastical minister, who lives alone with the Indians and knows their needs and relieves them as much as he is able. This must be done so that the destitute Indian orphans may live freely with their relatives. The governors often take from the Spaniards some Indians who are serving the Spaniards well, in order to keep them for themselves. They take them without compensation, or, in payment, give them a permit to go to the pueblos to look for other boys and girls and to take them by force.

It is requested that the Indians taken in wars, whatever their nation, may not be given as slaves or sentenced to personal service outside of New Mexico, as is prescribed by royal decrees. On the contrary, they should be placed in convents of the friars or in houses of Spaniards or Indians of exemplary conduct so that they may be taught our holy Catholic faith with all kindness in order that they may become Christians. If any of them should run away they will tell the people of their nations of the good treatment accorded them and they will become inclined to our life and religion. This assignment to a convent may not be in the nature of a sale, transfer, or any other material consideration or period of time, but simply as an act of charity to instruct and convert them, which is the only purpose for which we have gone there. They must always be free in their lands, as they are often taken in wars and on other occasions, placed with an individual for many years who then transfers them to another individual for a consideration for the remainder of the time the assignment is to last. This is often done by the governors through a third party, and under this pretext they take many Indians, both men and women, to Mexico and other places to be sold.

It is requested that the Spanish governors be forbidden from depriving any native Indian chief of his post or authority, because of the fact that the Indians greatly resent seeing their leaders and chieftains mistreated.

QUESTIONS

1. For what reasons does Benavides request restrictions on the amount of tribute and personal service that governors could demand of Indians? For what reasons does he request greater regulation of the Indian slave trade to and through New Mexico?
2. What kind of relationship among friars, governors, and Indians does Benavides seek?
3. What can you learn about Pueblo life and politics from Benavides's petition?

2.2. WILLIAM SIMMONDS, EXCERPTS FROM *THE PROCEEDINGS OF THE ENGLISH COLONIE IN VIRGINIA* (1612)

The difficulties that the Virginia Company of London encountered in trying to establish a colony at Jamestown and turn a profit from it generated a great deal of commentary on both sides of the Atlantic. The excerpt below comes from a narrative that William Simmonds published in Oxford, England, in 1612. A large portion of the work, which mostly provided an account of events in Virginia, came from John Smith himself and was sent to Simmonds by three friends of Smith, all of whom were in Virginia. At the beginning of the excerpt, these men have just finished recounting the difficulties that the English encountered in securing corn from Tsenacommacah's Algonquians to feed Jamestown.

Those temporall proceedings, to some maie seeme too charitable, to such a dailie daring trecherous people; to others unpleasant that we washed not the ground with their blouds, nor shewed such strange inventions in mangling, murdering, ransaking, and destroying (as did the Spaniards) the simple bodies of those ignorant soules; nor delightful, because not stuffed with relations of heaps and mines of gold and silver, nor such rare commodities as the Portugals[9] and Spaniards found in the East and West Indies. The want wherof hath begot us, that were the first undertakers, no lesse scorne and contempt, than their noble conquests and valiant adventures (beautified with it), praise and honor. Too much, I confesse, the world cannot attribute to their ever memorable merit. And to cleare us from the worlds blind ignorant censure, these fewe words may suffise to any reasonably understanding.

It was the Spaniards good hap[10] to happen in those parts where were infinite numbers of people, whose had manured the ground with that providence that it afforded victuall at all times; and time had brought them to that perfection [that] they had the vse of gold and silver, and [of] the most of such commodities as their countries affoorded: so that what the Spaniard got was only the spoile and pillage of those countrie people, and not the labours of their owne hands.

But had those fruitfull Countries beene as Salvage, as barbarous, as ill-peopled, as little planted laboured and manured, as *Virginia*; their proper labours, it is likely would have produced as small profit as ours. But had *Virginia* bin peopled, planted, manured, and adorned with such store of pretious Jewels and rich commodities as was the Indies: then, had we not gotten and done as much as by their examples might bee expected from us, the world might then have traduced us and our merits, and have made shame and infamy our recompence and reward.

But we chanced in a lande, even as God made it. Where we found only an idle, improvident, scattered people, ignorant of the knowledge of gold, or silver, or any commodities; and carelesse of anything but from hand to mouth, but for ba[u]bles of no worth; nothing to encourage us but what accidentally wee

Source: William Simmonds, *The Proceedings of the English Colonie in Virginia since Their First Beginning from England in the Yeare of our Lord, 1606 till This Present 1612, with All Their Accidents that Befell Them in the Journies and Discoveries* (Oxford, 1612), 76–78. Taken from Edward Arber, ed., *Captain John Smith: Works, 1608–1631,* (Birmingham, 1884), 147–48.

9. Portuguese.
10. Luck.

found nature afforded. Which ere wee could bring to recompence our paines, defray our charges, and satisfie our adventurers; we were to discover the country, subdue the people, bring them to be tractable civil and industrious, and teach them trades that the fruits of their labours might make us recompence, or plant such colonies of our owne that must first make provision how to live of themselves ere they can bring to perfection the commodities of the countrie: which doubtless will be as commodious for England as the west Indies for Spaine, if it be rightly managed; notwithstanding all our home-bred opinions that will argue the contrarie, as formerly such like have done against the Spaniards and Portugals.

But to conclude, against all rumor of opinion I only say this for those that the three first yeares began this plantation: notwithstanding al their factions, mutenies, and miseries, so gently corrected and well prevented, peruse the Spanish *Decades*, the relations of *Master Hacklu[y]t*; and tell mee how many ever, with such smal meanes as a barge of 2 Tunnes, sometimes with 7. 8. 9, or but at most 15 men, did ever discover so many faire and navigable rivers, subject so many severall kings people and nations to obedience and contribution, with so little bloud shed.

And if in the search of those Countries, wee had hapned where wealth had beene, we had as surely had it, as obedience and contribution; but if wee have overskipped it, we will not envy them that shall chance to finde it. Yet can wee not but lament it was our ill fortunes to end, when wee had but only learned how to begin, and found the right course how to proceed.

QUESTIONS

1. In what terms do the authors discuss the Spanish conquest of much of the Americas? In what ways does their discussion reflect the "Black Legend" of Spanish conquest that was then circulating in the Anglo-Atlantic world? Does their discussion undermine the "Black Legend" in some way? If so, how so? If not, why not?

2. In what ways did the precarious finances of the Virginia Company and concerns about the reputation of its employees in Virginia influence the tone and content of the narrative you've just read?

2.3. JEAN DE BRÉBEUF, "INSTRUCTIONS FOR THE FATHERS OF OUR SOCIETY WHO SHALL BE SENT TO THE HURONS" (1637)

French Jesuits served as a linchpin of the alliances that French officials sought to forge with Indians in order to sustain the fur trade and uphold French claims to North America. The most valuable ally to the French were the Wendats, whom the French called Hurons. Under the terms of an agreement reached between the French and the Hurons, Jesuits founded a mission among the Hurons in 1634. Father Jean de Brébeuf spent the next 15 years attached to that mission before he was taken captive and killed by Iroquois warriors. Brébeuf penned the document below, which was published and circulated in France as one of a series of reports from North America that historians call the "Jesuit Relations."

Source: Edna Kenton, *Jesuit Relations and Allied Documents: Travels and Explorations of the Jesuit Missions in North America (1610–1791)* (New York: Vanguard Press, 1954), 118–21.

The Fathers and Brethren whom God shall call to the holy Mission of the Hurons ought to exercise careful foresight in regard to all the hardships, annoyances, and perils that must be encountered in making this journey, in order to be prepared betimes for all emergencies that may arise.

You must have sincere affection for the Savages[11],— looking upon them as ransomed by the blood of the son of God, and as our Brethren with whom we are to pass the rest of our lives.

To conciliate the Savages, you must be careful never to make them wait for you in embarking.

You must provide yourself with a tinder box or with a burning mirror, or with both, to furnish them fire in the daytime to light their pipes, and in the evening when they have to encamp; these little services win their hearts.

You should try to eat their *sagamité*[12] or salmagundi in the way they prepare it, although it may be dirty, half-cooked, and very tasteless. As to the other numerous things which may be unpleasant, they must be endured for the love of God, without saying anything or appearing to notice them.

It is well at first to take everything they offer, although you may not be able to eat it all; for, when one becomes somewhat accustomed to it, there is not too much.

You must try and eat at daybreak unless you can take your meal with you in the canoe; for the day is very long, if you have to pass it without eating. The Barbarians eat only at Sunrise and Sunset, when they are on their journeys.

You must be prompt in embarking and disembarking; and tuck up your gowns so that they will not get wet, and so that you will not carry either water or sand into the canoe. To be properly dressed, you must have your feet and legs bare; while crossing the rapids, you can wear your shoes, and, in the long portages, even your leggings.

You must so conduct yourself as not to be at all troublesome to even one of these Barbarians.

It is not well to ask many questions, nor should you yield to your desire to learn the language and to make observations on the way; this may be carried too far. You must relieve those in your canoe of this annoyance, especially as you cannot profit much by it during the work. Silence is a good equipment at such a time.

You must bear with their imperfections without saying a word, yes, even without seeming to notice them. Even if it be necessary to criticise anything, it must be done modestly, and with words and signs which evince love and not aversion. In short, you must try to be, and to appear, always cheerful.

Each one should be provided with half a gross of awls, two or three dozen little knives called *jambettes* (pocket-knives), a hundred fish-hooks, with some beads of plain and colored glass, with which to buy fish or other articles when the tribes meet each other, so as to feast the Savages; and it would be well to say to them in the beginning, "Here is something with which to buy fish." Each one will try, at the portages, to carry some little thing, according to his strength; however little one carries, it greatly pleases the savages, if it be only a kettle.

You must not be ceremonious with the Savages, but accept the comforts they offer you, such as a good place in the cabin. The greatest conveniences are attended with very great inconvenience, and these ceremonies offend them.

Be careful not to annoy anyone in the canoe with your hat; it would be better to take your nightcap. There is no impropriety among the Savages.

Do not undertake anything unless you desire to continue it; for example, do not begin to paddle unless you are inclined to continue paddling. Take from the start the place in the canoe that you wish to keep; do not lend them your garments, unless you are willing to surrender them during the whole journey. It is easier to refuse at first than to ask them back, to change, or to desist afterwards.

Finally, understand that the Savages will retain the same opinion of you in their own country that they will have formed on the way; and one who has passed for an irritable and troublesome person will have considerable difficulty afterwards in removing this opinion. You have to do not only with those of your own canoe, but also (if it must be so stated) with all those of the country;

---

11. The French often referred to Indians as "savages," by which they meant "wild men."
12. A stew made from corn or corn meal.

you meet some today and others tomorrow, who do not fail to inquire, from those who brought you, what sort of man you are. It is almost incredible, how they observe and remember even the slightest fault. When you meet Savages on the way, as you cannot yet greet them with kind words, at least show them a cheerful face, and thus prove that you endure gayly the fatigues of the voyage. You will thus have put to good use the hardships on the way, and have already advanced considerably in gaining the affection of the Savages.

This is a lesson which is easy enough to learn, but very difficult to put into practice; for, leaving a highly civilized community, you fall into the hands of barbarous people who care but little for your Philosophy or your Theology. All the fine qualities which might make you loved and respected in France are like pearls trampled under the feet of swine, or rather mules, which utterly despise you when they see that you are not as good pack animals as they are. If you could go naked, and carry the load of a horse upon your back, as they do, then you would be wise according to their doctrine, and would be recognized as a great man, otherwise not. Jesus Christ is our true greatness; it is He alone and His cross that should be sought in running after these people, for, if you strive for anything else, you will find naught but bodily and spiritual affliction. But having found Jesus Christ in His cross, you have found the roses in the thorns, sweetness in bitterness, all in nothing.

QUESTIONS

1. What can you learn about Huron culture from the instructions that Brébeuf gave to his fellow Jesuits?
2. What can we learn about Jesuit culture from Brébeuf's advice? According to Brébeuf, in what ways and for what reasons would Jesuits who served in the Huron mission need to modify their expectations of others?

2.4. JOHN WINTHROP, EXCERPTS FROM "A MODELL OF CHRISTIAN CHARITY" (1630)

In 1630, John Winthrop, first governor of the Massachusetts Bay Company and occasional lay preacher in England, delivered the sermon "A Model of Christian Charity" to Puritans who were migrating to New England. We do not know whether Winthrop gave the sermon to departing colonists in England or en route to New England. Indeed, no written record of a person claiming to have heard it survives. It is likely that no one published Winthrop's sermon during the 17th century because few of the ideas would have struck its original audience as unusual or particularly noteworthy. Below are excerpts from the concluding section of the sermon, which has become one of the most famous examples of colonial literature.

God Almighty in his most holy and wise providence, hath soe disposed of the condition of mankind, as in all times some must be rich, some poore, some high and eminent in power and dignitie; others mean and in submission....

It rests now to make some application of this discourse, by the present designe, which gave the occasion of writing of it. Herein are 4 things to be propounded; *first* the persons, 2ly the worke, 3ly the end, 4thly the meanes. 1. For *the persons*. Wee are a company

Source: Collections of the Massachusetts Historical Society, 3rd Series, vol. 7 (Boston: Charles C. Little and James Brown, 1838), 33–48.

professing ourselves fellow members of Christ, in which respect onely though wee were absent from each other many miles, and had our imployments as farre distant, yet wee ought to account ourselves knitt together by this bond of love, and, live in the exercise of it, if wee would have comforte of our being in Christ. This was notorious in the practise of the Christians in former times; ... 2nly for the *worke* wee have in hand. It is by a mutuall consent, through a speciall overvaluing providence and a more than an ordinary approbation of the Churches of Christ, to seeke out a place of cohabitation and Consorteshipp under a due forme of Government both civill and ecclesiasticall. In such cases as this, the care of the publique must oversway all private respects, by which, not only conscience, but meare civill pollicy, dothe binde us. For it is a true rule that particular Estates cannot subsist in the ruin of the publique. 3ly The *end* is to improve our lives to doe more service to the Lord; the comforte and encrease of the body of Christe, whereof we are members; that ourselves and posterity may be the better preserved from the common corruptions of this evill world, to serve the Lord and worke out our Salvation under the power and purity of his holy ordinances. 4thly for the *meanes* whereby this must be effected. They are twofold, a conformity with the worke and end wee aime at. These wee see are extraordinary, therefore wee must not content ourselves with usuall ordinary meanes. Whatsoever wee did, or ought to have done, when wee lived in England, the same must wee doe, and more allsoe, where we goe. That which the most in theire churches maintaine as truthe in profession onely, wee must bring into familiar and constant practise; as in this duty of love, wee must love brotherly without dissimulation, wee must love one another with a pure hearte fervently. Wee must beare one anothers burthens. We must not looke onely on our owne things, but allsoe on the things of our brethren. Neither must wee thinke that the Lord will beare with such faileings at our hands as he dothe from those among whome wee have lived; and that for these 3 Reasons; 1. In regard of the more neare bond of mariage between him and us, wherein hee hath taken us to be his, after a most strickt and peculiar manner, which will make them the more jealous of our love and obedience. Soe he tells the people of Israell, *you onely have I knowne of all the families of the*

Earthe, therefore will I punishe you for your Transgressions. 2ly, because *the Lord will be sanctified in them that come neare him.* We know that there were many that corrupted the service of the Lord; some setting upp altars before his owne; others offering both strange fire and strange sacrifices allsoe; yet there came noe fire from heaven, or other sudden judgement upon them, as did upon Nadab and Abihu, whoe yet wee may think did not sinne presumptuously. 3ly When God gives a speciall commission he lookes to have it strictly observed in every article, When he gave Saule a commission to destroy Amaleck, Hee indented with him upon certain articles, and because hee failed in one of the least, and that upon a faire pretense, it lost him the kingdom, which should have beene his reward, if hee had observed his commission. Thus stands the cause betweene God and us. We are entered into Covenant with Him for this worke. Wee haue taken out a commission. The Lord hath given us leave to drawe our own articles. Wee have professed to enterprise these and those accounts, upon these and those ends. Wee have hereupon besought Him of favour and blessing. Now if the Lord shall please to heare us, and bring us in peace to the place we desire, then hath hee ratified this covenant and sealed our Commission, and will expect a strict performance of the articles contained in it; but if wee shall neglect the observation of these articles which are the ends wee have propounded, and, dissembling with our God, shall fall to embrace this present world and prosecute our carnall intentions, seeking great things for ourselves and our posterity, the Lord will surely break out in wrathe against us; be revenged of such a [sinful] people and make us knowe the price of the breache of such a covenant.

Now the onely way to avoyde this shipwracke, and to provide for our posterity, is to followe the counsell of Micah, *to doe justly, to love mercy, to walk humbly with our God.* For this end, wee must be knitt together, in this worke, as one man. Wee must entertaine each other in brotherly affection. Wee must be willing to abridge ourselves of our superfluities, for the supply of other's necessities. Wee must uphold a familiar commerce together in all meekeness, gentlenes, patience and liberality. Wee must delight in eache other; make other's conditions our oune; rejoice together, mourne together, labour and suffer together, allwayes haueving before our eyes our commission and community in the worke, as members of the same body. Soe shall wee *keepe the unitie of the spirit in the bond of peace*. The Lord will be our God, and delight to dwell among us, as his oune people, and will command a blessing upon us in all our wayes. Soe that wee shall see much more of his wisdome, power, goodness and truthe, than formerly wee haue been acquainted with. Wee shall finde that the God of Israell is among us, when ten of us shall be able to resist a thousand of our enemies; when hee shall make us a prayse and glory that men shall say of succeeding plantations, "the Lord make it likely that of *New England*." For wee must consider that wee shall be as a citty upon a hill. The eies of all people are uppon us. Soe that if wee shall deale falsely with our God in this worke wee have undertaken, and soe cause him to withdrawe his present help from us, wee shall be made a story and a by-word through the world. Wee shall open the mouthes of enemies to speake evill of the wayes of God, and all professors for God's sake. Wee shall shame the faces of many of God's worthy servants, and cause theire prayers to be turned into curses upon us till wee be consumed out of the good land whither wee are a goeing.

QUESTIONS

1. What kind of relationship does Winthrop posit between his audience and God? In what ways does that relationship help to explain Massachusetts Bay colonists' belief that they should police each other's behavior?
2. Based on Winthrop's sermon, in what sense did colonists believe that they were about to create a "New" England in North America?

2.5. EXCERPTS FROM THE NARRAGANSETT ACT OF SUBMISSION TO CHARLES I, (1644)

During the Pequot War of 1636–1637, Narragansetts and Mohegans allied with Massachusetts Bay and Connecticut colonists against the Pequots. Six years later, the Narragansett sachem Miantonomi was killed in Mohegan custody after attempting to forge a regional pan-Indian alliance against colonists. The documents below are a letter sent to Charles I by Narragansett leaders and the Narragansett response to a summons sent by Massachusetts Bay authorities to the sachems Conanicus, Miantonomi's uncle, and Pessicus, Miantonomi's brother and successor, requesting their appearance in Boston. Rhode Island colonist Samuel Gorton, then enmeshed in a dispute with Massachusetts Bay officials over land that Miantonomi had deeded him, and three associates (all mentioned below) delivered the Narragansett letter to Charles I and probably helped to write it.

*T*he Act and Deed of the voluntary and free submission *of the chiefe Sachem, and the rest of the Princes, with the whole people of the Nanhigansets,*[13] *unto the Government and protection of that Honorable State of Old-England; set downe, here. verbatim.*

Know all Men, Colonies, Peoples, and Nations, unto whom the fame hereof shall come; that wee, the chiefe Sachems, Princes or Governors of the Nanhigansets (in that part of America, now called New-England), together with the joynt and unanimous consent of all

Source: John Russell Bartlett, ed., *Records of the Colony of Rhode Island and Providence Plantations in New England*, vol. 1 (Providence, RI, 1856), 134–38.

13. Narragansetts.

our people and subjects, inhabitants thereof, do upon serious consideration, mature and deliberate advise and counsell, great and weighty grounds and reasons moving us thereunto, whereof one most effectual unto us, is, that noble fame we have heard of that Great and mighty Prince, Charles, King of Great Britaine, in that honorable and princely care he hath of all his servants, and true and loyall subjects, the consideration whereof moveth and bendeth our hearts with one consent, freely, voluntarily, and most humbly to submit, subject, and give over ourselves, peoples, lands, rights, inheritances, and possessions whatsoever, in ourselves and our heires successively for ever, unto the protection, care and government of that worthy and royal Prince, Charles, King of Great Britaine and Ireland, his heires and successors forever, to be ruled and governed according to the ancient and honorable lawes and customes, established in that so renowned realme and kingdome of Old England; we do, therefore, by these presents, confesse, and most willingly and submissively acknowledge ourselves to be the humble, loving and obedient servants and subjects of his Majestie; to be ruled, ordered, and disposed of, in ourselves and ours, according to his princely wisdome, counsell and lawes of that honorable State of Old England; *upon condition of His Majesties' royal protection,* and wrighting us of what wrong is, or may be done unto us, according to his honorable lawes and customes, exercised amongst his subjects, in their preservation and safety, and in the defeating and overthrow of his, and their enemies; not that we find ourselves necessitated hereunto, in respect of our relation, or occasion we have, or may have, with any of the natives in these parts, knowing ourselves sufficient defence, and able to judge in any matter or cause in that respect; but have just cause of jealousy and suspicion of some of His Majesty's pretended subjects. Therefore our desire is, to have our matters and causes heard and tried according to his just and equall lawes, in that way and order His Highness shall please to appoint: *Nor can we yield over ourselves unto any, that are subjects themselves in any case;* having ourselves been the chief Sachems, or Princes successively, of the country, time out of mind; and for our present and lawfull enacting hereof, being so farre remote from His Majestie, wee have, by joynt consent, made choice of foure of his loyall and loving subjects, our trusty and well-beloved friends, Samuel Gorton, John Wickes, Randall Houlden and John

Warner, whom we have deputed, and made our lawfull Attornies or Commissioners, not only for the acting and performing of this our Deed, in the behalfe of his Highnesse, but also for the safe custody, carefull conveyance, and declaration hereof unto his grace: being done upon the lands of the Nanhigansett, at a Court or Generall Assembly called and assembled together, of purpose, for the publick enacting, and manifestation hereof.

And for the further confirmation, and establishing of this our Act and Deed, wee, the abovesaid Sachems or Princes, have, according to that commendable custome of Englishmen, subscribed our names and sett our seals hereunto, as so many testimonies of our fayth and truth, our love and loyalty to that our dread Soveraighne, and that according to the Englishmen's account.

Dated the nineteenth day of April,
one thousand six hundred and forty-four.

PESSICUS, his marke, Chief Sachem, and
successor of that late deceased Miantonomy.
The marke of that ancient CONANICUS,
Protector of that late deceased Miantonomy,
during the time of his nonage.
The marke of MIXAN, son and heire
of that abovesaid Conanicus.

Witnessed by two of the chiefe counsellors to Sachem Pessicus.

AWASHOOSSE, his marke,
TOMANICK, his marke.
Indians

Sealed and delivered, in the presence of these persons:

CHRISTOPHER HELME,
ROBERT POTTER,
RICHARD CARDER.
English

Here followeth a copy of a letter sent to the Massachusetts, by the Sachems of the Narragansetts, (shortly after their subjection to the State and Government of Old England) they being sent unto by the Massachusetts, to make their appearance at their General Court, then approac[h]ing.

We understand your desire is, that we should come downe into the Massachusetts, at the time of your Courte, now approaching. Our occasions at this same time are very great; and the more because of the loss (in that manner) of our late deceased brother, upon which occasion, if we should not stir ourselves, to give testimony of our faithfulness unto the cause of that our so unjust deprivation of such an instrument as he was amongst us, for our common good, we should fear his blood would lie upon ourselves; so that we desire of you, being we take you for a wise people, to let us know your reasons why you seem to advise us as you do, not to go out against our so inhuman and cruel adversary, who took so great a ransom to release him, and his life also, when that was done. Our brother was willing to stir much abroad to converse with men, and we see a sad event at the last thereupon. Take it not ill, therefore, though we resolve to keep at home, (unless some great necessity calls us out,) and so, at this time, do not repair unto you, according to your request. And the rather because we have subjected ourselves, our lands and possessions, with all the rights and inheritances of us and our people, either by conquest, voluntary subjection or otherwise, unto that famous and honorable government of that Royal King, Charles, and that State of Old England, to be ordered and governed according to the laws and customs thereof; not doubting of the continuance of that former love that hath been betwixt you and us, but rather to have it increase, hereby being subjects now (and that with joint and voluntary consent), unto the same King and State yourselves are. So that if any small things of difference should fall out betwixt us, only the sending of a messenger may bring it to right again; but if any great matter should fall (which we hope and desire will not, nor may not), then neither yourselves, nor we are to be judges; and both of us are to have recourse, and repair unto that honorable and just Government; and for the passage of us or our men, to and again amongst you, about ours or their own occasions, to have commerce with you, we desire and hope they shall have no worse dealing or entertainment than formerly we have had amongst you, and do resolve accordingly to give no worse respect to you or yours, than formerly you have found amongst us, according to the condition and manner of our country.

Narrangansett, this present May the 24th, 1644.
PESSICUS, His marke.
CONANICUS, His marke.

QUESTIONS

1. On what grounds and for what reasons did Conanicus, Pessicus, and the Narragansetts submit to the authority of Charles I? On what grounds and in what terms did the sachems characterize their relationship to Massachusetts Bay Colony?

2. In what ways did the Narragansetts use ideas brought to North America by the English to defend their own sovereignty?

2.6. VISUAL DOCUMENT: SIMON VAN DE PASSE AND COMPTON HOLLAND, PORTRAIT OF POCAHONTAS (1616)

In 1616, Pocahontas, along with her husband John Rolfe, their infant son Thomas, an advisor to Powhatan named Uttamatomakin, and at least six Algonquian attendants, visited England. Officials of the struggling Virginia Company saw an opportunity to publicize the firm's work and shore up its precarious finances. They commissioned a Dutch-German artist, Simon Van de Passe, to sketch Pocahontas's portrait, from which Compton Holland made the engraving shown below. The English inscription underneath the engraving translates the Latin words that surround her image and also identifies her as a Christian convert married to John Rolfe and her father as "Emperor of Attanoughskomouck," which the English usually called Tsenacommacah. Although the engraving claims that she was 21 years old at the time of its making, she was probably only 19.

QUESTIONS

1. In what ways does Pocahontas's portrait differ from that of Eiakintomino in Chapter 2 of the text? Remember that the Virginia Company either used or sought to use both images for promotional purposes, and that its officials considered Pocahontas to be "nobility."

2. Did Pocahontas influence how Van de Passe portrayed her? What elements of the portrait and its captions suggest that she did?

Source: Virginia Historical Society, Richmond, Virginia, USA/The Bridgeman Art Library.

CHAPTER 3

FORGING TIGHTER BONDS, 1640 TO THE 1690s

3.1. BARBADOS ASSEMBLY, EXCERPTS FROM "AN ACT FOR THE BETTER ORDERING AND GOVERNING OF NEGROES" (1661)

Barbados became a black majority colony in the early 1660s, only two decades after the boom in sugar production that transformed the island began. Below are excerpts from a law that Barbados legislators passed in 1661 to address those developments. It was the first comprehensive slave code created in English North America and as such served as the model for the slave codes of several other colonies, including Jamaica, Antigua, South Carolina, and Georgia.

*W*hereas heretofore many good Laws and ordinances have been made for the governing, regulating and ordering the Negroes, Slaves in this Isle, and sundry punishments appointed to many their misdemeanour, crimes, and offences which yet not met the effect hath been desired and might have been reasonably expected had the Master of Families and other the Inhabitants of this Isle been so careful of their obedience and compliance with the said Laws as they ought to have been. And these former Laws being in many clauses imperfect and not fully comprehending the true constitution of this Government in relation of their Slaves their Negroes an heathenish brutish and an uncertain dangerous pride of people to whom if surely in any thing we may extend the legislative power given us of punishionary[1] Laws for the benefit and good of this plantation, not being contradictory to the Laws of England, there being in all the body of that Law no track to guide us where to walk nor any rule set us how to govern such Slaves, yet we well know by the right rule of reason and order, we are not to leave

Source: Stanley Engerman, Seymour Drescher, and Robert Paquette, eds., *Slavery* (New York: Oxford University Press, 2001), 105–13. The editors transcribed the excerpt from "An Act for the Better Ordering and Governing of Negroes" (Barbados, 1661), CO 30/2/16–26 (Public Record Office, Kew, United Kingdom), 25–28, 32–33.

1. Punitive.

them to the Arbitrary, cruel, and outrageous wills of every evil disposed person, but so far to protect them as we do many other goods and Chattels, and also somewhat further as being created Men though without the knowledge of God in the world, we have therefore upon mature and serious Consideration of the premises thought good to renew and revive whatsoever we have found necessary and useful in the former Laws of this Isle concerning the ordering and governing of Negroes and to add thereunto such further Laws and ordinances as at this time we think absolute needful for the public safety and may prove to the future behoveful to the peace and utility of this Isle by this Act repealing and dissolving all other former Laws made concerning the said Negroes and for the time to come.

CLAUSE I

Be it enacted published and declared...that no Master, Mistress, Commander, or Overseer of any family within this Island shall give their Negroes leave on Sabbath days, Holy days or at any other time to go out of their plantations except such Negroes as usually wait upon them at home and abroad, and them with a ticket under his Master, Mistress, Commander, or Overseers' hand, the said Ticket specifying the time of his or her coming from the plantation and the time allowed for his or her return, and no other Negroes except upon necessary business, and then to send a Christian or Negroes' Overseer along with them with a Ticket as aforesaid upon forfeiting for every Negro so limited to go abroad 500 pounds of Muscavado sugar....And if any Master, Mistress, Commander or Overseer of any plantation shall find any Negro or Negroes at any time in their plantation with out a Ticket and business from his said Master and not apprehend them or endeavour so to do, and having apprehended them and shall not punish them by a moderate whipping, shall forfeit 500 pounds of the like sugar to be disposed of as aforesaid....

CLAUSE 2

...if any Negro man or woman shall offer any Violence to any Christian as by striking or the like, the Negro shall for his and their first offence, by

information given to the next Justice of the Peace, be severely whipped by the Constable by order of the said Justice, for the serious offence of that nature by order of the said Justice of Peace he shall be severely whipped, his nose slit and be burned in face and for his third offence he shall receive by order of the Governor and Council such greater Corporal punishment as they shall think meet to inflict, providing always that such striking or conflict be not in the Lawful defence of their Master, Mistress or owner of their families, or of their goods.

CLAUSE 3

...the Negroes shall have clothes to cover their nakedness once every year (that is to say) drawers and caps for men and petticoats for women; And whereas the inhabitants of the Isles have much suffered by the running away of the Negroes and by the keeping such Runaways or fugitive Negroes by several persons in their plantations.

CLAUSE 4

...that all persons that are now possessed of any fugitive or Runaway Negroes do within six days after publication of this Act in the parish Church bring them in, and to their proper owners or into the custody of the Provost Marshall for the time being or his appointed deputy at the Town of St Michael's upon pain of paying of ten thousand pounds of good merchantable Muscavado sugar for damage unto the owner....And if any Christian Servant so possessed of any such Negro or Negroes not acquainting his Master thereof do neglect or fail to bring them before the time limited as is before enjoined, the said Servant shall immediately upon Conviction thereof receive nine and thirty lashes upon his naked back...and after Execution of his time of service shall serve the owner of the said Negro...seven years....

CLAUSE 5

...that all overseers of plantations do twice every week search their Negro houses for Runaway Negroes and what overseer shall neglect to do the same shall forfeit 100 pounds of sugar for every default....

CLAUSE 6

...whosoever hereafter shall take up any Runaway Negro...shall with forty eight hours after bring the said Runaway to his proper owner or to the Provost Marshall or his deputy upon pain of forfeiting for every day they shall keep such Negro or Negroes beyond the said forty-eight hours and thereof be convicted by Confession or Verdict the sum or quantity of one thousand pounds of merchantable Muscavado sugar, to be levied...upon the person so neglecting to bring the said Runaway upon his Lands, goods, or Chattels....And if the said person or persons informing be Servant or Servants to the party so delivering the said Negro that the said person or persons so informing shall be from thenceforth absolutely free and clear from his service any Indenture or Contract to the contrary notwithstanding....

CLAUSE 11

...that every overseer of a family in this Isle shall cause all his Negro houses to be searched diligently and effectually once every fourteen days for clubs, wooden swords, or other mischievous weapons and finding any to take them away and cause them to be burned....

CLAUSE 17

...that if any Negro shall make Insurrection or rise in rebellion against the place or people or make preparation of Arms, powder or offensive Weapons or hold any Council or conspiracy for raising Mutinies or rebellion in the Isle as hath been formerly attempted, that then for the speedy remedy thereof the Governor of the Isle or the superior officer for the time being appoint a Colonel and the field officers of the Regiment of the Island or any four of them to meet in Council and proceed by Martial Law against the Actors, Contrivers, raisers, fomenters and Concealers of such Mutiny or rebellion and them punish by death or other pain as their Crimes shall deserve. And as the aforesaid Colonel or field officers or any four of them shall seem fit.

And that no Master, Mistress or Commander of a family should be frighted by fear of loss to search into and discover their own Negroes so evilly intended.

CLAUSE 18

It is further enacted and ordained that the loss of Negroes so executed shall be born by the public and when the present Treasury is not sufficient to satisfy the loss, a public Levy to be presently made upon the Inhabitants for reparation of the same.

And whereas diverse Negroes are and long since have been Runaway into Woods and other fastness of the Isle do continually much mischief to several the Inhabitants of this Island hiding themselves sometimes in one place and sometimes in another so that with much difficulty they are to be found unless by some sudden surprise.

CLAUSE 19

...it shall, and may be lawful for any Justice of the peace, Constable or Captain of a Company within this Isle that shall have notice of the residence or hiding-place of any Runaway Negro, fugitive and outlaws to raise any Number of Men not exceeding twenty, to apprehend or take them either alive or dead. And for every Negro which they shall take alive being Runaway from the said Master above six Months they shall receive five hundred pounds of sugar. And for every Negro which hath been Runaway above [blank in text] Months one thousand pounds of sugar from the owner, Master, or Commander of the said Negro if killed they shall receive five hundred pounds of Muscavado sugar from the public....

CLAUSE 20

...that if any Negro under punishment of his Master or his Order for running away or any other Crimes or misdemeanour towards his said Master shall suffer in life or in Member, no person whatsoever shall be accomptable to any Law therefore, But if any Man whatsoever shall of wantonness or only mindedness and cruel intention wilfully kill any Negro of his own, he shall pay unto the public Treasury three thousand of Muscavado sugar, but if he shall kill another man's he shall pay unto the owner of the Negro double the value and into the public Treasure five thousand pounds of Muscavado sugar....But if any poor small freeholder or other person kill a Negro by night out of the Common path and stealing the provision, swine, or other goods he shall not be accomptable for it, any Law, Statute or ordinance to the contrary notwithstanding....

And because the Negroes of this Isle in these late years past are very much increased and grown to such a great number as cannot be safely or easily governed unless we have a considerable number of Christians to balance and equal their Strength and the richest Men in the Island looking for the present profit, stock themselves only with almost all Negroes neglecting Christians Servants and so consequently their own and public safety.

CLAUSE 22

Be it therefore enacted...that within twelve Months after publication hereof every freeholder provide himself of one Christian Servant for every twenty Acres of Land that he enjoys or possesses. And from the said twelve Months forward that every freeholder possessed of thirty Acres of land or more keep no less than one Man Servant for twenty Acres of Land he is Master,

owner or occupier of, upon the penalty of forfeiting three thousand pounds of Muscavado sugar....

QUESTIONS

1. On what grounds do the authors of this legislation argue that it was necessary? On what precedents do they draw to draft the law?

2. Compare the language used to describe enslaved people and distinguish them from others in this document and the language used in Azurara's narrative of the start of the Atlantic slave trade (Document 1.2). In what ways are they similar? Why, in your view, are they similar, and what does that reveal about white Barbadians' understanding of race in the 1660s?

3. What, judging from this legislation, were the chief concerns of the Barbados Assembly when its members sought to (to paraphrase them) "better order and govern" Africans and Afro-Barbadians? In what ways and by what means did the Assembly's members seek to enforce the law's provisions?

3.2. "THE TRAPPAN'D MAIDEN" (c. 1600s)

For most of the 17th century, colonists of means in Virginia and Maryland depended on indentured servants from England to sustain and expand their enterprises. Although the majority of indentured servants were young men between the ages of 16 and 24, as many as one in three were women, most of them young. Word of the rigors of American servitude crossed the Atlantic, where such news helped give rise to popular ballads like the one below, entitled "The Trappan'd Maiden." Ordinary Englishmen and women coined the term "trappaned" in the mid-17th century to describe someone who had been tricked or deceived into a situation that resulted in ruin or loss.

This Girl was cunningly Trappan'd, sent to Virginny from England, Where she doth Hardship undergo, there is no Cure it must be so: But if she lives to cross the Main, she vows she'll ne'r go there again.

Tune of *Virginny*, or, *When that I was weary, weary, O*.
Give ear unto a Maid, that lately was betray'd,
And sent into Virginny, O:

Source: C. H. Firth, *An American Garland, Being a Collection of Ballads Relating to America, 1563–1759* (Oxford: B. H. Blackwell, 1915), 51–53.

In brief I shall declare, what I have suffer'd there,
When that I was weary, weary, weary, weary, O.

[Since] that first I came to this Land of Fame,
Which is called Virginny, O,
The Axe and the Hoe have wrought my overthrow,
When that I was weary, weary, weary, weary O.

Five years served I, under Master Guy,
In the land of Virginny, O,
Which made me for to know sorrow, grief and woe,
When that I was weary, weary, weary, weary O.

When my Dame says "Go" then I must do so,
In the land of Virginny, O;
When she sits at Meat, then I have none to eat,
When that I am weary, weary, weary, weary, O.

The Cloath[e]s that I brought in, they are worn
      very thin,
In the land of Virginny, O,
Which makes me for to say, "Alas, and Well-a-day!"
When that I am weary, weary, weary, weary, O.

Instead of Beds of Ease, to lye down when I please,
In the Land of Virginny, O;
Upon a bed of straw, I lye down full of woe,
When that I am weary, weary, weary, weary, O.

Then the Spider, she, daily waits on me,
In the Land of Virginny, O;
Round about my bed, she spins her web [of thread],
When that I am weary, weary, weary, weary, O.

So soon as it is day, to work I must away,
In the Land of Virginny, O;
Then my Dame she knocks, with her tinder-box,
When that I am weary, weary, weary, weary, O.

I have play'd my part both at Plow and Cart,
In the Land of Virginny, O;
Billets from the Wood upon my back they load,
When that I am weary, weary, weary, weary, O.

Instead of drinking Beer, I drink the water clear,
In the Land of Virginny, O;
Which makes me pale and wan, do all that e'er I can,
When that I am weary, weary, weary, weary, O.

If my Dame says "Go!" I dare not say no,
In the Land of Virginny, O;

The Water from the Spring, upon my head I bring,
When that I am weary, weary, weary, weary, O.

When the Mill doth stand, I'm ready at
      command,
In the Land of Virginny, O;
The Morter for to make, which makes my heart
      to ake,
When that I am weary, weary, weary, weary, O.

When the Child doth cry, I must sing "By-a-by!"
In the Land of Virginny, O;
No rest that I can have, whilst I am here a Slave,
When that I am weary, weary, weary, weary, O.

A thousand woes beside, that I do here abide,
In the Land of Virginny, O;
In misery I spend my time that hath no end,
When that I am weary, weary, weary, weary, O.

Then let Maids beware, all by my ill-fare,
In the Land of Virginny, O;
Be sure to stay at home, for if you do here come,
You all will be weary, weary, weary, weary, O.

But if it be my chance, Homewards to advance,
From the Land of Virginny, O;
If that I, once more, land on English Shore,
I'll no more be weary, weary, weary, weary, O.

QUESTIONS

1. What impressions of indentured servitude and
    Virginia does "The Trappan'd Maiden" convey,
    particularly to young women who might have con-
    templated journeying to North America? In what
    ways does the song contrast life in Virginia with
    life in England?

2. Does the song provide an accurate and representa-
    tive portrait of indentured servitude, especially for
    women, in Virginia? Use what you have learned
    from reading Chapters 2 and 3 of the text to con-
    struct your answer.

3. Imagine that Anne Orthwood were to add some
    lyrics to "The Trappan'd Maiden" to reflect her or-
    deal in Virginia. What would she say? Write at least
    one additional stanza, consistent with the style
    and language of the ballad, that would express
    Orthwood's experience.

3.3. COMMITTEE OF THE MASSACHUSETTS BAY GENERAL COURT, "A MEMORANDUM OF INDIAN CHILDREN PUT FORTH INTO SERVICE TO THE ENGLISH" (1676)

In the wake of King Philip's War, New England colonists forced many Indian captives to become bound laborers. Those deemed too dangerous to remain in New England—mostly men, but also some boys (likely including Metacom's son)—were enslaved and sold in the West Indies. Indian children, including many orphaned by their parents' death in conflict or by execution by colonial authorities, became indentured servants. Below is a memorandum prepared by a committee that Massachusetts Bay legislators charged to bind out Indian children to colonists. One committee member, Daniel Gookin Sr., openly sympathized with the plight of Christian Indians during and after the war.

Beeing of those indians that came in & submitted with John Sachem of Packachooge, with the names of the persons with whome they were placed & the names and age of the children & the names of their relations & the places they Did belong to, By Mr Daniel Gookin Sen[r], Thomas Prentis Capt' & M[r] Edward Oakes, who were a comittee appointed by the Counsel to mannage y[t2] affayr. The termes & conditions vpon w[ch] they are to serve is to be ordered by the Gen[ll] Court who are to provide y[t] the children bee religiously educated & taught to read the English tounge

2 Boy A maid	To Samuel Simonds Esq. a boy named John his father named Alwitankus late of quantisit his father & mother p[r]ent[3] both consenting the boys age about 12 years To him a girle named Hester her father & mother dead late of Nashaway her age ten years her onkel named John woosumpigin of Naticke
1 Boy	To Thomas Danforth esq a boy aged about 13 yeares his name John
1 Boy	To Leift Jonathan Danforth of [Billericay?] a boy aged twelve yeares, son to papamech alius David late of Warwick or Cowesit.
2 Boyes	To Mathew Bridge of CamBridge two Boyes the one named Jabez aged about ten yeares the other named Joseph aged six yeares their father named woompthe late of Packachooge ☞ one or both these boyes is away with his father 8 ber[4] 17th 1676
3 A boy & two Girls	To M[r] Jerimiah Shepard of Rowley a boy named Absolom his father of the same name late of Manehage aged about ten yeares. To him a girle sister to the Lad named Sarah aged eleven yeares. These [illegible] of

Source: Proceedings of the Colonial Society of Massachusetts 19 (1918): 25–28.

2. that.
3. An abbreviation for "present."
4. October.

Naticke.

To him another girle aged about 8 yeares her named Jane her father & mother dead.

1 Mayd — To Mʳˢ Mitchell of Cambridg widow a maid named Margaret aged about twelve yeares, her father named Suhunnick of quantisit her mother dead.

1 Boy — To Thomas Jacob of Ipswich a boy aged ten yeares, on wennaputanan his guardian & on upacunt of quantisitt his grand mother was present. The Boy [illegible].

1 Boy — To on Goodman Read a Tanner of cambridge a Boy named John aged about thirteen yeares his father Dead.

1 Boy — To Mʳ Jacob Green of Charel Towne a boy aged about seaven yeares his parrents Dead Late of quantisit but his mother of Narraganset.

1 Boy — To Thomas Woolson of Wattertowne a boy aged about 14 yeares his name John his father dead who was of Cowesit or warwick, his mother pʳsent.

1 Boy — To Ciprian Steuens of Rumny Marsh but late of Lancaster a boy aged about six yeares son to nohanet of Chobnakonkonon. The Boy named Samuel.

1 Mayd — To Thomas Eliot of Boston a carpenter a maid aged about ten yeares her name Rebecka.

1 Boy — To Jacob Green Junior of Charles towne a Boy named Peter aged nine years his father dead his mother pʳsent named nannantum of quantisit.

1 Boy — To on Goodman Greenland a carpenter of Charles towne on misticke side a boy named Tom aged twelve yeares his father named santeshe of Pakachooge.

1 Girle — To Mʳ Edmund Batter of Salem a maid named Abigal aged sixteen her mother a widow named quanshishe late of Shookannet Beyond mendon.

2 a Boy A girle — To Daniel Gookin Senʳ A Boy named Joshua aged about eight yeares son to William wunuko late of magunkoog; his father dead.

To him a girle aged about six yeares daughter to the widdow quinshiske late of Shookanet beyond mendon

1 Girle — To Andrew Bordman Tayler of cambridge a girle named Anne sister to yᵉ Last named.

1 Boy — To Thomas Prentis Junior son to Capt Prentis of Cambridge village a boy named John son to William Wunnako late of magnkoy that was executed for Thomas Burney, aged thirteen.

1 Boy — To Benjamin Mills of Dedham a boy aged about six years is [named?] Joseph Spoonans late of Marlboro.

1 Boy — To Mʳ Edward Jackson a Boy named Joseph aged about 12 yeares Late of magalygook cosen[5] to Pyambow of Naticke.

1 Mayd — To Widdow Jackson of Cambridge village a girle named Hope aged nine yeare her parents dead who wer of Narraganset.

1 Boy — To old Goodman Myles of Dedham a boy of [ ] yeares old. son to Annaweeken Decesed who was late of Hassanamesit his mother pʳsent.

1 Boy — To Capt. Thomas Prentis a Boy named Joseph son to Annaweken decesed Brother to the last named aged about 11 yeares ☞ this boy was after taken from Capt Prentice & sent up Mʳ Stoughton for [ ] Capt Prentis is to bee considered about it for hee has taken more care & paynes about those indians.

1 Boy — To John Smith of Dedham a boy aged about eight yeares his father dead late of Marlborow hee is Brother to James Printers wife

1 Mayd — To Mʳ John Flint [?] of Concord a mayd aged about [ ] yeares [illegible]

1 Boy — To Mʳ Jonathan Wade of mistick a Boy named Tom Aged about 11 yeares sonne to William Wunakhow of Magunkgog deceased

1 Mayd — To Mʳ Nathaniel Wade of mistick a maid aged about ten years daughter to Jame Natomet [?] late of Packachooge her father & mother dead

---

5. Cousin.

It is humbly proposed to the Honble Generall Court, to set the time these children shall serve; & if not less y^n[6] till they come to 20 yeares of age. unto wch those y^t had relations seemed willing. and also that the Court lay som penalty upon them if they runne away before the time expire & on their parents or kindred y^t shall entice or harborr & conceale y^m[7] if they should runne away.

Signed By the Comitee

Above named   Daniel Gookin Senr Edward Oakes.

Cambridge
8 ber 28 1676

1. Under what terms were the Indian children bound out to colonists to serve?
2. What can you learn about the lives of Indian children from this memorandum? What does it tell you about the circumstances that brought them to be bound out and the lives that they might have lived once they became servants?
3. In what ways are the information contained and the values expressed in this memorandum similar to those in the *repartimiento* order for Indians on Española in 1514 (Document 1.4)? In what ways do they differ?

3.4. EXCERPTS FROM THE INTERROGATIONS OF JOSEPHE AND PEDRO NARANJO ON THE PUEBLO WAR FOR INDEPENDENCE (1681)

According to contemporary accounts, the coordinated attacks that drove the Spanish colonists from New Mexico in 1680 took the Spanish by surprise. As they regrouped after having fled for their lives, Spanish leaders, included the colony's governor Antonio de Otermín, sought to collect as much information as they could about what had happened. A key part of that process was the interrogation of Pueblo prisoners. Below are excerpts from the interrogation of two such prisoners, conducted in late 1681.

DECLARATION OF JOSEPHE, SPANISH-SPEAKING INDIAN

[Place of the Río del Norte, December 19, 1681.]

...[O]n the 19th day of the month of December, 1681,...his lordship caused to appear before him an Indian prisoner named Josephe, able to speak the Castilian language, a servant of Sargento Mayor Sebastián de Herrera who fled from him and went among the apostates....

Asked what causes or motives the said Indian rebels had for renouncing the law of God and obedience to his Majesty, and for committing so many kinds of crimes, and who were the instigators of the rebellion, and what he had heard while he was among the apostates, he said that the prime movers of the rebellion

---

Source: Charles Wilson Hackett, ed., *Revolt of the Pueblo Indians of New Mexico and Otermín's Attempted Reconquest 1680–1682*, vol. 9 (Albuquerque: University of New Mexico Press, 1942), 238–42, 245–49.

6. Than.
7. Them.

were two Indians of San Juan, one named El Popé and the other El Taqu, and another from Taos named Saca, and another from San Ildefonso named Francisco. He knows that these were the principals, and the causes they gave were alleged ill treatment and injuries received from the present secretary, Francisco Xavier, and the maestre de campo, Alonso García, and from the sargentos mayores, Luis de Quintana and Diego López, because they beat them, took away what they had, and made them work without pay. Thus he replies.

Asked if he has learned or it has come to his notice during the time that he has been here the reason why the apostates burned the images, churches, and things pertaining to divine worship, making a mockery and a trophy of them, killing the priests and doing the other things they did, he said that he knows and has heard it generally stated that while they were besieging the villa the rebellious traitors burned the church and shouted in loud voices, "Now the God of the Spaniards, who was their father, is dead, and Santa María, who was their mother, and the saints, who were pieces of rotten wood," saying that only their own god lived. Thus they ordered all the temples and images, crosses and rosaries burned, and this function being over, they all went to bathe in the rivers, saying that they thereby washed away the water of baptism. For their churches, they placed on the four sides and in the center of the plaza some small circular enclosures of stone where they went to offer flour, feathers, and the seed of maguey, maize, and tobacco, and performed other superstitious rites, giving the children to understand that they must all do this in the future. The captains and chiefs ordered that the names of Jesus and of Mary should nowhere be uttered, and that they should discard their baptismal names, and abandon the wives whom God had given them in matrimony, and take the ones that they pleased. He saw that as soon as the remaining Spaniards had left, they ordered all

the *estufas*[8] erected, which are their houses of idolatry, and danced throughout the kingdom the dance of the *cazina*[9], making many masks for it in the image of the devil....

...He said that what he has stated in his declaration is the truth and what he knows, under charge of his oath, which he affirms and ratifies, this, his said declaration, being read to him. He did not sign because of not knowing how, nor does he know his age. Apparently he is about twenty years old.

DECLARATION OF PEDRO NARANJO OF THE QUERES NATION

[Place of the Río del Norte, December 19, 1681.]

In the said plaza de armas...his lordship caused to appear before him an Indian prisoner named Pedro Naranjo, a native of the pueblo of San Felipe, of the Queres nation, who was captured in the advance and attack upon the pueblo of La Isleta. He makes himself understood very well in the Castilian language and speaks his mother tongue and the Tegua....

Asked whether he knows the reason or motives which the Indians of this kingdom had for rebelling, forsaking the law of God and obedience to his Majesty, and committing such grave and atrocious crimes, and who were the leaders and principal movers, and by whom and how it was ordered; and why they burned the images, temples, crosses, rosaries, and things of divine worship, committing such atrocities as killing priests, Spaniards, women, and children, and the rest that he might know touching the question, he said that since the government of Señor General Hernando Ugarte y la Concha they have planned to rebel on various occasions through conspiracies of the Indian sorcerers, and that although in some pueblos the messages were accepted, in other parts they would not agree to it....Finally, in the past years, at the summons of an Indian named Popé who is said to

---

8. By "estufas" the interrogators meant kivas, the cave-like structures in which Pueblos held religious ceremonies and reenacted their creation.

9. Katsinas, the ancestral and otherworldly beings whom the Pueblos believed brought rain and harmony.

have communication with the devil, it happened that in an estufa of the pueblo of Los Taos there appeared to the said Popé three figures of Indians who never came out of the estufa. They gave the said Popé to understand that they were going underground to the lake of Copala. He saw these figures emit fire from all the extremities of their bodies...and these three beings spoke to the said Popé, who was in hiding from the secretary, Francisco Xavier, who wished to punish him as a sorcerer. They told him to make a cord of maguey fiber and tie some knots in it which would signify the number of days that they must wait before the rebellion. He said that the cord was passed through all the pueblos of the kingdom so that the ones which agreed to it [the rebellion] might untie one knot in sign of obedience, and by the other knots they would know the days which were lacking; and this was to be done on pain of death to those who refused to agree to it....The said cord was taken from pueblo to pueblo by the swiftest youths under the penalty of death if they revealed the secret. Everything being thus arranged, two days before the time set for its execution, because his lordship had learned of it and had imprisoned two Indian accomplices from the pueblo of Tesuque, it was carried out prematurely that night, because it seemed to them that they were now discovered; and they killed religious, Spaniards, women, and children. This being done, it was proclaimed in all the pueblos that everyone in common should obey the commands of their father whom they did not know, which would be given through El Caydi or El Popé. This was heard by Alonso Catití, who came to the pueblo of this declarant to say that everyone must unite to go to the villa to kill the governor and the Spaniards who had remained with him, and that he who did not obey would, on their return, be beheaded; and in fear of this they agreed to it. Finally the señor governor and those who were with him escaped from the siege, and later this declarant saw that as soon as the Spaniards had left the kingdom an order came from the said Indian, Popé, in which he commanded all the Indians to break the lands and enlarge their cultivated fields, saying that now they were as they had been in ancient times, free from the labor they had performed for the religious and the Spaniards, who could not now be alive.

He said that this is the legitimate cause and the reason they had for rebelling, because they had always desired to live as they had when they came out of the lake of Copala....

Asked for what reason they so blindly burned the images, temples, crosses, and other things of divine worship, he stated that the said Indian, Popé, came down in person, and with him El Saca and El Chato from the pueblo of Los Taos, and other captains and leaders and many people who were in his train, and he ordered in all the pueblos through which he passed that they instantly break up and burn the images of the holy Christ, the Virgin Mary and the other saints, the crosses, and everything pertaining to Christianity, and that they burn the temples, break up the bells, and separate from the wives whom God had given them in marriage and take those whom they desired. In order to take away their baptismal names, the water, and the holy oils, they were to plunge into the rivers and wash themselves with amole, which is a root native to the country, washing even their clothing, with the understanding that there would thus be taken from them the character of the holy sacraments. They did this, and also many other things which he does not recall, given to understand that this mandate had come from the Caydi and the other two who emitted fire from their extremities in the said estufa of Taos, and that they thereby returned to the state of their antiquity, as when they came from the lake of Copala; that this was the better life and the one they desired, because the God of the Spaniards was worth nothing and theirs was very strong, the Spaniard's God being rotten wood. These things were observed and obeyed by all except some who, moved by the zeal of Christians, opposed it, and such persons the said Popé caused to be killed immediately. He saw to it that they at once erected and rebuilt their houses of idolatry which they call estufas, and made very ugly masks in imitation of the devil in order to dance the dance of the cacina; and he said likewise that the devil had given them to understand that living thus in accordance with the law of their ancestors, they would harvest a great deal of maize, many beans, a great abundance of cotton, calabashes, and very large watermelons and cantaloupes; and that they could erect their houses and enjoy abundant health and leisure. As he has said, the people were very much pleased, living at their ease in this life of their antiquity, which was the chief cause of their falling into such laxity. Following what has already been stated, in order to terrorize them further and cause them to observe the diabolical commands, there came to them a pronouncement from the three demons already described, and from El Popé, to the effect that he who might still keep in his heart a regard for the priests, the governor, and the Spaniards would be known from his unclean face and clothes, and would be punished.

...His declaration being read to him, he affirmed and ratified all of it. He declared himself to be eighty years of age, and he signed it with his lordship and the interpreters and assisting witnesses, before me, the secretary.

QUESTIONS

1. What, according to Josephe and Pedro Naranjo, prompted the uprising that drove the Spanish from New Mexico?
2. What did the Pueblos hope to achieve after they won their independence?

3.5. GERMANTOWN QUAKER MEETING, "REASONS WHY WE ARE AGAINST THE TRAFFIC OF MEN-BODY" (1688)

As Pennsylvania's population and economy grew rapidly during the 1680s, so did the nascent colony's population of enslaved Africans and African Americans, a development that alarmed some. In 1688, four German colonists who belonged to the Germantown Quaker Meeting penned the petition below and requested that the monthly meeting consider it. Included as well are that meeting's response and the responses of the quarterly meeting in Philadelphia and the monthly meeting in Burlington, New Jersey. As Chapter 5 discusses, Pennsylvania Quakers did spearhead an antislavery initiative in the Anglo-Atlantic world, but not until the 1760s.

This is to the monthly meeting held at Richard Worrell's:

These are the reasons why we are against the traffic of men-body, as followeth: Is there any that would be done or handled at this manner? viz., to be sold or made a slave for all the time of his life? How fearful and faint-hearted are many at sea, when they see a strange vessel, being afraid it should be a Turk, and they should be taken, and sold for slaves into Turkey. Now, what is *this* better done, than Turks do? Yea, rather it is worse for them, which say they are Christians; for we hear that the most part of such negers are brought hither against their will and consent, and that many of them are stolen. Now, though they are black, we cannot conceive there is more liberty to have them slaves, as [than] it is to have other white ones. There is a saying, that we should do to all men like as we will be done ourselves; making no

Source: George H. Moore, *Notes on the History of Slavery in Massachusetts* (New York, 1866), 75–78.

difference of what generation, descent, or colour they are. And those who steal or rob men, and those who buy or purchase them, are they not all alike? Here is liberty of conscience, which is right and reasonable; here ought to be likewise liberty of the body, except of evil-doers, which is another case. But to bring men hither, or to rob and sell them against their will, we stand against. In Europe, there are many oppressed for conscience-sake; and here there are those oppressed which are of a black colour. And we who know that men must not commit adultery—some do commit adultery *in* others, separating wives from their husbands, and giving them to others: and some sell the children of these poor creatures to other men. Ah! do consider well this thing, you who do it, if you would be done at this manner—and if it is done according to Christianity! You surpass Holland and Germany in this thing. This makes an ill report in all those countries of Europe, where they hear of [it,] that the Quakers do here handel men as they handel there the cattle. And for that reason some have no mind or inclination to come hither. And who shall maintain this your cause, or plead for it? Truly, we cannot do so, except you shall inform us better hereof, viz.: that Christians have liberty to practise these things. Pray, what thing in the world can be done worse towards us, than if men should rob or steal us away, and sell us for slaves to strange countries; separating husbands from their wives and children. Being now this is not done in the manner we would be done at, [by]; therefore, we contradict, and are against this traffic of men-body. And we who profess that it is not lawful to steal, must, likewise, avoid to purchase such things as are stolen, but rather help to stop this robbing and stealing, if possible. And such men ought to be delivered out of the hands of the robbers, and set free as in Europe. Then is Pennsylvania to have a good report, instead, it hath now a bad one, for this sake, in other countries: Especially whereas the Europeans are desirous to know in what manner *the Quakers* do rule in *their* province; and most of them do look upon us with an envious eye. But if this is done well, what shall we say is done evil?

If once these slaves (which they say are so wicked and stubborn men,) should join themselves—fight for their freedom, and handel their masters and mistresses, as they did handel them before; will these masters and mistresses take the sword at hand and war against these poor slaves, like, as we are able to believe, some will not refuse to do? Or, have these poor negroes not as much right to fight for their freedom, as you have to keep them slaves?

Now consider well this thing, if it is good or bad. And in case you find it to be good to handel these blacks in that manner, we desire and require you hereby lovingly, that you may inform us herein, which at this time never was done, viz., that Christians have such a liberty to do so. To the end we shall be satisfied on this point, and satisfy likewise our good friends and acquaintances in our native country, to whom it is a terror, or fearful thing, that men should be handelled so in Pennsylvania.

This is from our meeting at Germantown, held ye 18th of the 2d month, 1688, to be delivered to the monthly meeting at Richard Worrell's.

Garret Henderich,
Derick op de Graeff,
Francis Daniel Pastorius,
Abram op de Graeff.

At our monthly meeting, at Dublin, ye 30th 2d mo., 1688, we having inspected ye matter, above mentioned, and considered of it, we find it so weighty that we think it not expedient for us to meddle with it *here*, but do rather commit it to ye consideration of ye quarterly meeting; ye tenor of it being related to ye truth.

On behalf of ye monthly meeting, Jo. Hart.

This above mentioned, was read in our quarterly meeting, at Philadelphia, the 4th of ye 4th mo., '88, and was from thence recommended to the yearly meeting, and the above said Derrick, and the other two mentioned therein, to present the same to ye above said meeting, it being a thing of too great weight for this meeting to determine.

Signed by order of ye meeting.
Anthony Morris.

The minutes of the Yearly Meeting, held at Burlington in the same year, record the result of this first effort among the Quakers.

At a Yearly Meeting, held at Burlington the 5th day of the 7th Month, 1688.

A paper being here presented by some German Friends Concerning the Lawfulness & Unlawfulness of Buying & Keeping of Negroes It was adjudged not to be so proper for this Meeting to give a Positive Judgment in the Case It having so general a Relation to many other Parts & therefore at present they Forbear It.

QUESTIONS

1. On what grounds do Pastorius and his peers oppose slavery and the Atlantic slave trade? Keep in mind as you answer that they were Quaker men writing to other Quakers in 1688.
2. What became of the Germantown petition? In what manner did superior meetings respond to it?
3. Are there similarities in the ideas expressed in this petition, which opposes slavery, and the Barbados law (Document 3.1), which sought to strengthen it? If so, what are they and what explains those similarities? If not, why not?

3.6. VISUAL DOCUMENT: RICHARD FORD, *A NEW MAP OF THE ISLAND OF BARBADOES* (1674)

In 1674, Richard Ford made the map below of the island of Barbados. Published in England, it was the first economic map of an English American colony ever printed and soon became part of an atlas of maps that England's Office of Trade and Plantations compiled in the 1680s. Ford's map features the name of each plantation, usually named after its owner, as well as the sugar mills that produced the island's main export.

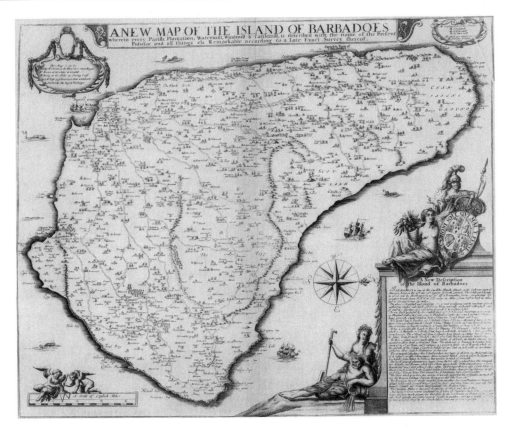

QUESTIONS

1. What can you learn about Barbados in the 1670s from Ford's map? What impression of Barbados did Ford seek to give English users of his map?

2. After closely examining the map and reading the captions that accompany it, what features of life and society in Barbados did Ford choose to ignore or leave out?

Source: Courtesy of the John Carter Brown Library at Brown University.

CHAPTER 4

ACCELERATING THE PACE OF CHANGE, c. 1690–1730

4.1. EXCERPTS FROM SAUKAMAPPEE'S ACCOUNT OF THE ADVENT OF HORSES AND GUNS TO THE BLACKFEET, AS TOLD TO DAVID THOMPSON (1787–1788)

Fur trader David Thompson spent part of the winter of 1787–1788 living among the Piegans, who belonged to the Blackfoot Confederacy and lived in what is today Montana. While there, he met Saukamappee, a Cree whom the Piegans had adopted. Saukamappee, then probably in his late seventies, told Thompson about his youth and Piegan history. Here Saukamappee recalls a battle that took place around 1730 between the Piegans and their allies, who were armed with guns and metal weapons, and their longtime foes, the Shoshones (whom Saukamappee and his people called "Snakes"), who fought on horseback. He also recounts what the Piegans did after their victory.

By this time the affairs of both parties had much changed; we had more guns and iron headed arrows than before; but our enemies the Snake Indians and their allies had Misstutim (Big Dogs, that is, Horses) on which they rode, swift as the Deer, on which they dashed at the Peeagans, and with their stone Pukamoggan knocked them on the head, and they had thus lost several of their best men. This news we did not well comprehend and it alarmed us, for we had no idea of Horses and could not make out what they were. Only three of us went and I should not have gone, had not my wife's relations frequently intimated, that her father's medicine bag would be honored by the scalp of a Snake Indian. When we came to our allies, the great War Tent [was made] with speeches, feasting and dances as before; and when the War Chief had viewed us all it was found between us and the Stone Indians we had ten guns and each of us about thirty balls, and powder for the war, and we were considered the strength of the battle. After a few days march our scouts brought us word that the enemy was near in a large war party, but had no Horses with them, for at that time they had very few of them. When we came to meet each other, as usual, each displayed their

Source: Richard Glover, ed., *David Thompson's Narrative, 1784–1812* (Toronto: Champlain Society, 1962), 241–43.

numbers, weapons and shiel[d]s, in all which they were superior to us, except our guns which were not shown, but kept in their leathern cases, and if we had shown [them], they would have taken them for long clubs. For a long time they held us in suspense; a tall Chief was forming a strong party to make an attack on our centre, and the others to enter into combat with those opposite to them; We prepared for the battle the best we could. Those of us who had guns stood in the front line, and each of us [had] two balls in his mouth, and a load of powder in his left hand to reload.

We noticed they had a great many short stone clubs for close combat, which is a dangerous weapon, and had they made a bold attack on us, we must have been defeated as they were more numerous and better armed than we were, for we could have fired our guns no more than twice; and were at a loss what to do on the wide plain, and each Chief encouraged his men to stand firm. Our eyes were all on the tall Chief and his motions, which appeared to be contrary to the advice of several old Chiefs, all this time we were about the strong flight of an arrow from each other. At length the tall chief retired and they formed their long usual line by placing their shields on the ground to touch each other, the shield having a breadth of full three feet or more. We sat down opposite to them and most of us waited for the night to make a hasty retreat. The War Chief was close to us, anxious to see the effect of our guns. The lines were too far asunder for us to make a sure shot, and we requested him to close the line to about sixty yards, which was gradually done, and lying flat on the ground behind the shields, we watched our opportunity when they drew their bows to shoot at us, their bodies were then exposed and each of us, as opportunity offered, fired with deadly aim, and either killed, or severely wounded, every one we aimed at.

The War Chief was highly pleased, and the Snake Indians finding so many killed and wounded kept themselves behind their shields; the War Chief then desired we would spread ourselves by two's throughout the line, which we did, and our shots caused consternation and dismay along their whole line. The battle had begun about Noon, and the Sun was not yet half down, when we perceived some of them had crawled away from their shields, and were taking to flight. The War Chief seeing this went along the line and spoke to every Chief to keep his Men ready for a charge of the whole line of the enemy, of which he would give the signal; this was done by himself stepping in front with his Spear, and calling on them to follow him as he rushed on their line, and in an instant the whole of us followed him, the greater part of the enemy took to flight, but some fought bravely and we lost more than ten killed and many wounded; Part of us pursued, and killed a few, but the chase had soon to be given over, for at the body of every Snake Indian killed, there were five or six of us trying to get his scalp, or part of his clothing, his weapons, or something as a trophy of the battle. As there were only three of us, and seven of our friends, the Stone Indians, we did not interfere, and got nothing.

The next morning the War Chief made a speech, praising their bravery, and telling them to make a large War Tent to commemorate their victory, to which they directly set to work and by noon it was finished.

The War Chief now called on all the other Chiefs to assemble their men and come to the Tent. In a short time they came, all those who had lost relations had their faces blackened; those who killed an enemy, or wished to be thought so, had their faces blackened with red streaks on the face, and those who had no pretensions to the one, or the other, had their faces red with ochre. We did not paint our faces until the War Chief told us to paint our foreheads and eyes black, and the rest of the face of dark red ochre, as having carried guns, and to distinguish us from all the rest. Those who had scalps now came forward with the scalps neatly stretched on a round willow with a handle to the frame; they appeared to be more than fifty, and excited loud shouts and the war whoop of victory. When this was over the War Chief told them that if any one had a right to the scalp of an enemy as a war trophy it ought to be us, who with our guns had gained the victory, when from the numbers of our enemies we were anxious to leave the field of battle; and that ten scalps must be given to us; this was soon collected, and he gave to each of us a Scalp.

QUESTIONS

1. How, according to Saukamappee, did the Piegans initially react to Shoshone use of horses, and how did the Shoshones initially react to Piegan use of firearms?
2. How did their use of firearms influence the ways that Piegans regarded Saukamappee and other Crees?

4.2. SUPERIOR COUNCIL OF LOUISIANA, EXCERPTS FROM DEBATES ON WHETHER TO INTERVENE IN A CHOCTAW-CHICKASAW WAR (1723)

In the early years of French Louisiana, the small colony needed to maintain good relations with Indians, and above all, Choctaws, who were often foes of Chickasaws, many of whom allied themselves with English colonists in South Carolina. In July and August 1723, the Superior Council of Louisiana, led by Governor Jean Baptiste Le Moyne, Sieur de Bienville, considered whether to intervene in an ongoing conflict between the two Indian nations. Below are excerpts from their deliberations. A few weeks later, the Council decided to endorse Bienville's recommendations.

Representation made by Mr. de Bienville to the Council, July 23, 1723.

By the letter of the Commissaries . . . it appears that these gentlemen are distressed because of the commerce of the Mississippi to see that we have war with the Chickasaws, and even seem to desire that we grant them peace. However on the representations that I have made them on this subject they are leaving the Council free to decide on war and peace.

That is the reason it is advisable that the Council deliberate seriously on this affair. My opinion is not at all that peace should be granted to this restless and faithless nation, for three reasons. The first is that the Choctaws who are our friends and our allies are pledged to declare war on the Chickasaws only on condition that we should listen to no sort of proposal of peace and [they have promised] that they would continue the war until the entire destruction of this nation, so it would be difficult not to say impossible, to make them change. I have even written to my brother de Chateaugué at Mobile in order to sound them, but they replied [asking] whether I had forgotten my promise and [saying] that now that they had avenged us they intended to avenge the deaths of several Honored Men whom they have lost in this war;

that even if they were given three houses full of presents they would never consent to peace.

The second reason is not less essential than the first. It consists of the danger that there would be in seeing these two large and numerous nations agitated, and we should have to fear that they might combine against us and in that case the mischief would be beyond remedy.

The third reason is not less obvious. If the Chickasaws became our allies and our friends, they would have to renounce all commerce with the English to trade with the French. It is impossible for us to do this because, in addition to the fact that we never have enough merchandise, the English furthermore trade for their peltries at a rate far higher than that at which the French receive them. This would doubtless produce discontentment among these Indians and we should see ourselves every day on the verge of some rupture, and it is even to be feared that if we are still unable to establish at the Choctaws the small warehouse that the Commissaries order in order to supply that nation with the things it needs, they will abandon us. Even as early as last summer they sent some principal chiefs to Carolina to invite the English to come and establish some warehouses among them and

Source: Dunbar Rowland and Albert Godfrey Sanders, eds., *Mississippi Provincial Archives, 1704–1743: French Dominion*, vol. 2 (Jackson, MS: Mississippi Department of Archives and History, 1932), 355–60.

this was promised to them, and recently my brother de Chateaugué informed me that the Emperor of the Kawitas who came to see me assured him that the English were preparing to go next September, six traders with sixty horses loaded with all sorts of merchandise that the Indians like.

When all these considerations have been well thought over and well examined I do not doubt that the Council will be of my opinion since that concerns the preservation of the colony which will always be uncertain and in continual alarms.

The Council is informed that four Chickasaw chiefs have been with me for more than two months who brought back to us one of the two French prisoners whom they had in the hope that that would induce us to grant peace to them more willingly. The other who was hunting when they departed from their village must now be at the Yazoos according to the information about him that has been given me by Mr. Delivilliers, the lieutenant who is in command there. These chiefs in return ask for one of their children eleven to twelve years of age and a woman who is related to them, who are here as slaves. The child still belongs to the Company and the woman has been sold on credit to a German. I do not think that the Council will refuse this exchange which appears to me so much the more just because two of these chiefs are known to all the French as being very fond of us. They made it known in 1720 when their nation declared war on us, [and] when they pillaged and undertook to kill all the Frenchmen who were trading among them. These [chiefs] by their influence saved them and themselves conducted them to the Choctaws. He thinks that such an indication of friendship deserves some compensation on our part, so much the more because it was these two chiefs who stripped themselves of all their goods in order to save the lives of the two Frenchmen when they were brought as prisoners to their village, and as a similar thing might happen in the future if the war with them continues, it is always to be desired that the unfortunate ones who fall into the hands of these barbarians may find a few good Indians who will snatch them from the fire.

At New Orleans, July 23, 1723.
Signed, Bienville.

On the representation above and from other sources, which was not communicated to me by the secretary of the Council until the first of the present month, . . . on the subject of the war that we have stirred up between the Choctaws and the Chickasaws in order to avenge the death of several Frenchmen killed by the said Chickasaws, my opinion is in the situation in which we are because of the few troops that there are in the colony and the posts so remote from each other that they cannot give each other mutual assistance, not one fort in a state of defence, the warehouses unprovided with all provisions and merchandise, a prevalent illness that has attacked everybody in general, to maintain this war between these two nations and to give the Choctaws, a nation that contains nearly eight thousand men, this bone to gnaw, [a nation] which since it is naturally warlike might with the assistance of the English disturb us in the future, and it is to be hoped for the welfare of the colony that all these strong nations may one after another become aroused against each other in order that their destruction may make it impossible for them to unite against us as might happen sooner or later. This opinion appears to me to be so much the more correct because Mr. de Chateaugué has said several times that he did not feel safe at Mobile against the Choctaws although at war with the Chickasaws. It is for this reason above all [others] that I decide to favor the continuation of this war in order to divert these two populous nations, until we are in a position to provide for it otherwise.

At New Orleans, August 3, 1723.
Signed, Le Blond de La Tour.

August 3, 1723.

After having maturely examined and considered the representation of Mr. de Bienville made to the Council on the twenty-third of last July concerning the Chickasaws for deliberation as to whether we ought to continue the war with the said nation or grant them peace as the Commissaries wish to do, the reasons that Mr. de Bienville presents are too strong with reference to the Choctaws who are our friends and allies for [me] not to be of his opinion until different orders are given by my said gentlemen the Commissaries, though I do not doubt that they will approve of it when they are informed of the consequences that are involved in supporting it, which force us to-day to keep our word to the Choctaws if we wish to avoid being at war with them. Nothing furthermore appears more just than to grant the four Chickasaw chiefs one of their children eleven or twelve years of age and a woman related to them, who are slaves here, and even a reward for their zeal for the French whom they have protected and caused to be saved by their influence; all in order to retain them constantly in our friendship and in order that if we continue the war with them the unfortunates who may fall into their hands may find the same favor that the others have had.

Signed, Fazende.

On August 3, 1723.

On the proposal to make war or peace with the Chickasaws I approve heartily Mr. de Bienville's reasons and my opinion is to leave the Choctaws free to make war on them. It appears to me that we owe this latter nation this satisfaction in consideration of the generous manner in which they have conducted themselves in avenging us and who besides it would be a great blessing if it were entirely destroyed. As for the four chiefs who are with Mr. de Bienville, as we have a peculiar obligation to them, my opinion is not to confuse them with the rest of their nation and to show the same consideration to them that they have shown to us. I approve that in gratitude for the Frenchmen whom they have saved or have brought to us they be granted their young boy and their woman relative; that they be escorted to a place of safety and even if it were possible that we should recommend to the Choctaws to spare them since it appears that it was without their consent that their nation attacked us.

Signed, Perry.

On August 3, 1723.

After having examined the representation of Mr. de Bienville on the subject of the war with the Chickasaws the reasons that he sets forth in it are very well calculated to make [us] decide to continue the war. It is to be feared that the Choctaws, a restless nation which is absolutely unwilling to hear any talk of peace and wishes to avenge its dead warriors, seeing itself unoccupied, may decide upon some other course which would be disadvantageous to us. There is only one thing to be observed, by no means to advance much to them. It will be necessary to give them powder and bullets, we cannot avoid it, but as for merchandise, it must not be paid until after the war or when they bring scalps and slaves; so my opinion is, with these observations, to continue the war.

In the matter of these Chickasaws who are here, the exchange that is requested is only too just and Mr. de Bienville has very prudently kept these slaves in order to return [them] to them. It will be necessary to recover from the German the woman whom he has and to promise the said Chickasaws to exchange with them every day their most noteworthy men and women prisoners for the Frenchmen who, having had the misfortune to fall into their hands, will be restored to us if that should happen in the future, without telling them that we wish to make war on them.

As for the two chiefs who were deprived of their merchandise and have always been inclined to the French [and] saved the life of some one and to whom it would be advisable to give some presents in gratitude, I do not know what is right for them. Mr. de Bienville who knows the taste and character of people of this sort perfectly will take the trouble, if he pleases, to have the memorandum drawn up and I will gladly sign it.

This is my opinion on the representation of Mr. de Bienville of the twenty-third of last July. I defer to the majority of the votes and to those that will be found to be better and in greater numbers.

Signed, Fleuriau.

QUESTIONS

1. What do these deliberations reveal about French attitudes toward Indians?
2. What reasons do Bienville and other members of the council give to justify their decision? In what ways do their deliberations reflect concerns about Choctaw power and English influence in the region?
3. Why did the Chickasaw chiefs decide to intervene to save the lives of the French traders? What did they hope to gain by doing so? In what ways do the council's deliberations illustrate the importance of captives to the practice of diplomacy in southeastern North America?

4.3. *BOSTON NEWS-LETTER*, EDITORIAL FAVORING INDENTURED SERVITUDE OVER SLAVERY (1706)

Although relatively few enslaved Africans and African Americans lived in Massachusetts in the early 18th century, the black population there was growing, largely because of Massachusetts merchants' engagement in the Atlantic slave trade. In 1706, an anonymous author composed and published an editorial on slavery in the *Boston News-Letter*, North America's first established newspaper. It was perhaps the first editorial to appear in a North American newspaper, and it is reprinted below in its entirety.

By last Years Bill of Mortality for the Town of Boston in Numb 100 *News Letter*,[1] we are furnished with a List of 44 Negroes dead last year, which being computed one with another at 30 *l*. per Head, amounts to the Sum of One Thousand three hundred and Twenty Pounds, of which we would make this Remark: That the Importing of Negroes into this or the Neighbouring Provinces is not so beneficial either to the Crown or Country, as White Servants would be.

For Negroes do not carry Arms to defend the Country as Whites do:

Negroes are generaly Eye-Servants[2], great Thieves, much addicted to stealing, Lying, and Purloining.

They do not People our Country as Whites would do whereby we should be strengthened against an Enemy.

By Encouraging the importing of White Men Servants, allowing somewhat to the importer, most Husbandmen in the Country might be furnished with Servants for 8, 9, or 10 *l*. a Head, who are not able to Launch out 40 or 50 *l*. for a Negro the now common Price.

A Man then might buy a White Man Servant we suppose for 10 *l*. to Serve 4 years, and Boys for the same price to Serve 6, 8 or 10 years: If a White Servant die, the Loss exceeds not 10 *l*. but if a Negro dies 'tis a very great Loss to the Husbandman. Three years Interest of the price of the Negro, will near upon if not altogether purchase a White Man Servant.

If Necessity call for it, that the Husbandman must fit out a man against the Enemy; if he has a Negro he cannot send him, but if he has a White Servant, 'twill answer the end, and perhaps save his Son at home.

Were Merchants and Masters Encouraged as already said to bring in Men Servants, there needed not be such complaint against Superiors Impressing our Children to the War, there would then be Men enough to be had without Impressing.

The bringing in of such servants would much enrich this Province, because Husbandmen would not only be able far better to manure what Lands are already under Improvement, but would also improve a great deal more that now lyes waste under Woods, and enable this Province to set about raising of Naval Stores, which would be greatly advantagious to the Crown of England, and this Province....

Suppose the Government here should allow Forty Shillings per head for five years, to such as should Import every of those years 100 White Men Servants, and each to serve 4 Years, the cost would be but 200 *l*. a

---

Source: Elizabeth Donnan, ed., *Documents Illustrative of the History of the Slave Trade to America*, vol. 3 (Washington, DC: Carnegie Institution of Washington, 1932), 21–23.

1. *Boston News Letter*, March 18, 1706.
2. A servant whom one must supervise constantly.

year, and a 1000 for the five years: the first 100 servants being free the 4th year, they serve the 5th for Wages, and the 6th there is 100 that goes out into the Woods, and settles a 100 Families to strengthen and Baracade us from the Indians, and so a 100 Families more every year successively.

And here you see that in one year the Town of Boston has lost 1320 *l.* by 44 Negroes, which is also a Loss to this Country in general, and for a less Loss, (if it may improperly be so called) for a 1000 *l.* the Country may have 500 Men in 5 years time for the 44 Negroes dead in one year.

A certain person within these 6 years had two Negroes dead computed both at 60 *l.* which would have procured him six white Servants at 10 *l.* per head to have Served 24 years, at 4 years a piece, without running such a great risque, and the Whites would have strengthened the Country, that Negroes do not.

'Twould do wel[l] that none of those Servants be liable to be Impressed during their Service of Agreement at their first Landing.

That such Servants being Sold or Transported out of this Province during the time of their Service, the person that buys them be liable to pay 3 *l.* into the Treasury.

QUESTIONS

1. On what grounds does the author favor indentured servitude over slavery? In what ways did then-current events probably influence the content and tone of the editorial?
2. This editorial and the petition of the Germantown Quaker Meeting express antislavery views. Do this editorial writer and the Germantown Quakers oppose slavery for similar reasons? If so, what are they? If not, why not?

4.4. VICE-ADMIRALTY COURT, BOSTON, EXCERPTS FROM THE TRIAL OF WILLIAM WHITE, JOHN ROSE ARCHER, AND WILLIAM TAYLOR AND THE EXECUTION OF WHITE AND TAYLOR (1724)

In 1696, Parliament passed a Navigation Act, under which the Board of Trade, the body charged to enforce that law's terms, established vice-admiralty courts in English North America and the Caribbean. Between 1700 and 1730, particularly in the 1710s and 1720s, the vice-admiralty courts served as one of the British Empire's chief weapons in its war on pirates. Below are excerpts from the 1724 trial of William White, John Rose Archer, and William Taylor, conducted at Boston's vice-admiralty court. Also included are documents related to the executions of White and Archer. The body of the latter was hung in chains on an island in Boston Harbor to, as the *Boston Gazette* put it, "be a Spectacle, and so a Warning to others."

Source: John Franklin Jameson, ed., *Privateering and Piracy in the Colonial Period: Illustrative Documents* (New York: Macmillan Company, 1923), 338–42, 344–45.

May the 13th day A.M.

The Court met according to Adjournmt. and was opened by Proclamation. Present The Hono'ble William Dummer, Esqr., etc. President.

William Tailer
Nathaniel Norden
Samuel Sewall
Thos. Hutchinson
Penn Townsend
Samuel Browne
Edwd. Bromfield
Thomas Fitch
John Cushing
Adam Winthrop
Spencer Phipps

Esqrs., of the Council of the Massachusetts Bay.

John Menzies
Thomas Durell
Thomas Lechmere
John Jekyll

Esqrs., Commissioners appointed in His Majesties Commission, etc.

A Warrant issued out for the bringing into Court William White, John Archer, otherwise Called John Rose Archer, and William Tailer, and they were brought to the Bar accordingly and arraigned upon the several articles Exhibited against them for Piracy Robbery and Felony.

At a Special Court of Admiralty for Tryal of Pyrates held at Boston within His maj'ties Province of the Massachusetts Bay in New England on the twelfth day of May In the Tenth year of the Reign of our sovereign Lord George, by the Grace of God of Great Britain, France and Ireland King, Defender of the Faith, etc., Annoq Domini 1724—

Articles of Pyracy, Robbery and Felony Exhibited then and there against William White, John Archer, otherwise Called John Rose Archer, and William Taylor, Marriners—

You stand Accused by His Majesties Advocate General of Felony, Pyracy and Robbery

First, For that the said William White, together with John Phillips, John Nutt, Samuel Ferne and

James Sparks, on or about the beginning of September last past, by force and Arms, in a Certain harbour near St. Peters in Newfoundland, upon the high sea, within the Jurisdiction of the Admiralty of Great Britain, piratically and Feloniously did surprise, seise, take and Carry away a Certain scooner named—, then and there being and belonging to His Maj'ties good subjects, and on the fifth day of the sd. month, being on board the sd scooner as aforesd., with force as aforesd., and on the high sea, within the Jurisdiction aforesd., near Newfoundland did Pyratically and Feloniously surprise, seize and take three fishing vessels belonging to His Majesties good subjects and in manner as aforesd. did take out of one of them an Indian Man named Isaac Lassen; and afterward, viz. on or about the middle of the sd Month of September, on the high sea and within the Jurisdiction aforesd., he the sd William White, in Conjunction as aforesd. with divers others, with force and arms Pyratically and Feloniously did surprise, seize and take a Certain scooner named—, one Furber, belonging to His Majesties good subjects and of the value of Five hundred pounds, and then and there within the Jurisdiction aforesd. out of her did seize, take and Carry away a quantity of provision and Cloaths of the Value of fifty pounds.

Lastly, For that the sd. William White, John Archer, als Rose Archer, and William Taylor, in Conjunction as aforesd., on or about the fourteenth of April last past, on the high sea and within the Jurisdiction aforesd., with force and Arms Did Feloniously and Pyratically surprise, seize and take a Sloop named the *Squirrel*, Andrew Harradine Master, of the Value of Three hundred pounds and belonging to His Maj'ties good subjects and on the fifteenth following with force and Feloniously and pyratically did Enter with all their Guns, ammunition and provision on board the sd Sloop. All which Actings of Pyracy, robbery and Felony were by you and Each of you done and Committed in manner as aforesd., Contrary to the Statutes and the Laws in that Case made and Provided.

Rob. Auchmuty, Adv. Genl.

Then the Kings Evidences were Called and sworn.

John Filmore Deposeth and Saith That he was in the harbour of St. Peters when Mr. Minotts scooner was run away with, by which scooner he was afterwards taken. That when he was Carried on board, he there saw William White upon Deck. That White told this Depont. he Came out upon that design, which this Depont. understood to be Pyracy, but that he was in Drink and he was sorry for it. That White went armed on board a Virginia Ship, that he had his Share of some Shirts that were taken out of a Portuguese Brigantine, That John Rose Archer and William Taylor (when a Brigantine whereof One Read was Master, in which the sd Archer and White were, was taken), Voluntarily Joyned with the Pyrates, That in a short time after Archer was Chosen Quarter-master and after he was so, he went on board every Vessel they took, armed, That William Taylor was very Great with Phillips, Nutt and Burrill, being Admitted into the Cabbin, upon any Consultation they had together.

Edward Cheesman Deposed That White told him he was [one] of the first five that run away with Mr. Minotts Scooner, [That] they made him Drink, and that he was sorry for it now. That in taking several Vessels White was more Active than others, who pretended to be forced men. That John Rose Archer, to this Deponts. certain knowledge, by force and Arms Entred into several vessels they took and aided and assisted in plundering the same and sharing part thereof, And that William Taylor was as active on board as any of them; That this Depont Saw him once take a great Coat and heard him then say, he would not willingly hurt a Man, but he was upon the Account, and he must not go Naked.

Isaac Lassen Deposeth That White told him three days [after] he was taken, that he was sorry he Came out upon the [Accot.], That this Depont. saw him go on board a snow armed, and that he shared part of the plunder.

Henry Giles Deposed That White was one of the four that went on board the Ship this Depont. was taken out of, that he was Armed with a Cutlass and Shared part of the plunder, That he also Saw him go on board a French ship armed with a Cutlass, out of which Ship they took Eight Great Guns: That Archer also was one of the four that went on board their ship armed with a Cutlash, and as this Depont. was going over the side Archer threatned to Cut him in sunder if he did not make hast and go on board the Pyrate with his Books and Instruments.

William Lancy Deposed That he was taken by the Pyrate Phillips sometime in April last, That Archer the Quarter Master was one of those who came on board his scooner and that he was armed with sword or Cutlash; that the sd. Archer went on board all or most of the vessels they took while this Depont. was with them, Armed with sword or Cutlass; That Archer told him that he was one of Teaches men and went into South Carolina upon the Act of Grace. That White told this Depont. he was sorry he came out upon the Accot. and if he Could he would get away before they went off the Coast. That he heard William Taylor say they were Carrying him to Virginia to be sold and they met with these honest Men, meaning the Pyrates, and he listed himself to go with them.

After the Kings Evidences had been severally Examined the Prisoners at the Bar were asked what they had to say in their own Defence. William White says he is sorry he should Commit such a sin, that he was in Drink when he went away with Phillips, Nutt, etc., in Mr Minotts scooner. John Archer and Willm Taylor say they were forced Men, and Archer, being asked how he Came to be Quarter Master, Answered that the Company thought him the fittest Man for a Quarter master and so Chose him.

Then the Kings Advocate General summed up the nature of the Evidence against the Prisoners, and the Prisoners were taken from the Bar, and the Court cleared and in private.

Then the Court Maturely weighed and Considered the Evidences and the Prisoners Cases, and Unanimously found William White, John Rose Archer, and William Taylor Guilty of Pyracy, robbery and Felony according to the Articles Exhibited against them. Then the Prisoners were brought to the Bar and the President acquainted them that the Court by a Unanimous Voice had found them Guilty....

BILL OF ROBERT DOBNEY, JUNE 2, 1724

The Province of the Massachusetts Bay by Order of Edward Stanbridge is Dr

   1724
   June 2d
   To Makeing of the Chaines for John Rose

archer one of the Pyrats and the hire of a
man to help fix him on the Gebbet att Brid
[Bird] Island   £12.10

per me
Robert Dobney

BILL OF EDWARD STANBRIDGE, JUNE 2, 1724

June 2d 1724   The Province of the
Massachusetts Bay to Edwd. Stanbridge, Dr
    for Sundrys by him Expended being Marshall
And by Order of A Speciall Cort of Admiralty for the
Execution of John Rose Archer and William White
two Pirates, Viz.

To the Executoner for his Service I
paid   £12.00.
him   0

To Mr Joseph Parsons for Cordage
I
paid his Bill   £2.17.6

To Boat hire and Labourers to help

Sett
the Gibet And there attendance at the
Execution and Diging the Grave for
White   3.10.8

To Expences on the Sheriefs officers
and
Cunstables after the Exicution att
Mrs.
Mary Gilberts her Bill   3.15.8
                                             _____
                                             22.3.10

To Georg Mayo, Blockmaker, his
Bill   1.5.00
                                             _____
                                             23.8.10

QUESTIONS

1. What evidence or testimony, in your view, led the
    court to convict White, Archer, and Taylor?
2. What does the testimony given in this case reveal
    about the maritime world of the early 18th
    century?

4.5. REVEREND JAMES MCGREGOR, PETITION TO SAMUEL SHUTE, GOVERNOR OF MASSACHUSETTS AND NEW HAMPSHIRE (1720)

In the late 1710s, thousands of migrants left Ulster for North America. Many headed to New England, particularly to areas of southern New Hampshire that both New Hampshire and Massachusetts claimed. The Ulsterite Presbyterian founders of Nutfield suffered violent harassment from Massachusetts colonists and officials, which prompted the petition below from Rev. James McGregor to Samuel Shute, the governor of both Massachusetts and New Hampshire. Shute subsequently accorded Nutfield residents the right to choose their own leaders, and New Hampshire officials soon granted the town, which residents renamed Londonderry, legal recognition. Massachusetts officials and colonists disputed the Ulsterites' claims until 1740, when the British Empire confirmed that New Hampshire should govern the disputed area.

Source: Kerby A. Miller, Arnold Schrier, Bruce D. Boling, and David N. Doyle, eds., *Irish Immigrants in the Land of Canaan: Letters and Memoirs from Colonial and Revolutionary America, 1675–1815* (New York: Oxford University Press, 2003), 438–39.

Rev. James McGregor, Nutfield, New Hampshire,

to Governor Samuel Shute, Boston, Massachusetts,
27 February 1720

The Humble Apology of the People of Nutfeild to His Exelency Sam^ll Shute Generall Govern^r. and Commander in Cheife of his Majesties Provinces of the Massachusetts Bay and New Hampsh^r in New England—

May it Please Y^r Exelency

The Subscribers having Seen a copy of Y^r Exelencys Lettr. To Capt: White & Capt: Kembell, find themselves undr. a Nessessity of Vindicating themselves from the Charges given in against them; it being alowable by the Law of Nature & of Nations, to ye greatest Criminalls to Defend them selves when they Justly plead in their Own Vindication. We were Surprised to hear our Selves termed *Irish People* when we So frequently ventured our all for the Brittish Crown and Liberties against the Irish papists & gave all tests of our Loyalty wch the Government of Ireland Required and are always ready to do the Same here w^n demanded. Tho we Settled att Nutfeild yett we Used no Violence in the manr. of our Settlement, Seing no body in the Least offered to hinder us to Sett down in a desolate Wilderness; and we were So fare from hindering the English that Really had a mind to Plant wth. us, that, many of them are now incorporated wth. us. after our Settlement we found that two or three Different parties Claimed Nutfeild, by virtue of Indian deeds, and we were Given to understand, that it was Nessesary for us to *hold the Soil by Some Right purchased from the Natives* accordingly we made applycation to the Honble. Coll. Wheelwright of Wells, and Obtained his Indian right; wch we have to Shew, his Deed being of Ninety Years Standing, and Conveyed from the Cheife Sagamores between the Rivers of Merimack and Piscattaqua, wth the Consent of the whole Tribe of the Indian Nation, and well Executed, is the most authentic we have Seen; and the Subscribers Could not in reason think that a deed wch is not twenty years Old, of Land wch is not Sufficiently butted and bounded, from an Obscure Indian, Could Give any Right to Land wch had been Sold So many years before, by the Right owners. And the Subscribers hope they will be Excused, from Giving away So Good a Title, for Others that cannot pretend Rationally to be So well Supported; and wch they always refused to Warrantee and make Good, ag^st other Claimes. The Dutifull Applications wch we have made to both Courts, If we be inCorporated, in whatSoEver Province we fall to be, will Witness for our respect to his Majesty's gov^rmt. If Affidavits have been Given agst one of our Number as useing Some threttning Expressions, we hope it will not be Imputed to the Community. If our accusers be permitted to Come up in troops, as they have done, and violently demolish'd one of our houses, and destroyed part of our hay, and threttned and Insulted us wth impunity, to the Great terror of our wives and Children, when we Suffered patiently, and then accuse us to our Rulers of violence, Injustice, fraud, force, insolence, Cruelty, dishonour of his Majesties Governt, & disturbance of his Majesties Subjects, injuries, and Offences to the English, and the like, when we know our Selves to be Innocent, we think it hard measure; and must have Recourse to God, who forbideth to take up a bad report ag^st our Neighbour, and will, we hope, bring forth our Righteousness as the Light, and our Judgment as the Noon day. If we be Guilty of these disorders, we know we are Liable to a Legall Tryall and are not So weak as to Suppose our Selves to be out of the reach of Your Exelencys Government. The Subsscribers hope that If any other accusations come in ag^st them they will be allowed an Equall hearing before they be condemned; and as we Enjoy the liberty of the Gospell here, wch is So Great a mercy [we] Shall Improve it, for Gods Glory; and as he has taught us be Dutifull to his Majesties Governt, Sett over us, and If possible live peaceably wth all men, Shall be Desierous of Peaceable Neighbours, that want to Settle wth us, and to help us to Subdue a part of this vast and uncultivated Wilderness; and we Shall not Cease to pray for the Divine blessing on Yr Exelency's person and Govt.

Done at Nutfield Feb: 27: 1719/20 & Subscribed by——

James McGregore &c

QUESTIONS

1. What do McGregor and the residents of Nutfield mean when they call their petition to Governor Shute a "humble apology?" In what ways does their petition reflect the influence of royalism in British North America politics in the early 18th century?

2. On what grounds do McGregor and his flock assert that they have a valid claim to the disputed lands? What is their response to assertions that they do not belong in Nutfield?

4.6. VISUAL DOCUMENT: STUDIO OF GODFREY KNELLER, PORTRAIT OF LUCY PARKE BYRD WITH UNIDENTIFIED BLACK WOMAN (c. 1716)

Sometime around 1716, Lucy Parke Byrd visited London and sat for the portrait presented below. Born in 1685 to a prominent Virginia planter family, she married planter William Byrd II in 1706 and had four children with him, only two of whom survived infancy. Parke Byrd died of smallpox in London in 1716. To judge from the diary that William Byrd kept, the couple had a tempestuous marriage, partly because of his controlling behavior towards her, which included what she considered his trespassing on her efforts to manage their household, and because of his infidelity. One of the ways in which Parke Byrd expressed her frustration with her husband was by abusing the enslaved women who attended her.

QUESTION

1. In what ways are gentility and slavery associated in this portrait?

Source: Virginia Historical Society, Richmond, Virginia, USA/Anonymously lent to the Virginia Historical Society/The Bridgeman Art Library.

CHAPTER 5

BATTLING FOR SOULS, MINDS, AND THE HEART OF NORTH AMERICA, 1730–1763

5.1. FUTURE RESIDENTS OF GRACIA REAL DE MOSE, FLORIDA, LETTER TO PHILIP V, KING OF SPAIN (1738)

During the 18th and early 19th centuries, enslaved Africans and African Americans in South Carolina and Georgia sought freedom by fleeing south to Spanish-ruled Florida. Even though royal orders dating back to 1693 granted refuge and freedom to enslaved people who converted to Catholicism, Spanish colonists sometimes re-enslaved the fugitives. Francisco Menéndez, an African man who had escaped slavery in South Carolina, wrote petitions in Spanish that implored Philip V to intervene. In 1738, the royal governor recognized the freedom of all Carolina runaways, which prompted the letter of thanks to Philip V that appears below.

My lord,

All the Black people who escaped from the English plantations, obedient and loyal slaves to Your Majesty, declare that Your Majesty has done us true charity in ordering us to be given freedom for having come to this country and for being Christian and following the true religion that saves us.

Disobeying a very high and sacred law, they bound us and made us slaves for many years, putting us through many miseries and much hunger. But obeying laws which Your Majesty decreed, the present Governor, Don Manuel de Montiano, has set us free, for which we greatly appreciate Your Majesty and thank him for this most royal kindness.

Likewise, the Governor has offered and assured us that he will establish a place for us, which is called Gracia Reál, where we may serve God and Your Majesty, cultivating the land so that there may be fruit in this country.

We promise Your Majesty that, whenever the opportunity arises, we will be the cruelest enemies to the English and will risk our lives in the service of Your Majesty, even to spilling the last drop of blood, in defense of the great crown of Spain and our holy faith.

Source: Kathleen DuVal and John DuVal, eds., *Interpreting a Continent: Voices from Colonial America* (Lanham, MD: Rowman & Littlefield, 2009), 179–80. Translated from Audiencia de Santo Domingo 844, fol. 607, reel 15, P. K. Yonge Library, University of Florida, Gainesville.

Thus Your Majesty may order any amount of service from us because we are his faithful slaves all of our life and we will always pray Our Lord to guard Your Majesty's life and the life of all the Royal Family throughout the slow years that we poor people need.

Saint Augustine, Florida, 10 June 1738.

QUESTIONS

1. What did the authors of this letter promise Philip V? Why did they make such a promise?
2. Carefully examine the language used by the Afro-Floridians. In what ways does it resemble the language used in the petition of the Ulsterite residents of Nutfield (Document 4.5)? In what ways does it differ from the language of that petition?

5.2. PEDRO TAMARÓN Y ROMERAL, BISHOP OF DURANGO, EXCERPTS FROM REPORT ON PASTORAL VISIT TO NEW MEXICO (1760)

In late 1759, Pedro Tamarón y Romeral, the Roman Catholic bishop of the Diocese of Durango, Mexico, embarked upon the first tour of his diocese, of which one of the most remote parts was New Mexico. Born in Spain in 1695, Tamarón served in Caracas (capital of today's Venezuela) for about 30 years before being named Bishop of Durango. In this position, Tamarón journeyed to almost every Spanish town or Indian pueblo in New Mexico that had a church or a mission and made careful observations on social life, demography, and religion. Below are excerpts from his observations on visits to Pecos and Taos. It is worth noting that Tamarón, like many of his predecessors, sought to bring New Mexico's Franciscans under his authority, which likely shaped his impressions.

PECOS

A Franciscan missionary parish priest resides in this Indian pueblo. It is eight leagues from Santa Fe to the southeast. There are 168 families, with 344 persons, and 192 persons were confirmed.

Here the failure of the Indians to confess except at the point of death is more noticeable, because they do not know the Spanish language and the missionaries do not know those of the Indians. They have one or two interpreters in each pueblo, with whose aid the missionaries manage to confess them when they are in danger of dying. And although they recite some of the Christian doctrine in Spanish, since they do not understand the language, they might as well not know it.

This point saddened and upset me more in that kingdom than in any other, and I felt scruples about confirming adults. I remonstrated vehemently with the Father Custos and the missionaries, who tried to excuse themselves by claiming that they could not learn those languages. In my writs of visitation I ordered them to learn them, and I repeatedly urged them to apply themselves to this and to formulate catechisms and guides to confession, of which I would pay the printing costs....

Source: Eleanor B. Adams, ed., "Bishop Tamarón's Visitation of New Mexico, 1760," *New Mexico Historical Review* 28, no. 3 (July 1953): 206–08, 215–17.

It is a shame that most of those Indians lack the benefit of confession. I take little satisfaction in these confessions through an interpreter when the latter is an Indian or a negro. I had experience of this when I was a parish priest in Caracas with the negroes brought there under the English contract. Many died soon after they arrived. I made repeated experiments with those of their own nation who had been in the land for some time. Although we granted confession, I never felt reassurance when this means was used. And I attempted to accomplish something in New Mexico by using interpreters, and their version is nothing but confusion on the subject of catechism and confession. In trade and temporal business where profit is involved, the Indians and Spaniards of New Mexico understand one another completely. In such matters they are knowing and avaricious. This does not extend to the spiritual realm, with regard to which they display great tepidity and indifference. And because of their scanty store of virtue and sacred things, they will hurl themselves into such wickedness as I am about to relate.

TAOS

The titular patron of this Indian pueblo is San Jerónimo. To reach it we traveled through pine forests and mountains until we descended to the spacious and beautiful valley they call the valley of Taos. In this valley we kept finding encampments of peaceful infidel Apache Indians, who have sought the protection of the Spaniards so that they may defend them from the Comanches. Then we came to a river called Trampas, which carries enough water. The midday halt was made at the large house of a wealthy Taos Indian, very civilized and well-to-do. The said house is well walled in, with arms and towers for defense. In the afternoon the journey through that valley continued. Three rivers of similar current and water were crossed. The first one in particular provides abundant ditches for irrigation. They are about a league and a half from one another. And, crossing the last one, we entered the pueblo of Taos, where a Franciscan missionary parish priest resides....

I also put forth every effort there to induce those best acquainted with Spanish to perform the act of contrition and confess. I therefore left this group until last, confirming the children first. And in fact some did confess, and, encouraged to contrition, were confirmed. But since they do not know the catechism except in Spanish, I did not feel as pleased and easy in my mind as I should have liked. Therefore I reprimanded the mission father and duly reminded him of his duty, ordering him to continue receiving their confessions.

When I was in the pueblo two encampments of Ute Indians, who were friendly but infidels, had just arrived with a captive woman who had fled from the Comanches. They reported that the latter were at the Río de las Animas preparing buffalo meat in order to come to trade. They come every year to the trading, or fairs. The governor comes to those fairs, which they call *rescates*,[1] every year with the majority of his garrison and people from all over the kingdom. They bring captives to sell, pieces of chamois, many buffalo skins, and, out of the plunder they have obtained elsewhere, horses, muskets, shotguns, munitions, knives, meat, and various other things. Money is not current at these fairs, but exchange of one thing for another, and so those people get provisions. I left Taos on June 12, and a few days later seventeen tents of Comanches arrived. They make these of buffalo hide, and they say that they are good and well suited for defense; and a family occupies each one. And at the end of the said month of June seventy of these field tents arrived. This was the great fair.

The character of these Comanches is such that while they are peacefully trading in Taos, others of their nation make warlike attacks on some distant pueblo. And the ones who are at peace, engaged in trade, are accustomed to say to the governor, "Don't be too trusting. Remember, there are rogues among us, just as there are among you. Hang any of them you catch."

In that year, 1760, I left that kingdom at the beginning of July. And on the fourth day of August, according to what they say, nearly three thousand Comanche

---

1.   Barter, trade.

men waged war with the intention of finishing this pueblo of Taos. They diverted, or provoked, them from a very large house, the greatest in all that valley, belonging to a settler called Villalpando, who, luckily for him, had left that day on business. But when they saw so many Comanches coming, many women and men of that settlement took refuge in this house as the strongest. And, trusting in the fact that it had four towers and in the large supply of muskets, powder, and balls, they say that they fired on the Comanches. The latter were infuriated by this to such a horrible degree that they broke into different parts of the house, killed all the men and some women, who also fought. And the wife of the owner of the house, seeing that they were breaking down the outside door, went to defend it with a lance, and they killed her fighting. Fifty-six women and children were carried off, and a large number of horses which the owner of the house was keeping there. Forty-nine bodies of dead Comanches were counted, and other trickles of blood were seen.

As soon as the governor, Don Francisco Marín del Valle, learned about it, he summoned his men with all possible speed. He set out on their trail with a thousand men and pursued them almost two hundred leagues. By this time the Apache auxiliaries were tired and dispirited. Food supplies were running out. They returned. They spent forty days reconnoitering a large area without accomplishing anything.

It is said, and they told me, that this numerous, strong, warlike tribe of Comanches came and showed themselves on the New Mexico front in the years 1717 or 1718. And they said that it had taken them twelve moons to travel from their lands. The immensity of those unpopulated regions may be deduced from this.

QUESTIONS

1. What did Tamarón think of the Franciscan mission at Pecos? In what ways did his experiences in Caracas shape his observations? In what ways do his observations testify to the impact of the Pueblo War for Independence on life in New Mexico?
2. What does Tamarón's account reveal about the Indian slave trade and New Mexico's relations with Apaches and Comanches?

5.3. CANASSATEGO (ONONDAGA), EXCERPTS FROM HIS RESPONSE TO A DELAWARE COMPLAINT CONCERNING THE WALKING PURCHASE (1742)

In 1736, the Iroquois League and Pennsylvania officials agreed that the Iroquois League would speak on behalf of all Indians who lived between the Iroquois homeland (in today's Upstate New York) and Philadelphia. The following year, Delaware Indians ceded about 1,200 square miles of land to Pennsylvania under the terms of the "Walking Purchase." Delawares issued a stream of protests concerning the "Walking Purchase" over the next few years, arguing that Pennsylvania officials had violated their agreement by dispatching runners along cleared and marked paths to claim as much territory as possible. In 1742, Onondaga chief and Iroquois spokesman Canassatego appeared at a treaty conference in Philadelphia and issued the following response to the Delaware delegation.

Source: *Pennsylvania Colonial Records*, vol. 4 (Harrisburg, PA: 1851), 578–80.

At a Council held at the Proprietors, July 12th. Present: The Honble GEORGE THOMAS, Esqr, Lieutenant Governor.

James Logan,
Clement Plumsted,
Thomas Laurence,
Abraham Taylor,
Robert Strettel,,

Esqrs.

Mr. Richard Peters.

Canassatego,
Skick Calamy,

and sundry Chiefs of the six Nations.

Sassonan and Delawares.
Nutimus and ffork Indians.

Pisquetoman,
Cornelius Spring,
Nicholas Scull,

Interpreters to the ffork Indians.

Canassatego said,

"Brethren, the Governor, and Council:

"The other Day you informed Us of the Misbehaviour of our Cousins the Delawares with respect to their continuing to Claim and refusing to remove from some Land on the River Delaware, notwithstanding their Ancestors had sold it by Deed under their Hands & Seals to the Proprietors for a valuable Consideration, upwards of fifty Years ago, and notwithstanding that they them[s]elves had about—Years ago, after a long and full Examination, ratified that Deed of their Ancestors, and given a fresh one under their Hands and Seals, and then you requested Us to remove them, enforcing your Request with a String of Wampum. Afterwards you laid on the Table by Conrad Weiser our own Letters, some of our Cousins' Letters, and the several Writings to prove the Charge against our Cousins, with a Draught of the Land in Dispute. We now tell You we have Perused all these several Papers. We see with our own Eyes that they have been a very unruly People, and are altogether in the wrong in their Dealings with You. We have concluded to remove them, and Oblige them to go over the River Delaware, and to quit all Claim to any Lands on this side for the future, since they have received Pay for them and it is gone through their Guts long ago. To confirm to You that we will see your Request Executed, we lay down this String of Wampum in return for your's."

Then turning to the Delawares, holding a Belt of Wampum in his Hand, he spoke to them as followeth:

"Cousins:

"Let this Belt of Wampum serve to Chastize You; You ought to be taken by the Hair of the Head and shak'd severely till you recover your Senses and become Sober; you don't know what Ground you stand on, nor what you are doing. Our Brother Onas'[2] Case is very just and plain, and his Intentions to preserve ffriendship; on the other Hand your Cause is bad, your Heart far from being upright, and you are maliciously bent to break the Chain of ffriendship with our Brother Onas. We have seen with our Eyes a Deed signed by nine of your Ancestors above fifty Years ago for this very Land, and a Release Sign'd not many Years since by some of your selves and Chiefs now living to the Number of 15 or Upwards. But how came you to take upon you to Sell Land at all? We conquer'd You, we made Women of you, you know you are Women, and can no more sell Land than Women. Nor is it fit you should have the Power of Selling Lands since you would abuse it. This Land that you Claim is gone through Your Guts. You have been furnished with Cloaths and Meat and Drink by the Goods paid you for it, and now You want it again like Children as you are. But what makes you sell Land in the Dark? Did you ever tell Us that you had sold this Land? did we ever receive any Part, even the Value of a Pipe Shank, from you for it? You have told Us a Blind story that you sent a Messenger to Us to inform Us of the Sale but he never came amongst Us, nor we never heard any thing about it. This is acting in the Dark, and very different from the Conduct our six Nations observe in their Sales of Land. On such Occasions they give Publick Notice and invite all the

---

2. The Iroquois called William Penn "Onas" (which means "pen," a pun on his name) and also used the term to refer to subsequent leaders of Pennsylvania.

Indians of their united Nations, and give them a share of the Present they receive for their Lands. This is the behaviour of the wise United Nations, but we find you are none of our Blood. You Act a dishonest part not only in this but in other Matters. Your Ears are ever Open to slanderous Reports about our Brethren. You receive them with as much greediness as Lewd Woman receive the Embraces of Bad Men. And for all these reasons we charge You to remove instantly. We don't give you the liberty to think about it. You are Women; take the Advice of a Wise Man and remove imediately. You may return to the other side of Delaware where you came from, but we don't know whether, Considering how you have demean'd your selves, you will be permitted to live there, or whether you have not swallowed that Land down your Throats as well as the Land on this side. We, therefore, Assign you two Places to go—either to Wyomin or Shamokin. You may go to either of these Places, and then we shall have you more under our Eye, and shall see how You behave. Don't deliberate, but remove away and take this Belt of Wampum."

This being interpreted by Conrad Weiser into English, and by Cornelius Spring into the Delaware language, Canassatego taking a String of Wampum added further:

"After our just reproof and absolute Order to depart from the Land, you are now to take Notice of what we have further to say to you. This String of Wampum serves to forbid You, Your Children and Grand Children, to the latest Posterity, for ever medling in Land Affairs, neither you nor any who shall descend from You, are ever hereafter to presume to sell any Land, for which Purpose you are to Preserve this string in Memory of what your Uncles have this Day given You in Charge. We have some other Business to transact with our Brethren, and therefore depart the Council and consider what has been said to you."

QUESTIONS

1. Why did Canassatego begin or end each statement by presenting wampum to the party he was addressing?
2. What did Canassatego want the Delawares to do? On what grounds did he support Pennsylvania's side in the Walking Purchase dispute and assert the Iroquois League's influence over the Delawares?

5.4. BENJAMIN FRANKLIN, EXCERPTS FROM "OBSERVATIONS ON THE INCREASE OF MANKIND" (1751)

In 1751, Benjamin Franklin penned the essay "Observations on the Increase of Mankind," excerpts of which appear below. The passage of the Iron Act of 1750, which sought to restrict the development of colonial British North America's iron industry, seems to have prompted him to write it. Most of the essay focuses on population growth in the colonies, which, Franklin argued, made North America increasingly important to the economic development and strategic needs of the British Empire. The essay was first published in London in 1755. Franklin's political enemies capitalized on some of its contents a decade later, as Chapter 5 of the text discusses.

Source: Leonard W. Labaree, ed., *The Papers of Benjamin Franklin*, vol. 4 (New Haven, CT: Yale University Press, 1961), 225–34.

6. Land being thus plenty in America, and so cheap as that a labouring Man, that understands Husbandry, can in a short Time save Money enough to purchase a Piece of new Land sufficient for a Plantation, whereon he may subsist a Family; such are not afraid to marry; for if they even look far enough forward to consider how their Children when grown up are to be provided for, they see that more Land is to be had at Rates equally easy, all Circumstances considered.

7. Hence Marriages in America are more general, and more generally early, than in Europe. And if it is reckoned there, that there is but one Marriage per Annum among 100 Persons, perhaps we may here reckon two; and if in Europe they have but 4 Births to a Marriage (many of their Marriages being late) we may here reckon 8, of which if one half grow up, and our Marriages are made, reckoning one with another at 20 Years of Age, our People must at least be doubled every 20 Years.

8. But notwithstanding this Increase, so vast is the Territory of North-America, that it will require many Ages to settle it fully; and till it is fully settled, Labour will never be cheap here, where no Man continues long a Labourer for others, but gets a Plantation of his own, no Man continues long a Journeyman to a Trade, but goes among those new Settlers, and sets up for himself, &c. Hence Labour is no cheaper now, in Pennsylvania, than it was 30 Years ago, tho' so many Thousand labouring People have been imported.

9. The Danger therefore of these Colonies interfering with their Mother Country in Trades that depend on Labour, Manufactures, &c. is too remote to require the Attention of Great-Britain.

10. But in Proportion to the Increase of the Colonies, a vast Demand is growing for British Manufactures, a glorious Market wholly in the Power of Britain, in which Foreigners cannot interfere, which will increase in a short Time even beyond her Power of supplying, tho' her whole Trade should be to her Colonies: Therefore Britain should not too much restrain Manufactures in her Colonies. A wise and good Mother will not do it. To distress, is to weaken, and weakening the Children, weakens the whole Family. . . .

12. 'Tis an ill-grounded Opinion that by the Labour of Slaves, America may possibly vie in Cheapness of Manufactures with Britain. The Labour of Slaves can never be so cheap here as the Labour of working Men is in Britain. Any one may compute it. Interest of Money is in the Colonies from 6 to 10 per Cent. Slaves one with another cost £30 Sterling per Head. Reckon then the Interest of the first Purchase of a Slave, the Insurance or Risque on his Life, his Cloathing and Diet, Expences in his Sickness and Loss of Time, Loss by his Neglect of Business (Neglect is natural to the Man who is not to be benefited by his own Care or Diligence), Expence of a Driver to keep him at Work, and his Pilfering from Time to Time, almost every Slave being *by Nature* a Thief, and compare the whole Amount with the Wages of a Manufacturer of Iron or Wool in England, you will see that Labour is much cheaper there than it ever can be by Negroes here. Why then will Americans purchase Slaves? Because Slaves may be kept as long as a Man pleases, or has Occasion for their Labour; while hired Men are continually leaving their Master (often in the midst of his Business,) and setting up for themselves.

13. As the Increase of People depends on the Encouragement of Marriages, the following Things must diminish a Nation, viz. 1. The being conquered; for the Conquerors will engross as many Offices, and exact as much Tribute or Profit on the Labour of the conquered, as will maintain them in their new Establishment, and this diminishing the Subsistence of the Natives discourages their Marriages, and so gradually diminishes them, while the Foreigners increase. 2. Loss of Territory. Thus the Britons being driven into Wales, and crowded together in a barren Country insufficient to support such great Numbers, diminished 'till the People bore a Proportion to the Produce, while the Saxons increas'd on their abandoned Lands; 'till the Island became full of English. And were the English now driven into Wales by some foreign Nation, there would in a few Years be no more Englishmen in Britain, than there are now People in Wales. 3. Loss of Trade. Manufactures exported, draw Subsistence from Foreign Countries for Numbers; who are thereby enabled to marry and raise Families. If the Nation be deprived of any Branch of Trade, and no new Employment is found for the People occupy'd in that Branch, it will also be soon deprived of so many People. 4. Loss of Food. Suppose a Nation has a Fishery, which not only employs great Numbers, but makes the Food and

Subsistence of the People cheaper; If another Nation becomes Master of the Seas, and prevents the Fishery, the People will diminish in Proportion as the Loss of Employ, and Dearness of Provision, makes it more difficult to subsist a Family. 5. Bad Government and insecure Property. People not only leave such a Country, and settling Abroad incorporate with other Nations, lose their native Language, and become Foreigners; but the Industry of those that remain being discourag'd, the Quantity of Subsistence in the Country is lessen'd, and the Support of a Family becomes more difficult. So heavy Taxes tend to diminish a People.... 6. The Introduction of Slaves. The Negroes brought into the English Sugar Islands, have greatly diminish'd the Whites there; the Poor are by this Means depriv'd of Employment, while a few Families acquire vast Estates; which they spend on Foreign Luxuries, and educating their Children in the Habit of those Luxuries; the same Income is needed for the Support of one that might have maintain'd 100. The Whites who have Slaves, not labouring, are enfeebled, and therefore not so generally prolific; the Slaves being work'd too hard, and ill fed, their Constitutions are broken, and the Deaths among them are more than the Births; so that a continual Supply is needed from Africa. The Northern Colonies having few Slaves increase in Whites. Slaves also pejorate the Families that use them; the white Children become proud, disgusted with Labour, and being educated in Idleness, are rendered unfit to get a Living by Industry....

21. The Importation of Foreigners into a Country that has as many Inhabitants as the present Employments and Provisions for Subsistence will bear; will be in the End no Increase of People; unless the New Comers have more Industry and Frugality than the Natives, and then they will provide more Subsistence, and increase in the Country; but they will gradually eat the Natives out. Nor is it necessary to bring in Foreigners to fill up any occasional Vacancy in a Country; for such Vacancy (if the Laws are good, § 14, 16) will soon be filled by natural Generation. Who can now find the Vacancy made in Sweden, France or other Warlike Nations, by the Plague of Heroism 40 Years ago; in France, by the Expulsion of the Protestants; in England, by the Settlement of her Colonies; or in Guinea, by 100 Years Exportation of

Slaves, that has blacken'd half America? The thinness of Inhabitants in Spain is owing to National Pride and Idleness, and other Causes, rather than to the Expulsion of the Moors, or to the making of new Settlements.

22. There is in short, no Bound to the prolific Nature of Plants or Animals, but what is made by their crowding and interfering with each others Means of Subsistence. Was the Face of the Earth vacant of other Plants, it might be gradually sowed and overspread with one Kind only; as, for Instance, with Fennel; and were it empty of other Inhabitants, it might in a few Ages be replenish'd from one Nation only; as, for Instance, with Englishmen. Thus there are suppos'd to be now upwards of One Million English Souls in North-America, (tho' 'tis thought scarce 80,000 have been brought over Sea) and yet perhaps there is not one the fewer in Britain, but rather many more, on Account of the Employment the Colonies afford to Manufacturers at Home. This Million doubling, suppose but once in 25 Years, will in another Century be more than the People of England, and the greatest Number of Englishmen will be on this Side the Water. What an Accession of Power to the British Empire by Sea as well as Land! What Increase of Trade and Navigation! What Numbers of Ships and Seamen! We have been here but little more than 100 Years, and yet the Force of our Privateers in the late War, united, was greater, both in Men and Guns, than that of the whole British Navy in Queen Elizabeth's Time. How important an Affair then to Britain, is the present Treaty for settling the Bounds between her Colonies and the French, and how careful should she be to secure Room enough, since on the Room depends so much the Increase of her People?

23. ... And since Detachments of English from Britain sent to America, will have their Places at Home so soon supply'd and increase so largely here; why should the Palatine Boors be suffered to swarm into our Settlements, and by herding together establish their Language and Manners to the Exclusion of ours? Why should Pennsylvania, founded by the English, become a Colony of *Aliens*, who will shortly be so numerous as to Germanize us instead of our Anglifying them, and will never adopt our Language or Customs, any more than they can acquire our Complexion.

24. Which leads me to add one Remark: That the Number of purely white People in the World is proportionably very small. All Africa is black or tawny. Asia chiefly tawny. America (exclusive of the new Comers) wholly so. And in Europe, the Spaniards, Italians, French, Russians and Swedes, are generally of what we call a swarthy Complexion; as are the Germans also, the Saxons only excepted, who with the English, make the principal Body of White People on the Face of the Earth. I could wish their Numbers were increased. And while we are, as I may call it, *Scouring* our Planet, by clearing America of Woods, and so making this Side of our Globe reflect a brighter Light to the Eyes of Inhabitants in Mars or Venus, why should we in the Sight of Superior Beings, darken its People? why increase the Sons of Africa, by Planting them in America, where we have so fair an Opportunity, by excluding all Blacks and Tawneys, of increasing the lovely White and Red? But perhaps I am partial to the Complexion of my Country, for such Kind of Partiality is natural to Mankind.

QUESTIONS

1. What were Franklin's views on slavery? In what ways do these views resemble those of the Germantown Quaker Meeting and the editors of the *Boston News-Letter*? In what ways do his views on slavery differ from those expressed in those two documents?

2. Why did Franklin take such a dim view of German immigration? How does his opposition to German immigration and slavery relate to his case for a more prominent role for colonists within the British Empire?

5.5. DIARY OF HANNAH HEATON, EXCERPTS FROM HER RECOLLECTIONS OF THE GREAT AWAKENING (1750s)

Sometime in the 1750s, after she had married and resettled on a farm in North Haven, Connecticut, Hannah Heaton began to keep a diary in which she occasionally commented on her spiritual experiences and significant events such as the American Revolution. It seems that Heaton primarily saw the diary as a way to record and sustain her spiritual development. Later, she also came to view it as a way to instruct her children and have them remember her. Below are excerpts of Heaton's recollections of her conversion during the Great Awakening, when she was 20 years old.

Now after a while i went over to new haven in the fall just before that great work of god began which was in the year 1741. There i heard mr tennant and mr whitefeild preach which awakened me much. Mr whitefeild laid down the marks of an unconverted person. O strange it was such preaching as i never heard before. Dont you said he when you are at the house of god long service should be over that your minds may be about your worldly conserns and pleasures. Is it not a wearines to you said he if one days serving god is so wearisom to you. How could you endure to be in heaven with him forever where nothing but praises are.

Source: Barbara E. Lacey, ed., *The World of Hannah Heaton: The Diary of an Eighteenth-Century New England Farm Woman* (DeKalb, IL: Northern Illinois University Press, 2003), 6–9.

He said if you was carried to heaven in this condition the first prayer you would make would be that yould might go into hell for that would be more agreeable to your natures. O thot i i have found it a wearines to me many a time over and over again. Then i began to think my nature must be changed but how to attain it i knew not. When i was coming from meeting to my quarters which was about 6 miles my company began to worry me to sing. I put them of till i feard they would be offended.....I thot that was better than to sing a song but o they little thot how i felt. It was hard work for me to sing i felt in such distress in my mind but i went to frollicks all winter and stifeld the conviction i had of its being a soul ruining sin. I was much for fine cloaths and fashons. In the spring in may i went to middletown to keep election. One of the days while i was there i was at a tavern in a frolic. Then there come in a young man from long island belonging to the society that i did and told me how the work of god was carried on there and of several of my mates that was converted. My sister elisabeth also sent a letter. I trembled when i read it. She said her soul magnifyed the lord her spirit rejoysed in god her saviour. Her sighs was turned into songs the comforter is come. I had a strong impression upon my mind to go home which i did in a few days. As soon as i got into my fathers house young people come in and began to talk. Sister elisabeth began to cry over me because i had no intrest in christ. That i wonderd at but the next morning father examined me and i was forst to tell my experiences as wel as i could. He told me when i had done what a dreadful condition i was in. It took hold of my heart. I kept going to the meetings and was more and more concerned. And o what crying out there was among the people what shall i do to be saved....O how i did invi toads or any creature that had no souls to perish eternally. Many a time i kneeled down to pray and my mouth was as it were stopt and i did vent out my anguish with tears and groans and a few broken speches. Now it cut me to think how i had spent my precious time in vanity and sin against god. My not regarding the sabbath no more was bitter to me now....O how it cut me to think i could not get away from god but appear before him i must and i lived in daily expectation of it. Now sometimes it would be cast into my mind thus you need not be so conserned you are not so great a sinner as some are some have mur-dered and done dreadful things but you pray and go to meeting and god will not have a heart to send you to hell. This i thot was the devil trying to beat me of....

I was such a loathsome sinner and he such a holy god sometimes i thot i was willing but he was not. I could hear of others finding mercy but o how it would strike me for i feard greatly that while others was taken i should be left. Now the promises in the schriptures was terror to me for i thot they belonged to the children of god. I had no part in them and i felt such an enmity against the way of salvation by christ. I could see no way to escape damnation. Now i began to feel like one lost in the woods. I knew not what to do nor what course to take for my heart began to grow hard. Now i could not cry and pray as before when i thot of hell. It did not ter-rify me as before it use to. Me thot i envied the very dev-ils for they believed and trembled but i did not. Nothing now semd to help me. I grew worse and worse....I thot it must be a gone case with me and i thot so the more because father never spoke one word to me about my soul in particular as i remember after he first examined me till after i had found comfort which was about three weeaks after. It being in the year 1741 june 20 i was then i suppose in my twentieth year. It was the lord's day. I went to our separate meeting in the school house....

Meeting being done i got away to go home. I thot i would not go to the night meeting which was to be at thomas sanfords for it would do me no good. I remember in the lot as i went i see strawberries and these thots past through my mind. I may as wel go to picking strawberries now as not its no matter what i do its a gone case with me. I fear i have commit-ted the unpardonable sin and now herdned but as i was going home i considered at last. I turned and went to meeting. Soon after meeting began the power of god come down. Many were crying out the other side of the room what shall i do to be saved. I was immediately moved to pres through the multitude and went to them. A great melting of soul come up on me. I wept bitterly and pleaded hard for mercy mercy. Now i was brought to vew the justice of god due to me for my sin. It made me tremble my knees smote together then i thot of belshezer when he see the hand writing against him. It seemd to me i was a sinking down into hell. I thot the flor i stood on gave way and i was just a going but then i began to resign and as i resind my distres began to go of till i was perfectly easy quiet and calm. I could say lord it is just if i sink in to hell. I felt for a few moments like a creature dead. I was nothing i could do nothing nor i desired nothing. I had not so much as one desire for mercy left me but presently i heard one in the room say seek and you shall find come to me all you that are weary and heavy laden and i will give you rest. I began to feel a thirsting after christ and began to beg for mercy free mercy for jesus sake. Me thot i see jesus with the eyes of my soul stand up in heaven. A lovely god man with his arms open ready to receive me his face was full of smiles he lookt white and ruddy and was just such a saviour as my soul wanted every way suitable for me. O how it melted my heart to think he had been willing all this while to save me but i was not willing which i never believed before now. I cryed

from the very heart to think what a tender herted savior i had been refusing how often i turned a deaf ear to his gracious calls and invitations. All that had kept me from him was my will. Jesus appeared altogether lovely to me now.

My heart went out with love and thankfulness and admiration. I cryed why me lord and leave so many. O what a fulnes was their in christ for others if they would come and give up their all to him. I went about the room and invited people to come to him.

QUESTIONS

1. What, according to Heaton, prompted her conversion?
2. What did Heaton's conversion and the Great Awakening mean to her?

5.6. ARTIFACT: JOSEPH LEDDEL, SILVER BEAKER WITH ETCHING OF POPE'S DAY PROCESSION (c. 1750)

In the 1660s, Charles II decreed that November 5, the anniversary of the foiled attempt of the Catholic Guy Fawkes to blow up the king and Parliament in 1605, be considered a holiday in English America. Three decades later, residents of colonial port towns staged processions on November 5, often also called "Pope's Day," that featured displays of effigies of the pope. By the 1740s such processions also included effigies of the Stuart Pretender, a Roman Catholic and the heir of James III, who was deposed by the "Glorious Revolution" in 1688, as well as the devil. Below is an image of a silver beaker that was made in France in the early 1700s and engraved by Joseph Leddel in New York around 1750. The inscription shown here on the beaker reads: "I wish they were all hang'd in a rope, The Pretender, Devil, and Pope." Two other images on the beaker (not shown here) feature the Devil and the Pope and read, respectively, "Three mortal enemies Remember. The Devil Pope and the Pretender" and "Most wicked damnable and evil. The Pope Pretender and the Devil."

Source: Courtesy of Museum of the City of New York/The Art Archive at Art Resource.

QUESTIONS

1. What do the etching and inscription shown here indicate about the relationship that colonists drew between politics and religion?

2. In what ways do the etching and inscription echo sentiments expressed in the Nutfield petition of 1720 (Document 4.5)?

CHAPTER 6

EMPIRE AND RESISTANCE, 1763–1776

6.1. CHARLES III, KING OF SPAIN, APPOINTMENT OF JOSÉ DE GÁLVEZ AS VISITOR GENERAL TO NEW SPAIN (1765)

In this appointment as Visitor General, Charles III gave great authority to José de Gálvez to inspect financial, judicial, and governmental matters in New Spain. Gálvez's main assignment was to improve the flow of revenues from the colonies to Spain, but these instructions also granted him enough power to accomplish other colonial goals, such as the expansion of settlement in North America and the expulsion of the Jesuits from New Spain.

Instruction Reservada, March 14, 1765

The King: Don Joseph Galvez, of my Council, *Alcalde de mi Casa y Corte*, and honorary minister with seniority of the Council of the Indies; notwithstanding that I am well satisfied with the zeal, activity, prudence, and disinterest with which the branches and revenues of my royal patrimony are managed by my viceroy of New Spain and by the ministers of my real hacienda, the governors, and other subordinates who serve under their orders, it being necessary, on account of the large sums needed in attending to the obligations of my royal crown, to exhaust all means from the revenues to the end that the burden of imposing new contributions may be avoided, and to collect all legitimate duties as legally provided without altering established practice or dispensing voluntary favors, and to prevent abuses and all superfluous expenses not absolutely indispensable for the best administration of revenues:

I have deemed it convenient to my royal service to name you, Don Joseph Galvez—a minister in whom I have entire satisfaction and confidence, able, zealous, and skilled in the management of revenues—that you may, in the capacity of visitor-general to my real hacienda within the jurisdiction of the kingdom of New Spain, take cognizance of all of them, examine their proceeds, expenses, balances,

Source: Herbert Ingram Priestley, *José De Gálvez, Visitor-General of New Spain (1765–1771)* (Berkeley: University of California Press, 1916), 404.

and the whereabouts of their funds; demand any arrears in which the administrators, treasurers, lessees of revenues, or other persons who have managed rents, may be to my real hacienda; and regulate the system and management with which the revenues are to be administered in future, reducing expenses and salaries which can and ought to be lowered or abolished, so that the balances be not dissipated by unnecessary expense, but made more effective to their destined ends.

I grant you for all this, and for all that is to be expressed, the powers and jurisdiction which you need to give your commission entire fulfillment. To this end I desire that my viceroy and captain-general of New Spain shall take all measures which you ask and give you the assistance you need....

QUESTIONS

1. How did Charles III expect Galvez to raise royal revenues in New Spain?

2. What kind of power does this set of instructions grant to Galvez?

6.2. WILLIAM PITT, EXCERPTS FROM SPEECHES IN PARLIAMENT OPPOSING THE STAMP ACT (1766)

Whig politician William Pitt spoke out strongly in the House of Commons against the Stamp Act in two speeches on January 14, 1766. Pitt thought that taxing American colonists violated the concept of British liberty, but he did not support the idea that North American colonies should be independent of British control.

As to the late ministry [turning to Grenville who sat near him], every capital measure they have taken has been entirely wrong....The manner in which this affair will be terminated will decide the judgment of posterity on the glory of this kingdom and the wisdom of its government during the present reign....On a question that may mortally wound the freedom of three millions of virtuous and brave subjects beyond the Atlantic Ocean, I cannot be silent....It is my opinion that this kingdom has no right to lay a tax upon the colonies. At the same time, I assert the authority of this kingdom over the colonies to be sovereign and supreme, in every circumstance of government and legislation whatsoever. They are the subjects of this kingdom, equally entitled with yourselves to all the natural rights of mankind, and the peculiar privileges of Englishmen: equally bound by its laws and equally participating of the constitution of this free country. The Americans are the sons, not the bastards of England. As subjects they are entitled to the common right of representation and cannot be bound to pay taxes without their consent.

Taxation is no part of the governing power. The taxes are a voluntary gift and grant of the Commons alone...when therefore in this House we give and grant, we give what is our own. But in an American tax what do we do? We your Majesty's Commons of Great Britain give and grant to your Majesty—what? Our own property? No. We give and grant to your Majesty

Source: Basil Williams, *The Life of William Pitt, Earl of Chatham*, vol. 2 (New York: Longmans, Green, & Co., 1914), 190–95.

the property of your Majesty's Commons in America. It is an absurdity of terms....

The Commons of America represented in their several assemblies have ever been in possession of this their constitutional right of giving and granting their own money. They would have been slaves if they had not enjoyed it.... If this House suffers the Stamp Act to continue in force, France will gain more by your colonies than she ever could have done if her arms in the last war had been victorious....

[Pitt later rose and spoke again in the same debate.]

America is almost in open rebellion. I rejoice that America has resisted....

Upon the whole, I will beg leave to tell the House what is really my opinion. It is, that the Stamp Act be repealed absolutely, totally, and immediately; that the reason for the repeal should be assigned, because it was founded on an erroneous principle. At the same time, let the sovereign authority of this country over the colonies be asserted in as strong terms as can be devised, and be made to extend every point of legislation whatsoever: that we may bind their trade, confine their manufactures, and exercise every power whatsoever—except that of taking money out of their pockets without their consent.

QUESTIONS

1. Why does Pitt argue that the colonists should not be taxed by Parliament?
2. Pitt argues that Britain had "sovereign and supreme" authority over the colonies. How does he reconcile this belief with his opposition to the Stamp Act?
3. According to Pitt, who could tax the American colonists?

6.3. THOMAS HUTCHINSON, EXCERPTS FROM LETTERS TO GREAT BRITAIN DESCRIBING POPULAR UNREST (1768, 1769)

Thomas Hutchinson, a native of Massachusetts who served as the colony's lieutenant governor and chief justice, found himself facing the wrath of protesters during the imperial crisis of the 1760s. His house was demolished by a mob protesting his proposed enforcement of the Stamp Act in 1765. In this letter from 1768, he describes riots in Boston to authorities in Great Britain and worries about resistance in the event that British troops were housed with Boston residents.

Principles of government absurd enough spread thro' all the colonies; but I cannot think that in any colony, people of any consideration have ever been so mad as to think of a revolt. Many of the common people have been in a frenzy, and talk'd of dying in defence of their liberties, and have spoke and printed what is highly criminal, and too many of rank above the vulgar, and some *in public posts* have countenanced and encouraged them until they increased so much in their numbers and opinion of their importance as to submit to government no further than they have thought proper. The legislative powers have been influenced by them, and the executive powers intirely lost their force.... For four or five weeks past the distemper has been growing, and I confess I have been without some apprehensions for myself, but my friends had more for me....

Source: Copy of Letters Sent to Great Britain, by His Excellency Thomas Hutchinson, the Hon. Andrew Oliver, and Several Other Persons, Born and Educated among Us (Boston: Edes and Gill, 1773), 9–12, 16.

The last spring there had been several riots, and a most infamous libel had been published in one of the papers....Whilst we were in this state, news came of two regiments being ordered from Halifax, and soon after two more from Ireland. The minds of the people were more and more agitated, broad hints were given that the troops should never land, a barrel of tar was placed upon the beacon, in the night to be fired to bring in the country when the government troops appeared, and all the authority of the government was not strong enough to remove it. The town of Boston met and passed a number of weak but very criminal votes....

In this confusion the troops from Halifax arrived. I never was much afraid of the people's taking arms, but I was apprehensive of violence from the mob, it being their last chance before the troops could land. As the prospect of revenge became more certain their courage abated in proportion. Two regiments are landed, but a new grievance is now rais'd. The troops are by act of parliament to be quartered no where else but in the barracks untill they are full. There are barracks enough at the castle to hold both regiments....

The government has been so long in the hands of the populace that it must come out of them by degrees, at least it will be a work of time to bring the people back to just notions of the nature of government.

[In another letter from January 1769, Hutchinson appealed for more help to put down unrest in Boston. His letters were meant to be private, but copies were published in 1773, after Hutchinson had been appointed royal governor. They seriously damaged his reputation, and he fled to England after the American Revolution broke out.]

This is most certainly a crisis. I really wish that there may not have been the least degree of severity beyond what is absolutely necessary to maintain, I think I may say to you the *dependance [sic]* which a colony ought to have upon the parent state; but if no measures shall have been taken to secure this dependance, or nothing more than some declaratory acts or resolves, *it is all over with us....*

There must be an abridgment of what are called English liberties. I relieve myself by considering that in a remove from the state of nature to the most perfect state of government there must be a great restraint of liberty. I doubt whether it is possible to project a system of government in which a colony 3000 miles distant from the parent state shall enjoy all the liberty of the parent state....I wish the good of the colony when I wish to see some further restraint of liberty rather than the connexion with the parent state should be broken; for I am sure such a breach must prove the ruin of the colony.

QUESTIONS

1. How does Hutchinson characterize the actions of people from different social classes?
2. How does Hutchinson think the colonial unrest should be controlled?
3. Why did the publication of these letters contribute to Hutchinson's disgrace and exile?

6.4. JOHN DICKINSON, "THE LIBERTY SONG" (1768)

John Dickinson published these song lyrics, meant to be sung to the British tune "Heart of Oak," in the *Boston Gazette* in July 1768 and then in the *Boston Chronicle* on August 29, 1768. This song was one of many that were sung in the colonies during popular protests against the British. The appearance song lyrics in newspapers could also cement allegiance to the cause, and printed lyrics could be posted in public places, such as taverns, to rouse public support. Protest songs were also used as drinking songs to accompany toasts at political gatherings. This song references a "bumper," a glass full of alcohol that is raised in a toast.

Source: Boston Chronicle, August 29–September 5, 1768.

The LIBERTY Song

COME join hand in hand brave AMERICANS all,
And rouse your bold hearts at fair LIBERTY's call;
No tyrannous acts shall suppress your just claim
Or stain with dishonor AMERICA'S name

> In FREEDOM we're born—Let's give them a
> cheer—
> Our purses are ready
> Steady, Friends, steady,
> Not as SLAVES, but as FREEMEN our Money
> we'll give...

Then join Hand in Hand brave AMERICANS all,
By uniting we stand, by dividing we fall;
In so RIGHTEOUS a Cause let us hope to succeed,
For Heaven approves of each generous Deed.

> In FREEDOM we're born, etc.

All Ages shall speak with Amaze and Applause,
Of the Courage we'll shew in support of our
LAWS;
To die we can bear—but to serve we disdain.
For Shame is to FREEDOM more dreadful than
pain

In FREEDOM we're born, etc.
This Bumper I crown for our Sovereign's
Health,
And this for Britannia's Glory and wealth;
That Wealth and that glory immortal may be,
If she is but JUST—and if we are but FREE

> IN FREEDOM we're born, and in FREEDOM
> we'll live
> Our purses are ready,
> Steady, Friends, steady
> Not as SLAVES but as FREEMEN our Money
> we'll give.

QUESTIONS

1. How does this song define freedom and slavery?
2. Why would protestors who sang this song be willing to toast to King George III and "Britainnia's Glory" while simultaneously resisting "tyrannous" Parliamentary taxes?
3. Do you think a song like this could convince anyone to join the Non-Importation Movement?

6.5. ABIGAIL ADAMS, EXCERPTS FROM LETTERS TO JOHN ADAMS ABOUT THE BATTLE OF BUNKER HILL AND CONDITIONS IN BOSTON (1775)

Abigail Adams wrote several letters to her husband, John Adams, who was serving in the Continental Congress, to tell him about the Battle of Bunker Hill, which she had witnessed from across the Charles River. In the excerpts below, she reports on the death of Dr. Joseph Warren, a strong patriot who became known as the primary hero of Bunker Hill.

Source: Charles Francis Adams, ed., *Letters of Mrs. Adams* (Boston: Charles C. Little and James Brown, 1840), 39–40, 49, 52–53.

Sunday, 18 June, 1775

The day,—perhaps, the decisive day,—is come, on which the fate of America depends. My bursting heart must find vent at my pen. I have just heard, that our dear friend, Dr. Warren, is no more, but fell gloriously fighting for his country; saying, better to die honorably in the field, than ignominiously hang upon the gallows. Great is our loss. He has distinguished himself in every engagement, by his courage and fortitude, by animating the soldiers, and leading them on by his own example. A particular account of these dreadful, but I hope glorious days will be transmitted you, no doubt, in the exactest manner. . . .

Charlestown is laid in ashes. The battle began upon our intrenchments upon Bunker's Hill, Saturday morning about three o'clock, and has not cased yet, and it is now three o'clock Sabbath afternoon.

It is expected they will come out over the Neck tonight, and a dreadful battle must ensue. Almighty God, cover the heads of our countrymen, and be a shield to our dear friends! How many have fallen, we know not. The constant roar of the cannon is so distressing, that we cannot eat, drink, or sleep. May we be supported and sustained in the dreadful conflict. I shall tarry here till it is thought unsafe by my friends, and then I have secured myself a retreat at your brother's, who has kindly offered me part of his house. I cannot compose myself to write any further at present. I will add more as I hear further. . . .

5 July, 1775

I would not have you be distressed about me. Danger, they say, makes people valiant. I have been distressed, but not dismayed. I have felt for my country and her sons, and have bled with them and for them. Not all the havoc and devastation they have made, has wounded me like the death of Warren. We want him in the Senate; we want him in his profession; we want him in the field. We mourn for the citizen, the senator, the physician, and the warrior. May we have others raised up in his room.

16 July, 1775

The appointments of the generals Washington and Lee gives universal satisfaction. . . . I was struck with General Washington. You had prepared me to entertain a favorable opinion of him, but I thought the half was not told me. Dignity with ease and complacency, the gentleman and the soldier, look agreeably blended in him. . . .

As to intelligence from Boston. . . I heard yesterday, by one Mr. Roulstone, a goldsmith, who got out in a fishing schooner, that their distress increased upon them fast. Their beef is all spent; their malt and cider all gone. All the fresh provisions they can procure, they are obliged to give to the sick and wounded. . . . No man dared now to be seen talking to his friend in the street. They were obliged to be within, every evening, at ten o'clock, according to martial law; nor could any inhabitant walk any street in town after that time, without a pass from [British commander] Gage. He has ordered all the molasses to be distilled up into rum for the soldiers. . . .

Every article here in the West India way is very scarce and dear. In six weeks we shall not be able to purchase any article of the kind. I wish you would let Bass get me one pound of pepper, and two yards of black calamanco for shoes. . . . You can hardly imagine how much we want many common small articles, which are not manufactured amongst ourselves; but we will have them in time; not one pin to be purchased for love or money.

QUESTIONS

1. What qualities does Adams admire in patriots and military leaders?
2. What evidence do these letters offer regarding women's roles in the American Revolution?

CHAPTER 7

A REVOLUTIONARY
NATION, 1776–1789

7.1. VISUAL DOCUMENT: PIERRE LE BEAU, PORTRAIT OF BENJAMIN FRANKLIN (1780s)

Pierre Le Beau engraved this portrait of Benjamin Franklin after a portrait by Claude Desrais, and it was published in Paris in the 1780s. The caption notes that Franklin was "born in Boston in New England on 17 January 1706." The artist depicts Franklin in the

Source: Courtesy of the Library of Congress Prints and Photographs Division, LC-USZ62-28230.

fur hat that he was fond of wearing in Paris to portray himself as a "rustic" American. He is not wearing his trademark spectacles in this portrait, but his famous face would have been very recognizable to Parisians nonetheless. This engraving is typical of the scores of Franklin portraits that Parisians reproduced on paper, candy boxes, ceramics, and other items in the 1780s.

QUESTIONS

1. Why would Parisians want to buy an engraving of Franklin like this one?

2. How does Franklin's appearance in this image communicate a message about his reputation?

7.2. DIARY OF SURGEON ALBIGENCE WALDO, EXCERPTS DESCRIBING THE CONTINENTAL ARMY'S ENCAMPMENT AT VALLEY FORGE (1777)

Albigence Waldo was a physician from Pomfret, Connecticut, who served as a surgeon with the First Connecticut Infantry Regiment, a militia unit that joined the Continental Army in Pennsylvania in September 1777. Waldo's diary entries about the Continental Army's winter quarters in Valley Forge, Pennsylvania, at the end of 1777 paint a harrowing picture of the conditions that soldiers there faced.

Dec. 12th [1777].—A Bridge of Waggons made across the Schuylkill last Night consisting of 36 waggons, with a bridge of Rails between each....Militia and dragoons brought into Camp several Prisoners. Sun Set.—We are order'd to march over the River—It snows—I'm Sick—eat nothing—No Whiskey—No Forage—Lord—Lord—Lord. The Army were 'till Sun Rise crossing the River—some at the Waggon Bridge, & some at the Raft Bridge below. Cold & uncomfortable.

Dec. 13th—The army march'd three miles from the West side the River and encamp'd near a place call'd the Gulph and not an improper name neither, for this Gulph seems well adapted by its situation to keep us from the pleasure & enjoyments of this World, or being conversant with any body in it....

Dec. 14th—Prisoners & Deserters are continually coming in. The Army which has been surprisingly healthy hitherto, now begin to grow sickly from the continued fatigues they have suffered this Campaign. Yet they still show spirit of Alacrity & Contentment not to be expected from so young Troops. I am Sick—discontented—out of humour. Poor food—hard lodging—Cold Water—fatigue—Nasty Cloaths—nasty

Source: "Diary of Surgeon Albigence Waldo, of the Connecticut Line," *Pennsylvania Magazine of History and Biography* 21 (1897): 305–09.

Cookery—Vomit half my time—smoak'd out of my senses—the Devil's in't—I can't Endure it—Why are we sent here to starve and freeze—What sweet Felicities have I left at home; A charming Wife—pretty Children—Good Beds—good food—good Cookery—all agreeable—all harmonious. Here all Confusion—smoke Cold—hunger & filthyness—A pox on my bad luck. There comes a bowl of beef soup—full of burnt leaves and dirt, sickish enough to make a hector spue,—away with it Boys—I'll live like a Chameleon upon Air.... See the poor Soldier, when in health—with what cheerfulness he meets his foes and encounters every hardship—if barefoot, he labours thro' the Mud & Cold with a Song in his mouth extolling War & Washington—if his food be bad, he eats it notwithstanding with seeming content—blesses God for a good Stomach and Whistles it into digestion. But harkee Patience, a moment—There comes a Soldier, his bare feet are seen thro' his worn out Shoes, his legs nearly naked from the tatter'd remains of an only pair of stockings, his Breeches not sufficient to cover his nakedness, his Shirt hanging in Strings, his hair dishevell'd, his face meager; his whole appearance pictures a person forsaken & discouraged. He comes, and crys with an air of wretchedness & despair, I am Sick, my feet lame, my legs are sore, my body cover'd with this tormenting Itch—my Cloaths are worn out, my Constitution is broken, my former Activity is exhausted by fatigue, hunger & Cold, I fail fast I shall soon be no more! And all the reward I shall get will be—"Poor Will is dead!" People who live at home in Luxury and Ease, quietly possessing their habitations, Enjoying their Wives & families in peace, have but a very faint Idea of the unpleasing sensations, and continual Anxiety the Man endures who is in a Camp, and is the husband and parent of an agreeable family. These same People are willing we should suffer every thing for their Benefit & advantage, and yet are the first to Condemn us for not doing more!!...

Dec. 21st—Preparations made for hutts. Provision Scarce. Mr. Ellis went homeward—sent a Letter to my Wife. Heartily wish myself at home—my Skin & eyes are almost spoil'd with continual smoke.

A general cry thro' the camp this Evening among the Soldiers, "No Meat! No Meat!"—the Distant vales Echo'd back the melancholly sound—"No Meat! No Meat!" Immitating the noise of Crows & Owls, also, made a part of the confused Musick.

What have you for our Dinners Boys? "Nothing but Fire Cake & Water, Sir." At night, "Gentlemen the Supper is ready." What is your supper, Lads? "Fire Cake & Water, Sir." Very poor beef has been drawn in our Camp the greater part of this season.

QUESTIONS

1. How did his experience at Valley Forge give Waldo a sense of how military men are separated from civilians?
2. What were the causes of suffering at Valley Forge?

7.3. BOSTON KING, EXCERPTS FROM "MEMOIRS OF THE LIFE OF BOSTON KING: A BLACK PREACHER" (1798)

In his memoir, Boston King describes escaping from slavery to fight with the British in 1780 and his subsequent attempts to keep his freedom. The British moved King to Canada after the war, and he later emigrated to Sierra Leone with his family.

Source: Boston King, "Memoirs of the Life of Boston King: A Black Preacher (1798)," in *If We Must Die: African American Voices on War and Peace*, ed. Karin L. Stanford (New York: Rowman & Littlefield, 2008), 21–23.

My master being apprehensive that Charles-Town was in danger on account of the war, removed into the country, about 38 miles off. Here we built a large house for Mr. Waters, during which time the English took Charles-Town.... To escape his cruelty, I determined to go to Charles-Town, and throw myself into the hands of the English. They received me readily, and I began to feel the happiness of liberty, of which I knew nothing before, altho' I was much grieved at first, to be obliged to leave my friends, and reside among strangers. In this situation I was seized with small-pox, and suffered great hardships; for all the Blacks affected with that disease, were ordered to be carried a mile from the camp, lest the soldiers should be infected, and disabled from marching....

Being recovered, I marched with the army to Chamblem.... From thence I went to a place about 35 miles off, where we stayed two months: at the expiration of which, an express came to the Colonel to decamp in fifteen minutes. When these orders arrived I was at a distance from the camp, catching some fish for the captain that I waited upon; upon returning to the camp, to my great astonishment, I found all the English were gone, and had left only a few militia. I felt my mind greatly alarmed, but Captain Lewes, who commanded the militia, said, "You need not be uneasy, for you will see your regiment before 7 o'clock tonight." This satisfied me for the present, and in two hours we set off.

As [we] were on the march, the Captain asked, "How will you like me to be your master?"

I answered, that I was Captain Grey's servant. "Yes," said he; "but I expect that they are all taken prisoners before now; and I have been long enough in the English service, and am determined to leave them." These words roused my indignation, and I spoke some sharp words to him. But he calmly replied, "If you do not behave well, I will put you in irons, and give you a dozen stripes every morning." I now perceived that my case was desperate, and that I had nothing to trust to, but to wait the first opportunity for making my escape....

I tarried with Captain Grey about a year, and then left him, and came to Nelson's-ferry. Here I entered into the service of the commanding officer of that place. But our situation was very precarious, and we expected to be made prisoners every day; for the Americans had 1600 men, not far off; whereas our whole number amounted only to 250: But there were 1200 English about 30 miles off; only we knew not how to inform him of our danger, as the Americans were in possession of the country. Our commander at length determined to send me with a letter, promising me great rewards, if I was successful in the business....

Soon after I went to Charles-Town, and entered on board a man of war. As we were going to Chesapeak-bay, we were at the taking of a rich prize. We stayed in the bay two days, and then sailed for New-York, where we went on shore. Here I endeavored to follow my trade, but for want of tools was obliged to relinquish it, and enter service.... I then went out on a pilot-boat. We were at sea eight days, and had only provisions for five, so that we were in danger of starving. On the 9th day we were taken by an American whale-boat. I went on board them with a cheerful countenance, and asked for bread and water, and made very free with them...my mind was sorely distressed at the thought of being again reduced to slavery, and separated from my wife and family; and at the same time it was exceeding difficult to escape from my bondage....

[In 1783] the horrors and devastation of war happily terminated, and peace was restored between America and Great Britain, which diffused universal joy among all parties, except us, who had escaped from slavery, and taken refuge in the English army; for a report prevailed at New-York, that all the slaves, in number 2000, were to be delivered up to their masters, altho' some of them had been three or four years among the English.... The English had compassion upon us in the day of distress, and issued out the Proclamation, importing, That all slaves should be free, who had taken refuge in the British lines....Each of us received a certificate from the commanding officer at New-York, which dispelled all our fears, and filled us with joy and gratitude. Soon after, ships were fitted out, and furnished with every necessary for conveying us to Nova Scotia.

QUESTIONS

1. King relates how he found "the happiness of liberty" for the first time after his escape from slavery. Of what did his sense of "liberty" consist?
2. How did King use different kinds of work and labor to maintain his freedom?
3. Why was King so happy to go to Canada at the end of the war?

7.4. JAMES MADISON, EXCERPTS FROM "FEDERALIST NO. 51" (1788)

James Madison published this essay in the *New York Packet* on February 8, 1788. He wrote anonymously as "Publius" as part of the effort to convince the New York convention to ratify the U.S. Constitution. In this essay, Madison sought to reassure New Yorkers that the federal government would not grow too powerful.

To what expedient, then, shall we finally resort, for maintaining in practice the necessary partition of power among the several departments, as laid down in the Constitution? The only answer that can be given is...by so contriving the interior structure of the government as that its several constituent parts may, by their mutual relations, be the means of keeping each other in their proper places....In order to lay a due foundation for that separate and distinct exercise of the different powers of government, which to a certain extent is admitted on all hands to be essential to the preservation of liberty, it is evident that each department should have a will of its own; and consequently should be so constituted that the members of each should have as little agency as possible in the appointment of the members of the others. Were this principle rigorously adhered to, it would require that all the appointments for the supreme executive, legislative, and judiciary magistracies should be drawn from the same fountain of authority, the people, through channels having no communication whatever with one another....

It is equally evident, that the members of each department should be as little dependent as possible on those of the others, for the emoluments annexed to their offices. Were the executive magistrate, or the judges, not independent of the legislature in this particular, their independence in every other would be merely nominal.

But the great security against a gradual concentration of the several powers in the same department, consists in giving to those who administer each department the necessary constitutional means and personal motives to resist encroachments of the others....Ambition must be made to counteract ambition. The interest of the man must be connected with the constitutional rights of the place. It may be a reflection

Source: *The Federalist: A Commentary on The Constitution of the United States* (New York: G. P. Putnam's Sons, 1888), 322–25.

on human nature, that such devices should be necessary to control the abuses of government. But what is government itself, but the greatest of all reflections on human nature? If men were angels, no government would be necessary. If angels were to govern men, neither external nor internal controls on government would be necessary. In framing a government which is to be administered by men over men, the great difficulty lies in this: you must first enable the government to control the governed; and in the next place oblige it to control itself. A dependence on the people is, no doubt, the primary control on the government; but experience has taught mankind the necessity of auxiliary precautions....

But it is not possible to give each department an equal power of self-defense. In republican government, the legislative authority necessarily predominates. The remedy for this inconveniency is to divide the legislature into different branches; and to render them, by different modes of election and different principles of action, as little connected with each other as the nature of their common functions and their common dependence on society will admit....The weakness of the executive may require, on the other hand, that it should be fortified.

QUESTIONS

1. How would keeping the powers of the branches of government separate help in "the preservation of liberty," according to Madison?
2. Why was the independence of the judicial and executive branches from the legislative branch so important to Madison?
3. What roles do "interest" and "ambition" play in controlling government power, according to Madison?

7.5. MERCY OTIS WARREN, EXCERPTS FROM "OBSERVATIONS ON THE NEW CONSTITUTION, AND THE FEDERAL AND STATE CONVENTIONS BY A COLUMBIAN PATRIOT" (1788)

This pamphlet, anonymously published by playwright and historian Mercy Otis Warren, criticized the proposed U.S. Constitution for consolidating too much power in the federal government. Warren criticized the elitism and secrecy of the Constitutional Convention and called on the state ratification conventions to reject the Constitution. Warren's fear of power and conspiratorial tone were typical of many other Antifederalists.

Animated with the firmest zeal for the interest of this country, the peace and union of the American States, and the freedom and happiness of a people who have made the most costly sacrifices in the cause of liberty,—who have braved the power of Britain, weathered the convulsions of war, and waded thro' the blood of friends and foes to establish their independence and to support the freedom of the human mind; I cannot

Source: Richard Henry Lee, *An Additional Number of Letters from the Federal Farmer to the Republican*, reprint ed. (Chicago: Quadrangle Books, 1962).

silently witness this degredation without calling on them, before they are compelled to blush at their own servitude, and to turn back their languid eyes on their lost liberties.... Self defence is a primary law of nature, which no subsequent law of society can abolish; this primeval principle, the immediate gift of the Creator, obliges every one to remonstrate against the strides of ambition, and a wanton lust of domination, and to resist the first approaches of tyranny, which at this day threaten to sweep away the rights for which the brave sons of America have fought with an heroism scarcely paralleled even in ancient republicks....

The mode in which this constitution is recommended to the people to judge without either the advice of Congress, or the legislatures of the several states, is very reprehensible—it is an attempt to force it upon them before it could be the roughly understood, and may leave us in that situation, that in the first moments of slavery the minds of the people agitated by the remembrance of their lost liberties, will be like the sea in a tempest, that sweeps down every mound of security.

But it is needless to enumerate other instances, in which the proposed constitution appears contradictory to the first principles which ought to govern mankind; and it is equally so to enquire into the motives that induced to so bold a step as the annihilation of the independence and sovereignty of the thirteen distinct states.—They are but too obvious through the whole progress of the business, from the first shutting up the doors of the federal convention and resolving that no member should correspond with gentlemen in the different states on the subject under discussion; till the trivial proposition of *recommending* a few amendments was artfully ushered into the convention of the Massachusetts....

And the hurry with which it has been urged to the acceptance of the people, without giving time, by adjournments, for better information, and more unanimity has a deceptive appearance.... May the people be calm, and wait a legal redress; may the mad transport of some of our infatuated capitals subside; and every influential character through the States, make the most prudent exertions for a new general Convention, who may vest adequate powers in Congress, for all national purposes, without annihilating the individual governments, and drawing blood from every pore by taxes, impositions and illegal restrictions—This step might again re-establish the Union, restore tranquility to the ruffled mind of the inhabitants, and save America from distresses dreadful even in contemplation.... Though several State Conventions have assented to, and ratified, yet the voice of the people appears at present strong against the adoption of the Constitution...—by the imbecility of some, and the duplicity of others, a majority of the Convention of Massachusetts have been flattered with the ideas of amendments, when it will be too late to complain.

QUESTIONS

1. How does Warren contend that the proposed Constitution betrayed the legacy of the American Revolution?
2. What are Warren's objections to the way the Constitution was formed and ratified?
3. What solution does she propose?

CHAPTER 8

A NEW NATION FACING A REVOLUTIONARY WORLD, 1789–1815

8.1. *GREENLEAF'S NEW YORK JOURNAL*, ANONYMOUS LETTERS REPORTING ON CROWD PROTESTS AGAINST THE JAY TREATY IN PHILADELPHIA (1795)

On July 8, 1795, the editor of *Greenleaf's New York Journal* printed two conflicting accounts of a protest against the Jay Treaty, the highly controversial treaty stabilizing relations between the U.S. and Great Britain. In the summer of 1795, the terms of the treaty were kept secret while the Senate decided whether to ratify it. But the secrecy did nothing to stop popular opposition. The Federalists and Democratic Republicans battled not only over the treaty itself, but also over the specifics and meaning of protests like this one held by Philadelphia sailors.

Extract of a Letter from a respectable Citizen of Philadelphia, to his friend in this city. I must inform you of a circumstance which took place here on Saturday evening last. At eleven o'clock the ship-carpenters of Kensington, and a number of other citizens, about 500 armed with clubs, paraded the streets with a transparent painting of *Mr. Jay*; the figure in the attitude of presenting "THE TREATY" to an expecting, admiring Senate, with the left hand, and in the right, a pair of scales suspended—In the elevated scale, "*Virtue, Liberty and Independence*," were inscribed in large capitals; in the preponderating one "*British Gold*." After passing through several streets, they returned again to Kensington, where the painting was *committed to the flames*. A small party of the Light-Horse attempted to disperse them, but without effect; they were driven from the field amidst a shower of stones, by which some were severely hurt, but no lives lost. I was an eyewitness to the whole proceeding, you may therefore rely on this account.

[Extract of another letter of the same date.]

The 4th of July passed over in quietness, whatever you may have heard to the contrary.

Source: *Greenleaf's New York Journal*, July 8, 1795.

On the fourth [of] July a number of ship carpenters from Kensington, and some of the Democratic Society, intended to burn Mr. Jay's effigy opposite the president's house. They were warned not to attempt it, and the militia officers, light horse, artillery, &c. waited for them in Market-street, till ten o'clock, but deterred them from their design, they came down Second to Market, from thence to Front, about one o'clock Sunday morning, as silent as a funeral procession, till they got above Vine street, and supposing themselves out of danger, when they gave three cheers. I mention this in case it becomes the subject of conversation. You may know how to speak of it.

Not ten persons in all the streets they passed knew any thing of it.

QUESTIONS

1. Judging from these two opposing accounts, what is it possible to discern regarding the attitude of Philadelphia sailors and shipbuilders toward the Jay Treaty?
2. Which letter was likely written by a person with Democratic-Republican sympathies and which one by a person with Federalist sympathies?
3. Why would the New York newspaper publish these two conflicting accounts?

8.2. VISUAL DOCUMENT: ANONYMOUS CARTOONIST, *THE PROVIDENTIAL DETECTION* (c. 1797–1800)

In this, one of the earliest political cartoons published in the United States, an anonymous Federalist cartoonist uses a variety of images to paint a shocking picture of the Democratic-Republican front-runner in the 1800 election, Thomas Jefferson. The cartoon portrays him as a willing traitor to the United States who worships at the altar of revolutionary France—the "Altar of Gallic Despotism."

The eagle with the shield represents the United States as it swoops down to snatch the U.S. Constitution from a kneeling Jefferson before he can add the Constitution to the fire of French despotism. The French altar (which is supposed to recall similar altars to "Reason" that were used in high-profile radical revolutionary rituals in France) is surrounded by moneybags labeled "American Spoliations," "Plunder," "Sardinia," "Flanders," and with the names of other parts of Europe that France had invaded. A fire atop the altar is fed by radical writings—Democratic-Republican newspapers, including the *Aurora;* works by the English radical William Godwin; and French philosophical works by Rousseau and Voltaire. Falling from Jefferson's right hand is a copy of his famous letter to Philip Mazzei, an Italian diplomat and supporter of the French Revolution. The letter, which was published in a Paris newspaper in 1797, had criticized Federalists as monarchists and implied that George Washington was among them. The cartoon also contains religious imagery, showing the eye of Providence (God) looking down from the clouds and the Devil lurking behind the French altar.

Source: The Providential Detection. Courtesy American Antiquarian Society, Worcester, Massachusetts, USA/The Bridgeman Art Library.

QUESTIONS

1. How did the cartoonist communicate his belief that Jefferson was dangerous? Might any symbols or parts of the picture particularly move viewers?
2. Do you think the cartoon was effective? Could it have changed anyone's mind about the French Revolution? Did it probably appeal only to Federalists who already opposed Jefferson, or could it have had a broader appeal?
3. Why do you think the cartoonist decided to use a visual to make this argument about Jefferson, instead of writing a newspaper article or pamphlet?

8.3. JAMES BAYARD, EXCERPTS FROM A LETTER TO ALEXANDER HAMILTON DESCRIBING HIS DILEMMA IN THE DISPUTED PRESIDENTIAL ELECTION OF 1800 (JANUARY 7, 1801)

Delaware Congressman James Bayard was a loyal member of the Federalist Party. In this letter, he speculates to one of his party's leaders, Alexander Hamilton, about what might resolve the deadlocked presidential election and whether the Federalists in the House of Representatives would vote for Aaron Burr or Thomas Jefferson. When the ballots were cast in March, it was Bayard's vote that decided the election in favor of Jefferson.

I assure you, sir, there appears to be a strong inclination in a majority of the federal party to support Mr. Burr. The current has already acquired considerable force, and is manifestly increasing. The vote which the representation of a State enables me to give would decide the question in favor of Mr. Jefferson. At present I am by no means decided as to the object of preference. If the federal party should take up Mr. Burr, I ought certainly to be impressed with the most undoubting conviction before I separated myself from them. With respect to the personal qualities of the competitors, I should fear as much from the sincerity of Mr. Jefferson (if he is sincere), as from the want of probity in Mr. Burr. There would be really cause to fear that the government would not survive the course of moral and political experiments to which it would be subjected in the hands of Mr. Jefferson. But there is another view of the subject which gives me some inclination in favor of Burr. I consider the State ambition of Virginia as the source of present party. The faction who govern that State, aim to govern the United States. Virginia will never be satisfied but when this state of things exists. If Burr should be the President,

they will not govern, and his acceptance of the office, which would disappoint their views, which depend upon Jefferson, would, I apprehend, immediately create a schism in the party which would soon rise into open opposition.

I cannot deny, however, that there are strong considerations, which give a preference to Mr. Jefferson. The subject admits of many doubtful views, and before I resolve on the part I shall take, I shall wait the approach of the crisis which may probably bring with it circumstances decisive of the event. The federal party meet on Friday, for the purpose of forming a resolution as to their line of conduct. I have not the least doubt of their agreeing to support Burr.

QUESTIONS

1. What are Bayard's objections to Jefferson and Burr?
2. Does this document offer evidence that the Federalists had become a well-organized political party by 1801?

Source: Allen Johnson, ed., *Readings in American Constitutional History, 1776–1876* (New York: Houghton Mifflin Company, 1913), 214–15.

8.4. JAMES MATHER AND WILLIAM CLAIBORNE, EXCERPTS FROM LETTERS REGARDING CARIBBEAN MIGRANTS IN NEW ORLEANS (1809)

On July 18, 1809, James Mather, the mayor of New Orleans, wrote to Louisiana's territorial governor, William Claiborne, about refugees from the Haitian revolution who had come to New Orleans from Cuba. The emigrants, a mix of whites, free people of color, and slaves, presented a challenge to the city. Congress eventually passed a special exemption to the prohibition on the international importation of slaves to allow these slaves to be brought into the United States from Cuba.

In answer to your much esteemed [letter] of yesterday, I beg leave to enclose here in for the information of your Excellency, a general statement of the People brought here from the Island of Cuba by thirty four vessels.... It is hardly possible to form as yet a Judgement on the general character of the different classes.—It may however be inferred from their conduct since they have lived among us, as also from various other circumstances.

1stly In what regards the Blacks, they are trained up to the habits of strict discipline, and consist wholly of Africans bought up from guineamen in the island of Cuba, or of faithful slaves who have fled with their masters from St. Domingo as early as the year 1803.

2dly A few characters among the free People of Color have been represented to me as dangerous for the peace of this Territory; I must however own your Excellency that in every other Territory but this, the most part of them would not, I think, be viewed under the same light if due attention should be paid to the effects of the difference of language, and if it should be considered that these very men possess property, and have useful trades to live upon[1].... In the mean time there has not been one single complaint that I know of; against any of them concerning their conduct since their coming to this place.

3rdly The white persons, consisting chiefly of Planters, and merchants of St. Domingo who took refuge on the shores of Cuba about six years ago, appear to be an active, industrious People.... They have suffered a great deal from the want of Provisions both at sea, and in the River.—Several of them have died, and many are now yet a prey to diseases originating, as it appears, from the use of unwholesome food and from the foul air they have breathed, while heaped up together with their slaves, in the holds of small vessels during their passage from Cuba....

I know of no provision established by our Laws, to prevent free white persons who have means for their living, to come and settle in the United States....

[On November 5, 1809, William Claiborne wrote to Secretary of State Robert Smith to express his suspicion and concern about the refugees from Haiti who had come into New Orleans through Cuba and Jamaica.]

At all times, the *utmost vigilance* on the part of the officers of the Government in this Territory, is essential, but it is particularly so at the present period, when foreigners and *Strangers* are daily arriving among us; of *whom*, many are of doubtful character and desperate fortunes, and may (probably) become willing

Source: Dunbar Rowland, ed., *Official Letter Books of W. C. C. Claiborne, 1801–1816*, reprinted. (New York: AMS Press, 1976), 4:387–88, 422–23; 5: 1–2.

1. The free people of color were required to post bond and leave the territory within a set amount of time.

instruments in the hands of those unprincipled, intriguing individuals, who would wish to disturb the *peace, and Union* of the American States....

You are already acquainted with the difficulty and anxiety which the Emigrants from Cuba occasioned me; —I anticipate like difficulties with the French Emigrants from Sto. Domingo and Jamaica, who I suspect will repair hither with their slaves.

[Just days later, on November 12, 1809, Claiborne again wrote to Secretary Smith about refugees from Haiti who were entering New Orleans from Cuba and Jamaica and bringing slaves with them. He feared that the city could not handle the influx of people, and that the international slave trade would be reopened, despite its being outlawed by Congress the previous year.]

Two or three vessels from the City of Sto. Domingo via Jamaica have recently arrived in the Mississippi, with passengers and some slaves on board and others are expected.—

Already New Orleans and its vicinity are crowded with the unfortunate refugees from Cuba, and if the French of St. Domingo, Jamaica (& perhaps Guadeloupe, for I am told it is about to [be] attacked) should also seek an asylum here, I shall deem it alike unfortunate for them and for us; —for independent political considerations, this society will be totally unable to furnish conveniences for so numerous and sudden an emigration, or to supply the wants of the poor and distressed. I am particularly desirous to discourage the Emigrants from bringing slaves with them.—Motives of humanity induce me to permit the Refugees from Cuba to land their slaves, but this indulgence cannot be extended much farther, for already Sir, it is represented to me, that Negro's purchased from the Jails of Jamaica, have been smuggled into the Territory, and I suspect if it was understood, that Negro's brought by the French of St. Domingo were permitted to be landed, that a Negro trade hither would be immediately commenced.— These considerations Sir, induced me to write the Letters to our Consuls at Havanah and Jamaica, and I hope the same will be approved by the President.—

QUESTIONS

1. What problems do the mayor and the governor anticipate that the Caribbeans will bring with them to New Orleans?
2. Why did government officials accept these refugees if they were so troublesome?
3. What evidence does this document present about the ways that Caribbean emigrants confused and challenged Americans' racial attitudes?

8.5. VISUAL DOCUMENT: JOHN WESLEY JARVIS, PORTRAIT OF CAPTAIN SAMUEL CHESTER REID (1815)

John Wesley Jarvis painted this portrait of Captain Samuel Chester Reid in 1815, just after the War of 1812. During the war, Reid captained a privateer, the *General Armstrong*, that raided in the Azores Islands, located about halfway between Portugal and the United States. In 1814, he engaged British naval forces bound for Jamaica and New Orleans, and Andrew Jackson claimed that Reid's actions slowed British naval reinforcements down sufficiently to aid his triumphal defense of New Orleans. Reid's naval heroism was publicly applauded and became the subject of popular engravings, some of which may have used this portrait as a source. In 1817, Reid designed the present pattern of the U.S. flag, with 13 stripes and one star for each state. The flag in the background of this portrait is a forerunner of his stars and stripes design.

Source: The William Hood Dunwoody Fund/Minneapolis Institute of Arts.

QUESTIONS

1. What visual aspects of this portrait indicate that Reid is a heroic figure?

2. What impression of naval warfare does this portrait offer?

3. Does this portrait reveal anything about American national identity, or is it better understood as simply a picture of one heroic man?

CHAPTER 9

AMERICAN PEOPLES ON THE MOVE, 1789–1824

9.1. ELI WHITNEY AND THOMAS JEFFERSON, LETTERS ON THE PATENTING OF THE COTTON GIN (1793)

On June 20, 1793, Eli Whitney wrote to Secretary of State Thomas Jefferson requesting a patent for the cotton gin that he had recently invented. Congress empowered the secretary of state to grant a patent to anyone who submitted a description of an invention, drawings, a model, and a fee. Whitney's letter and Jefferson's reply of November 16, 1793 are reproduced below.

That having invented a Machine for the Purpose of ginning Cotton, he is desirous of obtaining an exclusive Property in the same. Concerning which invention, your Petitioner alledges as follows (viz) first. That it is entirely new and constructed in a different manner and upon different principles from any, other Cotton Gin or Machine heretofore known or used for that purpose. 2d. That with this Ginn, if turned with horses or by water, two persons will clean as much cotton in one Day, as a Hundred persons could cleane in the same time with the gins now in common use. 3d. That the Cotton which is cleansed in his Ginn contains fewer broken seeds and impurities, and is said to be more valuable than Cotton, which is cleaned in the usual way. Your Petitioner, therefore Prays your Honor to Grant him the said Whitney, a Patent for the said Invention or Improvement....

[November 16, 1793]

Your favor of October 18, including a drawing [of] your cotton gin, was received....The only requisite of the law now uncomplied with is the forwarding of a model, which being received your patent may be made out & delivered to your order immediately. As the state of Virginia, of which I am, carries on household manufactures of cotton to a great extent, as I also do myself, and one of our great embarrassments in the cleaning the cotton of the seed, I feel a considerable interest in the success of your invention, for family use. Permit me therefore to ask information from you on these points, has the machine been thoroughly tried in the ginning of cotton, or is it as yet but a machine of theory? What quantity of cotton has it cleaned on an average of several days, & worked by

Sources: John Catanzariti, ed., *The Papers of Thomas Jefferson*, vol. 26 (Princeton, NJ: Princeton University Press, 1995); Eli Whitney Papers, Yale University Library.

hand, & by how many hands? What will be the cost of one of these made to be worked by hand? Favorable answers to these questions would induce me to engage one of them to be forwarded to Richmond for me.

1. What claims for improvement in cotton gin design does Whitney make?
2. What aspects of the new gin most interest Jefferson?

9.2. JOURNAL OF BENJAMIN CARPENTER, REFLECTIONS ON THE INDIA TRADE (1790)

Benjamin Carpenter captained his merchant ship, the *Ruby*, from Boston in 1789 hoping to trade at Port Louis in the Mauritius Islands, but when he arrived there, he found the French port in an upheaval caused by the French Revolution. He sailed to Ceylon (Sri Lanka) instead and then to India to continue trading first in Madras and then in Calcutta. Here, he comments in his ship journal about U.S. trade prospects in India.

On your arrival at Calcutta you will proceed as at Madras—the manner and customs are the same with this difference only—the inhabitants are more sociable and friendly. You will find them ready to assist you in everything. They are very liberal and deal on honorable terms. On my arrival at Bengal I was an utter stranger to every person there—and notwithstanding I was destitute of even a line of recommendation, I found the greatest hospitality and very soon became acquainted with the principal merchants there.

The produce and manufactories of Bengal are every way suited for the American market, but as the trade to this country is a very recent affair, they have not those goods on hand which we are most in want of. For this reason our ships are obliged to wait three or four months for a cargo. This inconvenience is easily remedied by a previous order. You may then be sure to have your goods in readiness on your arrival, and then your detention may not be more than three weeks or a month....

A voyage from America may be performed in fourteen months—and a person well acquainted with a suitable cargo will seldom fail to make a good voyage. Their sugar and niter will ballast your ship, you can fill her with dry goods. The sugar is of a superior quality to West India sugar and is sold at six rupees per maund of eighty-two pounds English. The country abounds with a great variety of drugs of the first qualities.... They are sold astonishingly cheap, and if care is taken in choosing them they will turn to very good account in Europe. There is many articles in Bengal which would answer well in America that we are not yet acquainted with. There are also many things [that are] the produce of America that would net good profit and would be a sure remittance in India....

America abounds with furs of different kinds, any quantity of the various species would very readily sell in Bengal at 100 percent profit. They purchase them to send to China, which is by far the best remittance they can make. It is a little surprising that [given] the

Source: Benjamin Carpenter, "From the Journal of the *Ruby*, 1789–1790," in *Yankee India: American Commercial and Cultural Encounters with India in the Age of Sail, 1784–1860*, ed. Susan S. Bean, 61–63 (Salem, MA: Peabody Essex Museum, 2001).

number of ships we have sent to China that none of them should think of furs. They are certainly the best article they can carry....

3000 barrels of whale oil would readily sell in Calcutta for 20 Rupees on the barrel which is double the price it sells at in America....

After duly considering the advantage arising from this trade, there is no one can venture to affirm that the commerce with India is prejudicial to America....

Having contracted for a quantity of chintz to be manufactured at Chandernagore (a French factory about 30 miles from Calcutta). In order to choose patterns and expedite matters, I this morning hired a buggerow and made an excursion up the river....

The navigation to Chandernagore is perfectly safe and there is a sufficient depth of water for a vessel of 1,000 tons to anchor within a cable's length of the shore. If we can conquer the silly jealousies subsisting between the American merchants and persuade them to unite their property to establish a factory here, I am fully persuaded they would realize forty percent per annum on their stock. This is certainly a far greater profit than they can gain on their Europe, West India or any other trade whatever.

QUESTIONS

1. What kinds of goods does this document show were involved in the U.S.–India trade?
2. Why would this description make the India trade sound attractive to prospective ship captains?

9.3. VISUAL DOCUMENT: TODDY JUG WITH PORTRAIT OF GEORGE WASHINGTON (c. 1800–1820)

This porcelain jug, made to serve hot alcoholic beverages, belonged to Edward Tilghman, a Philadelphia lawyer. Tilghman's uncle, Benjamin Chew Wilcocks, ordered the jug from China, where it was manufactured and hand decorated. The portrait on the jug copies an engraving made by David Edwin of a Gilbert Stuart portrait of Washington.

Source: The Metropolitan Museum of Art, New York, NY, U.S.A. Image copyright © The Metropolitan Museum of Art. Image source: Art Resource, New York.

QUESTIONS

1. Why would Americans want to have pictures of George Washington on household objects like this one?

2. What does this object tell us about the relationship that existed between the United States and China at the beginning of the 19th century?

9.4. SUSANNAH ROWSON, PREFACE TO *CHARLOTTE TEMPLE* (1794)

Novelist Susannah Rowson explained the purpose of her novel *Charlotte Temple* in the preface to the Philadelphia edition of the book. She argued that her novel should not be seen as dangerous for young women, as many novels were perceived to be at the turn of the 19th century. The publisher of this edition of the work, Matthew Carey, also preceded the novel with this review from a contemporary magazine:

"It may be a Tale of Truth, for it is not unnatural, and it is a tale of real distress—Charlotte, by the artifice of a teacher...is enticed from her governess, and accompanies a young officer to

Source: Susannah Rowson, *Charlotte: A Tale of Truth*, vol. 1, 2nd ed. (Philadelphia: Matthew Carey, 1794).

America.—The marriage ceremony, if not forgotten, is postponed, and Charlotte dies a martyr to the inconstancy of her lover and treachery of his friend.—The situations are artless and affecting—the descriptions natural and pathetic; we should feel for Charlotte, if such a person ever existed, who, for one error, scarcely, perhaps, deserved so severe a punishment. If it is a fiction, poetic justice is not, we think, properly distributed."

For the perusal of the young and thoughtless of the fair sex, this Tale of Truth is designed; and I could wish my fair readers to consider it as not merely the effusion of Fancy, but as a reality. The circumstances on which I have founded this novel were related to me some little time since by an old lady who had personally known Charlotte, though she concealed the real names of the characters, and likewise the place where the unfortunate scenes were acted: yet as it was impossible to offer a relation to the public in such an imperfect state, I have thrown over the whole a slight veil of fiction, and substituted names and places according to my own fancy. The principal characters in this little tale are now consigned to the silent tomb: it can therefore hurt the feelings of no one; and may, I flatter myself, be of service to some who are so unfortunate as to have neither friends to advise, or understanding to direct them, through the various and unexpected evils that attend a young and unprotected woman in her first entrance into life.

While the tear of compassion still trembled in my eye for the fate of the unhappy Charlotte, I may have children of my own, said I, to whom this recital may be of use, and if to your own children, said Benevolence, why not to the many daughters of Misfortune who, deprived of natural friends, or spoilt by a mistaken education, are thrown on an unfeeling world without the least power to defend themselves from the snares not only of the other sex, but from the more dangerous arts of the profligate of their own.

Sensible as I am that a novel writer, at a time when such a variety of works are ushered into the world under that name, stands but a poor chance for fame in the annals of literature, but conscious that I wrote with a mind anxious for the happiness of that sex whose morals and conduct have so powerful an influence on mankind in general; and convinced that I have not wrote a line that conveys a wrong idea to the head or a corrupt wish to the heart, I shall rest satisfied in the purity of my own intentions, and if I merit not applause, I feel that I dread not censure.

If the following tale should save one hapless fair one from the errors which ruined poor Charlotte, or rescue from impending misery the heart of one anxious parent, I shall feel a much higher gratification in reflecting on this trifling performance, than could possibly result from the applause which might attend the most elegant finished piece of literature whose tendency might deprave the heart or mislead the understanding.

QUESTIONS

1. How does Rowson argue that her novel can teach good morals to young women?
2. What does this document indicate about public opinion in the 1790s on the nature of women?

9.5. ANNE ROYALL, EXCERPTS FROM *LETTERS FROM ALABAMA* (1818)

The writer Anne Royall's *Letters from Alabama*, originally written as a series of letters to her friend Matt and later published as a book, recounts her travels around that state in the years after the War of 1812. She noted economic developments in the area and expressed sympathy for several Cherokee families, who had been forced off their farms. She also commented on Andrew Jackson's plantation.

Melton's Bluff, January 12th, 1818

Dear Matt,

It is unnecessary to state what you have learned from the newspapers, that this land was abandoned last Fall by the Indians. The fires were still smoking, when the white people took possession. Although I had travelled through a beautiful country, the two preceding days, and my mind had been raised to the highest pitch of expectation by repeated descriptions of this land; yet, it far exceeded all I anticipated. . . .

About ten o'clock we came in sight of the first Indian farm—but Indian farm no longer! The smoke was issuing slowly through the chimney. Why, these Indians have been like us!—could not be savage—cornfields—apple trees, and peach-trees. Fences like ours—but not so high—trusted to their neighbors' honesty—perhaps these being more civilized had more reason to fear their neighbor. . . . The house looked tight and comfortable; the fruit-trees are large, and show age—there the Indian sat under their shade, or stood up and plucked the apples—wonder he did not plant more—suppose he did not know how to make cider. . . .

Melton's Bluff, January 14th, 1818

Dear Matt,

Melton's Bluff is a town, and takes its name from John Melton, a white man . . . [who] became displeased with the white people; attached himself to the Cherokee Indians; married a squaw, and settled at this place many years ago. . . . He became immensely rich; owned a great number of slaves. . . .

When the Cherokee Indians abandoned this area last fall, some of them went up the river to the Cherokee nation, there to remain, till boats were provided for their removal to the west, by the government; others went directly down the river to Arkansas. . . . The order for their departure was sudden and unexpected. . . .

Here is a very large plantation of cotton and maize, worked by about sixty slaves, and owned by General Jackson, who bought the interest of Old Melton. . . . I took a walk with some ladies to-day, over the plantation, as we wished to hav[e] a nearer view of those snowy fields . . . together with orchards, gin houses, gardens, Melton's mansion, and a considerable negro town.

QUESTIONS

1. What relationship does Royall observe as existing among the Cherokee, slaves, and white people?
2. In 1818, Alabama was one of the fastest-growing areas of the country, and it was viewed as a place filled with natural resources. How do Royall's observations show that attitude toward Alabama's bounty?

Source: Anne Royall, *Letters from Alabama on Various Subjects* (Washington, DC: 1830), 54–60.

CHAPTER 10

MARKET REVOLUTIONS AND THE RISE OF DEMOCRACY, 1789–1832

10.1. EDITOR OF *THE EASTERN ARGUS*, EXCERPTS FROM COVERAGE OF FOURTH OF JULY CELEBRATIONS IN PORTLAND, MAINE (JULY 9, 1830)

The editor of *The Eastern Argus*, the Democratic-Republican newspaper in Portland, Maine, reported on Fourth of July celebrations that took place in that city in 1830 in partisan terms. Newspapers in the 1830s were an important organ of political party development and organization.

The Anniversary of American Independence was celebrated on Monday last, by the Republicans of Portland, in a style never equaled upon a like occasion in this State.

The illiberal and disingenuous course pursued in advance of the day, by the mangers of what has been called the *Town Celebration*, aroused a proper sense of self respect in Republicans, who resolved spontaneously, as it were, not to submit to the indignity of it....Preparations were consequently made for a celebration among themselves, in self defence....

The inside was tastefully decorated throughout with green boughs, evergreen and roses, historical paintings and engravings. Over the arched entrance from the street, stood erect, during the day, a beautiful, full grown, living American Eagle, whose fine appearance excited the admiration of thousands. Upon the face of the arch beneath, was inscribed the republican motto—VOX POPULI! On the inner side surrounded by other appropriate decorations, were two full rigged vessels in miniature suspended from the arch, and on the sides of the walk beneath were the portraits of Washington, Jefferson, and Jackson, as if to preside over and cheer the festivities of the occasion....

At noon a procession was formed....We believe we expose ourselves to the contradiction of no candid

Source: *The Eastern Argus*, July 9, 1830.

and disinterested man, in saying that this procession was decidedly the most numerous ever witnessed in this town, on any previous occasion. In passing through Middle Street the procession for the "town celebration" was met with, and the two parties passed each other under a military salute....

After the services at the Meeting-house were concluded, the procession re-organized and passed up Federal Street...to the bower, where five hundred and sixty eight persons partook of a dinner, provided by Mr. ATWOOD....

[Toasts were then given.]

By Gen. J. W. Smith, Vice President, *Those sacred Democratic principles of the party*, which in 1801 called forth the immortal Jefferson, and in 1829, the hero and illustrious patriot Jackson, to preside over this great and happy republic....

By Doct. B. H. Mace. V. P. *The Democracy of New Hampshire*—Founded on a rock—Firm as the *Hills*, its pillars stand unmoved....

By Mr. Daniel Robinson, V. P. *Andrew Jackson, President of the United States*—May he live to a good old age, for the benefit of the rising generation....

By Hon. Wm. Chadwick. *The Hon'ble John Anderson, our Representative in Congress*—His untiring industry and successful exertions in behalf of our commercial interests, justly entitle him to the warmest gratitude of his constituents....

By Hon. Luther Fitch. *The Fourth of July*—The anniversary of American Independence—the time to revert to the essential principles of the republic—to impress them upon the mind and the heart, that they may never be forgotten or abandoned.

QUESTIONS

1. How did this celebration seek to link Portland's Democratic Republicans to the glory of America's past?
2. What were the partisan elements of the celebration? Which parts seemed to be purely patriotic?

10.2. WILLIAM SAMPSON, EXCERPTS FROM *PEOPLE V. MELVIN* IN DEFENSE OF THE NEW YORK JOURNEYMEN SHOEMAKERS (1809)

Attorney William Sampson, a Jacobin émigré from France, defended New York's journeyman shoemakers when they were prosecuted in 1809 for illegally colluding to go on strike and win a wage increase. In this case, called *People v. Melvin*, Sampson made an eloquent speech that argued that the journeymen deserved a fair chance in the changing market economy.

Shall all others, except only the industrious mechanic, be allowed to meet and plot; merchants to determine their prices current, or settle the markets, politicians to electioneer, sportsmen for horseracing and games, ladies and gentlemen for balls, parties and bouquets; and yet those poor men be indicted for combining against starvation? I ask again, is this repugnant to the rights of man? If it be, is it not repugnant to our

Source: John R. Commons, Ulrich B. Phillips, Eugene A. Gilmore, Helen L. Sumner, and John B. Andrews, eds., *Documentary History of American Industrial Society*, vol. 3 (Cleveland, OH: Arthur H. Clark Company, 1910), 279–80, 299–300.

constitution? If it be repugnant to our constitution, is it law? And if it is not law, shall we be put to answer to it?

If it be said, they have wages enough, or too much already, I do not think any man a good witness to that point but one who has himself laboured. If either of the gentlemen opposed to us will take his station in the garret or cellar of one of these industrious men, get a leather apron and a strap, a last, a lap-stone and a hammer, and peg and stitch from five in the morning till eight in the evening, and feed and educate his family with what he so earns, then if he will come into court, and say upon his corporal oath that he was, during that probation too much pampered or indulged, I will consider whether these men may not be extortioners....

Like most other societies of the same nature, the journeymen shoemakers' society is a charitable institution.

They raise a fund, which is sacred to the use of their helpless or unfortunate members, and to the relief of the widows and orphans of their departed brethren....And to induce every one to join the society, while by his labour he may make something to spare for their fund, they refuse to work with any one who is so wanting in charity as not to join them....Who will

say that an association of this nature is illegal?...The masters were in the habit of crowding their shops with more apprentices than they could instruct. Two was thought as many as one man could do justice by. The journeymen shoemakers therefore determined to set their faces against the rapacity of the masters, and refused to work for those who were so unjust as to delude with the promise of instruction which it was impossible they could give....

It is to be observed, that neither of these counts charge that the design of the defendants was to raise their wages. And though it should be admitted that a conspiracy to raise their wages would subject the defendants to an indictment, yet I doubt if any authority can be found to support an indictment for charges like these.

QUESTIONS

1. What is the basis for Sampson's defense of the journeymen shoemakers?
2. Does this document show evidence that the journeymen were developing a sense of belonging to a working class that was separate from the master craftsmen for whom they worked?

10.3. VISUAL DOCUMENT: PAPER ELECTION TICKET FOR MARYLAND GENERAL ASSEMBLY (1828)

This paper election ticket allows us to understand what it was like to take part in the new democratic politics of the 1820s. The ticket was printed in Baltimore in 1828 to promote the Democratic candidacy of John Van Laer McMahon and George H. Steuart for the Maryland legislature. One of the tools of Democratic Party electioneering that was beginning to take place in 1828 was the distribution of paper ballots like this one, which associated the local candidates with both presidential candidate Andrew Jackson and past Democratic-Republican president Thomas Jefferson. Although

Source: Broadside Collection/Library of Congress Rare Book and Special Collections Division.

campaigning and voting had both gained a heightened importance among white men in 1828, the process was not identical to that which occurs in the 21st century. Because secret ballots were not required in the United States until 1888, elections were conducted in public. States did not print official ballots, and voters could cast their votes on highly partisan ballots like this one, which were often distributed by party bosses, labor unions, and other campaign workers.

QUESTIONS

1. How does the ballot use text and images to link the local candidates to Jackson and Jefferson? Why would that appeal to many voters?

2. Other Democratic tickets printed for the 1828 election featured mottos like "Jackson Ticket: Agriculture, Commerce, and Manufactures" and "Jackson Ticket: Firm united let us be, Rallying round our Hickory tree." To which groups of voters would these tickets appeal the most?

3. Would seeing and touching a physical object like this election ticket make a voter a better participant in an election, or did party control of the ballot decrease individual choice?

10.4. BASIL HALL, EXCERPTS FROM *TRAVELS IN NORTH AMERICA IN THE YEARS 1827 AND 1828* (1829)

In 1829, Basil Hall, a British Naval officer from a Scottish aristocratic family, published a book recounting his travels in North America in the previous two years. In this selection, Hall describes parts of upstate New York and western Massachusetts, where he met people with many ideas about how to improve American transportation and trade.

On the 3d of October, 1827, we left Stockbridge, and proceeded across the country to Northampton, another of those beautiful New England villages, which it is impossible to overpraise. Our road was conducted through ravines, over mountain passes, and occasionally along the very summit of ridges, from whence we commanded a view of sufficient beauty to redeem, in the course of one morning, all the flatness and insipidity of our previous journey. The greater part, indeed, of the country which we had yet seen—always, of course, excepting the beautiful Lake George, and delightful Hudson—consisted either of ploughed fields, or impenetrable forests, or it was spotted over with new villages, as raw and unpicturesque as if they had just stepped out of a saw-pit. The towns of Massachusetts, on the contrary, were embellished with ornamental trees and flower gardens, while the larger features of the landscape owed their interest to the more vigorous accompaniments of rocks, mountains, waterfalls, and all the varied lights and shades of Alpine scenery.

In the course of this agreeable day's journey, we traversed a considerable portion of the route over which it has been seriously proposed, I was assured, to carry a rail-road between the cities of Boston and Albany. No single State, still less any Section of the Union, it seems, likes to be outdone by any other State; and this feeling of rivalry, stimulated by the success of the great Erie Canal—is an undertaking highly favoured by nature—has, I supposed suggested the visionary project in question. In answer to the appeals frequently made to my admiration of this scheme, I was compelled to admit, that there was much boldness in the conception; but I took the liberty of adding, that I conceived the boldness lay in the conception alone; for, if it were executed, its character would be changed into madness.

Albany and Boston lie nearly east and west of each other; while much of the intermediate space is so completely ribbed over by a series of high ridges running north and south, that the rail-way in question would have to pass along a sort of gigantic corduroy road, over a country altogether unsuited for such an undertaking. Besides which, several navigable rivers, and more than one canal, lying along the intermediate valleys, connect the interior with the sea, and thus afford far readier means of exporting or importing goods to or from New York, Albany, or Boston, than any rail-way can ever furnish.

The same reasoning might be applied to a hundred other projects in the United States, many of them not less impracticable, but which, although existing only on paper, are, nevertheless assumed completed, and cast into the balance of American greatness, till the imaginary scale, loaded with anticipated magnificence, makes the Old World kick the beam, to the great satisfaction of

Source: Basil Hall, *Travels in North America in the Years 1827 and 1828*, vol. 2 (Edinburgh: Cadell and Co., 1829), 93–94, 100–101.

the inhabitants of this country, and the admiration of distant lands, who know nothing of the matter. . . .

At Worcester I met a remarkably intelligent person, with whom I fell into conversation on the subject of manufactures, and the measure which was then in agitation, and has since been carried, of protecting, as it is called, the domestic industry of that country by a new Tariff, or higher scale of duties on imported goods.

He contended that the manufactures of New England in particular, but also those of other parts of the Union, had grown up during the late war, when foreign goods were excluded, and had been enabled to flourish, more or less, ever since, in consequence of the protecting duties laid on foreign articles by the General Government.

QUESTIONS

1. Hall claims that Europeans are overly awed by American transportation and manufacturing, yet he seems impressed himself. Why?

2. How do Hall's observations offer evidence both of states working together to implement internal improvements and of jealousies between states?

10.5. ANDREW JACKSON, VETO OF THE BANK OF THE UNITED STATES (JULY 10, 1832)

When Andrew Jackson vetoed the reauthorization of the charter of the Second Bank of the United States in July 1832, he issued this message to explain his actions. Jackson later backed up his veto by withdrawing all federal funds from the bank and eventually triumphed in his political war with Nicholas Biddle, the bank's president.

A bank of the United States is in many respects convenient for the Government and useful to the people. . . . I sincerely regret that in the act before me I can perceive none of those modifications of the bank charter which are necessary, in my opinion, to make it compatible with justice, with sound policy, or with the Constitution of our country. . . .

Every monopoly and all exclusive privileges are granted at the expense of the public, which ought to receive a fair equivalent. The many millions which this act proposes to bestow on the stockholders of the existing bank must come directly or indirectly out of the earnings of the American people. . . .

It is to be regretted that the rich and powerful too often bend the acts of government to their selfish purposes. Distinctions in society will always exist under every just government. Equality of talents, of education, or of wealth can not be produced by human institutions. In the full enjoyment of the gifts of Heaven and the fruits of superior industry, economy, and virtue, every man is equally entitled to protection by law; but when the laws undertake to add to these natural and just advantages artificial distinctions, to grant titles, gratuities, and exclusive privileges, to make the rich richer and the potent more powerful, the humble members of society—the farmers, mechanics, and laborers—who

Source: Francis Newton, ed., *The Statesmanship of Andrew Jackson as Told in His Writings and Speeches* (New York: Tandy-Thomas Company, 1909), 155–76.

have neither the time nor the means of securing like favors to themselves, have a right to complain of the injustice of Government. There are no necessary evils in government. Its evils exist only in its abuses....

Nor is our Government to be maintained or our Union preserved by invasions of the rights and powers of the several States. In thus attempting to make our General Government strong we make it weak. Its true strength consists in leaving individuals and States as much as possible to themselves—in making itself felt, not in its power, but in its beneficence; not in its control, but in its protection; not in binding the States more closely to the center, but leaving each to move unobstructed in its proper orbit....

I have now done my duty to my country. If sustained by my fellow-citizens, I shall be grateful and happy; if not, I shall find in the motives which impel me ample grounds for contentment and peace. In the difficulties which surround us and the dangers which threaten our institutions there is cause for neither dismay or alarm. For relief and deliverance let us firmly rely on that kind of Providence which I am sure watches with peculiar care over the destinies of our Republic, and on the intelligence and wisdom of our countrymen.

QUESTIONS

1. What were Jackson's main objections to the bank charter?
2. What can you tell about Jackson's idea of democracy based upon his objections to the bank?

CHAPTER 11

NEW BOUNDARIES, NEW ROLES, 1820–1856

11.1. JOHN ROSS, EXCERPTS FROM "MEMORIAL AND PROTEST OF THE CHEROKEE NATION" (JUNE 21, 1836)

Since the 1820s, the state of Georgia had been working to eject the Cherokee, who occupied valuable lands where gold had been discovered. In 1835, a rump group within the Cherokee nation signed an agreement with the United States at New Echota to move to Oklahoma. John Ross, the principal chief, and the other elected Cherokee leadership did not sign or agree with the New Echota treaty, but the United States regarded the document as binding and sent the U.S. Army to forcibly evict the community in the summer of 1836.

Submitting the protest of the Cherokee nation against the ratification, execution, and enforcement of the treaty negotiated at New Echota, in December, 1835....

Read and referred to the Committee of the Whole House to which is committed the bill (R. H. No. 695), *making further appropriations for carrying into effect certain Indian treaties.*

To the honorable the Senate and House of Representatives of the United States of North America in Congress assembled:

It is the expressed wish of the Government of the United States to remove the Cherokees to a place west of the Mississippi. That wish is said to be founded in humanity to the Indians. To make their situation more comfortable, and to preserve them as a distinct people. Let facts show how this *benevolent* design has been prosecuted, and how faithful to the spirit and letter has the promise of the President of the United States to the Cherokees been fulfilled—that *"those who remain may be assured of our patronage, our aid, and good neighborhood."* The delegation are not deceived by empty professions, and fear their race is to be destroyed by the mercenary policy of the present day, and their lands wrested from them by physical force; as proof, they will

Source: John Ross, speaking to the U.S. House of Representatives, on June 21, 1836, *S. Doc. No. 286*, 24th Cong., 1st sess.

refer to the preamble of an act of the General Assembly of Georgia, in reference to the Cherokees, passed the 2d of December, 1835, where it is said, "from a knowledge of the Indian character, and from the present feelings of these Indians, it is confidently believed, that the right of occupancy of the lands in their possession should be withdrawn, *that it would be a strong inducement to them to treat with the General Government, and consent to a removal to the west*; and whereas, the present Legislature openly avow that their primary object in the measures intended to be pursued, *are founded on real humanity to these Indians*, and with a view, in a distant region, to perpetuate them with their old identity of character, *under the paternal care of the Government of the United States*; at the same time frankly disavowing *any selfish or sinister motives towards them in their present legislation.*" This is the profession. Let us turn to the practice of *humanity*, to the Cherokees, by the State of Georgia. In violation of the treaties between the United States and the Cherokee nation, that State passed a law requiring all white men, residing in that part of the Cherokee country, in her limits, to take an oath of allegiance to the State of Georgia. For a violation of this law some of the ministers of Christ, missionaries among the Cherokees, were tried, convicted, and sentenced to hard labor in the penitentiary. Their case may be seen by reference to the records of the Supreme Court of the United States.

Valuable gold mines were discovered upon Cherokee lands, within the chartered limits of Georgia, and the Cherokees commenced working them, and the Legislature of that State interfered by passing an act, making it penal for an Indian to dig for gold within Georgia, no doubt *"frankly disavowing any selfish or sinister motives towards them."* Under this law many Cherokees were arrested, tried, imprisoned, and otherwise abused. Some were even shot in attempting to avoid an arrest; yet the Cherokee people used no violence, hut humbly petitioned the Government of the United States for a fulfilment of treaty engagements, to protect them, which was not done, and the answer given that the United States could not interfere.... The Cherokee delegation have thus considered it their duty to exhibit before your honorable body a brief view of the Cherokee case, by a short statement of facts. A detailed narrative would form a history too

voluminous to be presented, in a memorial and prof [*illeg*]. They have, therefore, contented themselves with a brief recital, and will add, that in reviewing the past, they have done it alone for the purpose of showing what glaring oppressions and sufferings the peaceful and unoffending Cherokees have been doomed to witness and endure. Also, to tell your honorable body, in sincerity, that owing to the intelligence of the Cherokee people, they have a correct knowledge of their own rights, and they well know the illegality of those oppressive measures which have been adopted for their expulsion, by State authority. Their devoted attachment to their native country has not been, nor ever can be, eradicated from their breast. This, together with the implicit confidence, they have been taught to cherish, in the *justice, good faith, and magnanimity of the United States*, also, their firm reliance on the generosity and friendship of the American people, have formed the anchor of their hope and upon which alone they have been induced and influenced to shape their peaceful and manly course, under some of the most trying circumstances any people ever have been called to witness and endure. For more than *seven long years* have the Cherokee people been driven into the necessity of contending for their just rights, and they have struggled against fearful odds. Their means of defence being altogether within the grasp and control of their competitors, they have at last been trampled under foot. Their resources and means of defence, have been seized and withheld. The treaties, laws, and constitution of the United States, their bulwark, and only citadel of refuge, put beyond their reach; unfortunately for them, the protecting arm of the commander-in-chief of these fortresses has been withdrawn from them. The judgments of the judiciary branch of the government, in support of their rights, have been disregarded and prostrated; and their petitions for relief, from time to time before Congress, been unheeded. Their annuities withheld; their printing press, affording the only clarion through which to proclaim their wrongs before the American people and the civilized world, has been seized and detained, at the instance of an agent of the United States.... The faith of the United States being solemnly pledged to the Cherokee nation for the guarantee of the quiet and uninterrupted protection of their territorial possessions forever; and it being an unquestionable fact, that the Cherokees love their country; that no amount of money could induce them voluntarily to yield their assent to a cession of the same. But, when under all the circumstances of their peculiar situation and unhappy condition, the nation see the necessity of negotiating a treaty for their security and future welfare, and having appointed a delegation with full powers for that purpose, is it liberal, humane, or just, that a fraudulent treaty, containing principles and stipulations altogether objectionable, and obnoxious to their own sense of propriety and justice, should be enforced upon them? The basis of the instrument, the sum fixed upon, the commutation of annuities, and the general provisions of the various articles it contains, are all objectionable. Justice and equity demand, that in any final treaty for the adjustment of the Cherokee difficulties, that their rights, interests, and wishes should be consulted; and that the individual rights of the Cherokee citizens, in their possessions and claims, should be amply secured; and as freemen, they should be left at liberty to stay or remove where they please. Also, that the territory to be ceded by the United States to the Cherokee nation west of the Mississippi, should be granted to them by a patent in fee simple, and not clogged with the conditions of the act of 1830; and the national funds of the Cherokees should be placed under the control of their national council.

The delegation must repeat, the instrument entered into at New Echota, purporting to be a treaty, is deceptive to the world, and a fraud upon the Cherokee people. If a doubt exist as to the truth of their statement, a committee of investigation can learn the facts, and it may also learn that if the Cherokees are removed under that instrument, it will be by force. This declaration they make in sincerity, with hearts sickening at the scenes they may be doomed to witness; they have toiled to avert such a calamity; it is now with Congress, and beyond their control; they hope they are mistaken, but it is hope against a sad and almost certain reality. It would be uncandid to conceal their opinions, and they have no motive for expressing them but a solemn sense of duty. The Cherokees cannot resist the power of the United States, and should they be driven from their native land, then will they look in melancholy sadness upon the golden chains presented by President Washington to the Cherokee people as emblematical of the brightness and purity of the friendship between the United States and the Cherokee nation.

JNO. ROSS,
JOHN MARTIN,
JAMES BROWN,
JOSEPH VANN,
JOHN BENGE,
LEWIS ROSS,
ELIJAH HICKS,
RICH'D FIELDS,

Representatives of the Cherokee nation.
Washington City, 21st June, 1836.

QUESTIONS

1. Why do the Cherokee leaders use the language of treaties and law to make their case?
2. What do the Cherokee think is the cause of their expulsion?
3. What distinctions do the authors of this document draw between the conduct of Georgia and that of the United States?

11.2. JOSÉ ENRIQUE DE LA PEÑA, EXCERPTS FROM *WITH SANTA ANNA IN TEXAS* (1836)

In 1835, an independence movement composed of Spanish- and English-speaking residents of Mexico's northernmost state of Coahuila erupted. This movement attracted the attention of Americans, who fought on behalf of the rebels. Mexican forces, led by Antonio Lopez de Santa Anna, attacked the rebels, most famously at the Alamo, a former mission in San Antonio. De la Peña was a soldier with Santa Anna's army in the attack at the Alamo, in which all the defenders were killed.

On the 17th of February the commander in chief had proclaimed to the army: "Comrades in arms," he said, "our most sacred duties have brought us to these uninhabited lands and demand our engaging in combat against a rabble of wretched adventurers to whom our authorities have unwisely given benefits that even Mexicans did not enjoy, and who have taken possession of this vast and fertile area, convinced that our own unfortunate internal divisions have rendered us incapable of defending our soil. Wretches! Soon will they become aware of their folly! Soldiers, our comrades have been shamefully sacrificed at Anáhuac, Goliad, and Béjar, and you are those destined to punish these murderers. My friends: we will march as long as the interests of the nation that we serve demand. The claimants to the acres of Texas land will soon know to their sorrow that their reinforcements from New Orleans, Mobile, Boston, New York, and other points north, whence they should never have come, are insignificant, and that Mexicans, generous by nature, will not leave unpunished affronts resulting in injury or discredit to their country, regardless of who the aggressors may be."

This address was received enthusiastically, but the army needed no incitement; knowing that it was about to engage in the defense of the country and to avenge less fortunate comrades was enough for its ardor to become as great as the noble and just cause it was about to defend. Several officers from the Aldama and Toluca sappers were filled with joy and congratulated each other when they were ordered to hasten their march, for they knew that they were about to engage in combat. There is no doubt that some would have regretted not being among the first to meet the enemy, for it was considered an honor to be counted among the first. For their part, the enemy leaders had addressed their own men in terms not unlike those of our commander. They said that we were a bunch of mercenaries, blind instruments of tyranny; that without any right we were about to invade their territory; that we would bring desolation and death to their peaceful homes and would seize their possessions; that we were savage men who would rape their women, decapitate their children, destroy everything, and render into ashes the fruits of their industry and their efforts. Unfortunately they did partially foresee what would happen, but they also committed atrocities that we did not commit, and in this rivalry of evil and extermination, I do not dare to venture who had the ignominious advantage, they or we!

In spirited and vehement language, they called on their compatriots to defend the interests so dear to them and those they so tenderly cherished. They urged mothers to arm their sons, and wives not to admit their consorts in their nuptial beds until they had taken up arms and risked their lives in defense

Source: Carmen Perry, ed., *With Santa Anna in Texas: A Personal Narrative of the Revolution by José Enrique de la Peña* (College Station: Texas A&M Press, 1975), 38–57.

of their families. The word liberty was constantly repeated in every line of their writings; this magical word was necessary to inflame the hearts of the men, who rendered tribute to this goddess, although not to the degree they pretend.

When our commander in chief haughtily rejected the agreement that the enemy had proposed, Travis became infuriated at the contemptible manner in which he had been treated and, expecting no honorable way of salvation, chose the path that strong souls choose in crisis, that of dying with honor, and selected the Alamo for his grave. It is possible that this might have been his first resolve, for although he was awaiting the reinforcements promised him,[1] he must have reflected that he would be engaged in battle before these could join him, since it would be difficult for him to cover their entry into the fort with the small force at his disposal. However, this was not the case, for about sixty men did enter one night, the only help that came. They passed through our lines unnoticed until it was too late. My opinion is reinforced by the certainty that Travis could have managed to escape during the first nights, when vigilance was much less, but this he refused to do. It has been said that General Ramírez y Sesma's division was not sufficient to have formed a circumventing line on the first day, since the Alamo is a small place, one of its sides fronting the San Antonio River and clear and open fields. The heroic language in which Travis addressed his compatriots during the days of the conflict finally proved that he had resolved to die before abandoning the Alamo or surrendering unconditionally.

QUESTIONS

1. How does Santa Anna characterize the mission of the Mexican Army?
2. How does this characterization compare to the language that de la Peña attributes to the American commanders?
3. Who does de la Peña blame for the atrocities that occurred at the Alamo and the war in general?

11.3. AMBASSADOR A. I. DEIRISARRI, EXCERPTS FROM A REPORT TO LEWIS CASS ON WILLIAM WALKER (NOVEMBER 10, 1857)

William Walker was the most famous American "filibuster," or adventurer, of the 19th century. He invaded several South American republics, including Nicaragua, where he declared himself president and attempted to unseat the elected government. He was executed in Honduras in 1860. A. I. DeIrisarri served as ambassador for Guatemala and Salvador. Lewis Cass, to whom this letter was addressed, was at this time Secretary of State of the United States.

Source: A. I. DeIrisarri, reporting to U.S. House of Representatives, on November 10, 1857, House Executive Document No. 24, 35th Cong., 1st sess., 10–12.

1. Fannin was still expected to come with aid from Goliad. Not until several days after the Alamo fell was he ordered to Victoria instead.

Washington, November 10, 1857.

The undersigned, minister plenipotentiary of the republics of Guatemala and of Salvador, has the honor of imparting to the Hon. Secretary of State of the United States that he has seen, in the public papers printed in these States, a letter addressed to his excellency, and said to be written by the Sonora and Nicaragua adventurer, William Walker, who has unduly arrogated the name of president of Nicaragua, by which he has never been recognized in the States of Central America, in any of the Spanish American republics, in this government of the United States, or in any other government of the world, and who never could have been president of that republic, because the Nicaraguan constitution excludes any one not a native of Central America from the exercise of the executive power of that State....

Truly astonishing is the impudence with which this adventurer, expelled from Nicaragua by her forces and those of all the Central Americans, attempts to constitute himself the champion of Nicaragua. The man, whose course in that country was an exclusive one of assassination of the defenders of that country— the burner of whole villages, the spoiler of national property, the trampler on all rights, the plunderer of churches, the leader of the foreign stipendiaries which he gathered under his own banner—alone could have alleged his right of citizenship in Nicaragua, and thereby held as dunces all men else on earth.

This same man, without bitter insult on the common sense of mankind, could not have contrived a more absurd pretext under which to carry into effect the expedition, which he has levied to recover a treacherously usurped authority, than this claim, that his expedition is not one hostile to the country, but a peaceful colonizing enterprise! He himself has, time and again, and with characteristic impudence, published that his projected expedition looks to a recuperation of power in that country; whilst in the very letter attributed to him, and addressed to the honorable Secretary of the United States, he claims for himself the title of *"Lawful Executive Power of Nicaragua."*

This is ample to prove that the expedition, composed of spurious colonists, is, in reality, one of soldiers moving with the design of supporting this dream-begotten legitimate executive power of the country. But whatever may be the character of this colonizer and of those colonists, under a new patent, they cannot set foot on the territory which they are about to invade, nor be there received, save as real pirates; because, in Nicaragua and in Costa Rica, as well as in the other republics of Spanish America, Walker is held in no other light than that of a traitor to the party which he went to serve in Nicaragua, of an usurper of the sovereignty of that country, of a blood-shedder, whose object was to destroy the defenders of their country; whilst his satellites were nothing else than accomplices of his crimes. In proof of this I transmit to the Secretary of State the decree of the 31st of August last, officially communicated to me by the minister of foreign relations of Nicaragua, by which it will be clearly seen that the expedition which Walker intends to lead into that county, under the appellation of colonists, will be received as an expedition of pirates; in view of which communication through the isthmus has been ordered to be foreclosed.

Neither in Nicaragua, nor in any republic of Central America, is any colony desired, formed by Walker, or by any other adventurer, who, like him, has dreamed of mastery over its lands, to divide them among his foreign followers. Experience amply teaches there, as well as here, that the thousands of individuals shipped as colonists for Nicaragua from New York and New Orleans during the course of the last two years went there with the exclusive aim of waging war against the natives of the land, under the command of an intrusive usurper. And if, with miserable cunning, they can battle the laws of the United States, which forbid the citizens of those States to disturb the peace of friendly nations, they will certainly not deceive now, as they never have been able to deceive, the Central Americans; and they must not complain of the fate that may befall them, however hard it may appear to them. Natural law imposes on the Central Americans the duty of making an example of the incorrigible violators of the laws of all the nations.

Walker never was, nor can he ever be, president of Nicaragua, or a citizen of that republic, from the time that he was declared to be a traitor to it; nor can any men that may be led by him, or any one else in his name, fail to be received and treated in any other manner than that due to bandits and *pirates*, by *whatever name* they may be known, or from whatever quarter they may come. This is a fact which grows out of authentic documents from the true *executive power*, *national*, and not *foreign*, of Nicaragua; and to this should the citizens of the United States rivet their attention, so that they may not venture to follow the private banner of the adventurer of Sonora and of Nicaragua. . . . The undersigned, as minister plenipotentiary of Guatemala and of Salvador, and in his appointed capacity by the government of Nicaragua to represent her in the United States, cannot but protest against the contemplated expedition of colonization and peace to Nicaragua under the leadership of Walker; declaring that, as it cannot be received in that republic save as a hostile expedition, it shall be treated by the three

States, Guatemala, Salvador, and Nicaragua, as one of real pirates. This the undersigned has deemed it his duty to bring to the knowledge of the government of the United States.

The undersigned improves this opportunity to tender to the Hon. Secretary of State renewed assurances of his very high consideration.

A. I. DE IRISARRI.

QUESTIONS

1. How does DeIrisarri characterize Walker's actions?
2. To what extent does he feel that the U.S. government is responsible for Walker's actions?
3. What effect would this sort of behavior by Americans have had on relations with South American countries?

11.4. *THE PHALANX*, EXCERPTS FROM "THE STRIKE FOR WAGES" (NOVEMBER 4, 1843) AND "THE TEN HOUR SYSTEM" (MAY 18, 1844)

In the 1820s and 1830s, workers began going on strike to gain higher wages. When these efforts failed, labor leaders began advocating policy changes to protect laboring people. The *Phalanx* was one of many small workers' newspapers that flourished in northeastern cities.

THE STRIKE FOR WAGES

There has been a very general "turn-out" in all the Atlantic cities among the working classes. In every trade almost there has been a strike for higher wages, and generally the demands of the workmen have been complied with by the "masters." The reaction in the commercial world has stimulated business a little, which has increased slightly the demand for labor, and as the population of this country has not

yet become dense and excessive, the working classes by the subversive means of counter-coalitions to those which exist under our present false system of Industry and Commerce—leagues of wealth and industrial monopoly—are enabled to obtain a small advance of wages. But how trifling and pitiful an amount of benefit, after all, they receive, by such means, even when and for the time they do succeed; and how miserably inadequate to meet their wants and satisfy their rights,

Source: John R. Commons, Ulrich B. Phillips, Eugene A. Gilmore, Helen L. Sumner, and John B. Andrews, eds., *A Documentary History of American Industrial Society*, vol. 7 (Cleveland, OH: Arthur Clark, 1910), 231–33.

are such beggarly additions to their wages. Will not the working classes, the intelligent producers of this country, see what a miserable shift and expedient to better their condition is a "strike for wages?" Will they not see how uncertain the tenure by which they hold the little advantage they gain by it? Will they not see how degrading the position which forces them to appeal to and beg concessions of employers? Will they not see this and a thousand other evils connected with a false system of industry, and learn that the only remedy is a union among themselves to produce for themselves, to associate, and combine, and owning the land on which they live and the tools and machinery with which they work, enjoy the products of their own labor? We hope so, and then all such "civilized" false association, will be unnecessary....

THE TEN HOUR SYSTEM

The agitation of the subject of a reduction of the time of labor in factories is not, however, confined to England; in this country, the evils of the factory system in the exaction of an undue portion of the time of the laborer—twelve, fourteen, and even sixteen and eighteen hours out of the twenty-four, and in the excessive toil imposed on young children, have been severely felt. In a general way the subject has occupied the attention of politicians, from time to time, as elections were pending, and a vast deal of demagogism has been expended on it; but latterly it has been specially considered by the Legislature of Pennsylvania, and now in New England great feeling is manifested towards it in some of the manufacturing towns. An association of mechanics has been formed at Fall River, Massachusetts, for the special purpose of reducing the duration of labor to ten hours per day,

and to effect this object, has started a spirited little sheet called the *Mechanic*. We wish, however, that we could impress upon our countrymen the degrading littleness and insufficiency of this attempt at a compromise of their rights, for it is neither more nor less than a demeaning compromise and dastardly sacrifice of their rights, for them to make terms which only modifies the condition but does not change the terms of dependence on masters. In wretched England, where the laborer is indeed a poor, degraded, helpless being, it is well that any amelioration can be obtained; but here, where the laboring classes are intelligent and generally possess the ability to do full justice to themselves, it does appear to us to be excessively weak and trifling, if not disgraceful, for them to talk about a reform which at the most can relieve them temporarily of a few hours' oppressive toil—can convert them from twelve and fourteen to ten hour slaves—but cannot elevate them to the dignity of true independence! What a farce is boasted American freedom, if free-men are reduced to such beggarly shifts! Do they not see that they exhibit the badge of slavery in the very effort to mitigate its oppression? Free-men would not talk about terms which involve only a question of time of subjection to the authority and will of another—they would consult and act for their own good in all things without let or hindrance!

QUESTIONS

1. Why does the *Phalanx* argue against workers using strikes as a means of protest?
2. What is the newspaper's attitude toward a ten-hour workday?
3. What kind of solution does the paper recommend?

11.5. VISUAL DOCUMENT: FAN WITH VIEW OF FOREIGN FACTORIES AT CANTON (1790–1800)

In the late 18th century, European traders desperately tried to gain access to Chinese markets. The Chinese restricted their trading "factories" (or warehouses) to a confined section of Canton. This fan is one of many small consumer goods that would have been carried back to the United States.

QUESTIONS

1. What would American consumers have made of this object?
2. What does the array of European flags and facilities suggest about Chinese authority?
3. Why is the fence around the trading facility only present on the seaward side?

11.6. AMY MELENDA GALUSHA, LETTER TO AARON LELAND GALUSHA (APRIL 3, 1849)

The textile mills in Lowell, Massachusetts, housed one of the first large-scale industrial facilities in the United States. Many of the workers in the factory were young women.

Lowell, April 3, 1849

Dear Brother,

I do not know but you will blame me for not answering youre kind letter sooner but I think you will excuse me when I tell you the reason which is this I have been very sick with the vere Loyd[2] I do not know as you will know what that is so I will tell you it is the same as the small pox only it does not go quite so hard on account of being evaxionated[3] I was at the Hospital one week and I was sick enough I can tell you my face was swolen so that if you had seen me you would not have known me from Adam but I am getting pretty smart again I am not sorry that I have had it now it is over for I shall not fear the small pox any more but I had a pretty hard time I think I shall go to work again next week I expect my sickness will cost me about 15 dollers time and all which is quite a sum as low as wages are now you wanted I should write about mens wages in the mill mens wages are good but boys wages very low I do not think it will be best for you to try to work in the mill you will have to work a good many years before you will be a capable overseer and none but such can get good wages if you go into the mill now you will have to be very steady and I know that youre disposition will not admit of youre being confined from 5 in the morning till 7 at night in a noisey factory and luging around a great bas- ket of bobbins you would soon get tired of that fun I will promise you and then you must put up with a great many things which you never had to put up with before you would probably get scolded sometimes and that you know that you would not bear very patiently which would make it all the worse for you you would soom get weary and discontented and then you would not be much better off for what you had done a boy canot get along so easy in the mill with their work as the girls do with theirs for it is harder to learn it the girls have nothing to do but tend the work after it is all fixed and set to going the men have to keep the looms and machinery in order and put in the webs [—] and fix them all in order for weaving before the girls have anything to do with it which makes the mens work more trying and more particular a great deal than the girls when I come home I will tell you all about it more than I can write I should be very glad to have you here whare I can see you but I know in all reason Lele[4] it will not be for your best interest I think the best thing that you can do will be to go into some country town and learn a good trade get into some respectable shop and be steady and industrious and do what you think is perfectly right take youre bible keep it by you where you can get at it handy read a portion of it every day and follow its precepts every day be considerate in everything if any one asks you to do a thing stop and think if it is right you can easely tell whether a thing is

Source: Galusha Family Collection, Lowell National Historical Park, Center for Lowell History, University of Massachusetts Lowell Libraries, http://library.uml.edu/clh/All/Gal.htm.

2. Varioloid.
3. Vaccinated.
4. A nickname for Aaron Leland Galusha.

right or wrong by stopping to to think if you think it is wrong tell them at once that it is not right and that you will not do it and let that be the last of it do not stop to argue the point at all for they may be better skilled in argument then you are and by that I means you may weaken a strong point if you think it is wrong say so and that will be enough be independent do not be persuaded by any one however smart or rich or influential to do a wrong action you have a good mind enough for anybody if you will be guided by that do not let the evil spirit get the uper hand at any time if you can—t decide upon any question yourself go to someone that you know to be good for advise do not associate with any whose character is the least doubtful of either sex especialy the oposite Lealand for heavens sake let no fancy get the uper hands of reason do not be too ardent an admirer of outside apearances if you are attracted by a beautiful form or face stop and consider watch the actions and words with a jealous eye see if retiring modesty reigns there see if [*torn area*] place of all [*torn area*] of folly and frivalous actions there is anything like common sense to guide the bark or if its frail and delicate form is left pilotless upon the vast ocean of time to be driven by the winds of pride and folly to the gulf of distruction Leland I think of you a great deal and tremble for youre welfare for many a boy has been ruined when young by keeping bad company but my sheet (is almost full or I might say quite full you must answer my letter as soon as you receive it give my love to [JC] and [—ll] write to them soon write soon).

(Write as soon as you receive this I heard from Canada last night Jane Westover come down and Mrs Stark).

Amy L. Galusha

(dear Lele be kind to pa an ma do not do any thing to greive or hurt their feelings for you do not know how much they feel for youre welfare Lele the world is cold pitiless and miserliy what I have suffered no one knows but I have lived to find a calm a blessed calm in a land of strangers I know that youre feelings are tender like as mine were and capable of believing the insinuations of heartless wretches who will deceive you and then expose every little word and action and egreavate it to the highest pitch put no confidence in any one however friendly they may appear until you have thoroughly proved them).

(give my love to [—] enquiring friends give my love to Aunt I and L and J and all uncle Bens folks).

(you must not show this letter to any body except ma or pa it is written from the fountain of an overflowing and affectionate heart and must not be exposed to the scorn of an unfeeling world).

QUESTIONS

1. How does Amy compare the advantages and disadvantages of millwork for men and women?
2. What values does she believe a man should possess?
3. What kind of emotional relationship does Amy seem to have with her brother?

11.7. VISUAL DOCUMENT: GEORGE CALEB BINGHAM, *THE COUNTY ELECTION* (1852)

During Andrew Jackson's tenure in the White House (1828–1836), partisan politics emerged as a central feature of American life. Voting days assumed great importance, with the parties distributing ballots for their candidates and often serving liquor to supporters at the polling places. Voting was conducted in public, not through secret ballot.

QUESTIONS

1. How would the public nature of the voting process affect the way people voted?
2. Does the communal nature of the voting process suggest a deep involvement in politics?
3. How does the dispensing of alcohol (depicted in the left foreground) shape your opinion of what is happening in the painting?

Source: Saint Louis Art Museum, Missouri, USA/The Bridgeman Art Library.

11.8. LOUIS KOSSUTH, EXCERPTS FROM A SPEECH DELIVERED AT A DINNER GIVEN IN HIS HONOR BY THE U.S. CONGRESS (JANUARY 7, 1852)

During the European revolutions of 1848, the Hungarians mounted the strongest resistance to the Hapsburg Empire. Leaders of the Hungarian movement declared themselves an autonomous nation and elected Kossuth regent-president. Under military attack by the Hapsburgs, Kossuth fled the country in 1849. He was received abroad as one of the leading freedom fighters of his day.

Sir: As once Cineas the Epirote stood among the Senators of Rome, who, with an earnest word of self-conscious majesty, controlled the condition of the world, and arrested mighty kings in their ambitious march—thus, full of admiration and of reverence, I stand amongst you, legislators of the new capitol, that glorious hall of your people's majesty. The capitol of old yet stands, but the spirit has departed from it, and come over to yours, purified by the air of liberty. [*Applause.*] The old stands a mournful monument of the fragility of human things: yours, as a sanctuary of eternal right. The old beamed with the red lustre of conquest, now darkened by oppression's gloomy night; yours beams with freedom's bright ray. The old absorbed the world by its own centralized glory: yours protects your own nation against absorption, even by itself. [*Applause.*] The old was awful with irrestricted power; yours is glorious with having restricted it. At the view of the old, nations trembled; at the view of yours, humanity hopes. To the old, misfortune was only introduced with fettered hands to kneel at triumphant conquerors' heels. To yours, the triumph of introduction is granted to unfortunate exiles invited to the honor of a seat. And where Kings and Cæsars never will be hailed for their powers, might, and wealth, there the persecuted chief of a downtrodden nation is welcomed as your great Republic's guest, precisely because he is persecuted, helpless, and poor. [*Great applause and cheers.*] In the old, the terrible *væ victis!* was the rule. In yours, protection to the oppressed, malediction to ambitious oppressors, and consolation to a vanquished just cause. And, while out of the old a conquered world was ruled, you in yours provide for the common federative interests of a territory larger than the conquered world of the old. There sat men boasting their will to be the sovereign of the world; here sit men whose glory is to acknowledge the laws of nature and of nature's God, and to do what their sovereign, the people, wills. [*Applause.*]...

We Hungarians are very fond of the principle of municipal self-government, and we have a natural horror against the principle of centralization. That fond attachment to municipal self-government, without which there is no provincial freedom possible, is a fundamental feature of our national character. We brought it with us from far Asia a thousand years ago, and we conserved it throughout the vicissitudes of ten centuries. No nation has perhaps so much struggled and suffered from the civilized Christian world as we. [*Sensation.*] We do not complain of this lot. It may

Source: *Report of the Special Committee Appointed by the Common Council of the City of New York to Make Arrangements for the Reception of Gov. Louis Kossuth* (New York: Common Council, 1852), 418–32.

be heavy, but it is not inglorious. Where the cradle of our Saviour stood, and where his divine doctrine was founded, there now another faith rules, and the whole of Europe's armed pilgrimage could not avert this fate from that sacred spot, nor stop the rushing waves of Islamism absorbing the Christian empire of Constantine. *We* stopped those rushing waves. The breast of my nation proved a breakwater to them. [*Bravo! Bravo!*] We guarded Christendom, that Luthers and Calvins might reform it. [*Applause.*]... Our nation, through all its history, was educated in the school of municipal self-government; and in such a country ambition having no field, has also no place in man's character.

The truth of this doctrine becomes yet more illustrated by a quite contrary historical fact in France. Whatever have been the changes of government in that great country—and many they have been, to be sure—we have seen a Convention, a Directorate, Consuls, and one Consul, and an Emperor, and the Restoration, and the Citizen King, and the Republic; through all these different experiments centralization was the fundamental tone of the institutions of France—power always centralized; omnipotence always vested somewhere. And, remarkably indeed, France has never yet raised one single man to the seat of power who has not sacrificed his country's freedom to his personal ambition! [*Great applause.*]

It is sorrowful, indeed, but it is natural. It is in the garden of centralization where the venomous plant of ambition thrives. I dare confidently affirm, that in your great country there exists not a single man through whose brains has ever passed the thought that he would wish to raise the seat of his ambition upon the ruins of your country's liberty, if he could. Such a wish is impossible in the United States. [*Applause.*] Institutions react upon the character of nations. He who sows wind will reap storm. History is the revelation of Providence. The Almighty rules by eternal laws not only the material but the moral world; and every law is a principle, and every principle is a law. Men as well as nations are endowed with free will to choose a principle, but that once chosen the consequences must be abided.

With self-government is freedom, and with freedom is justice and patriotism. With centralization is ambition, and with ambition dwells despotism. Happy your great country, sir, for being so warmly addicted to that great principle of self-government. Upon this foundation your fathers raised a home to freedom more glorious than the world has ever seen. Upon this foundation you have developed it to a living wonder of the world. Happy your great country, sir! that it was selected by the blessing of the Lord to prove the glorious practicability of a federative union of many sovereign States, all conserving their State rights and their self-government, and yet united in one—every star beaming with its own lustre, but all together one constellation on mankind's canopy. [*Great applause and cheers.*]

Upon this foundation your free country has grown to a prodigious power in a surprisingly brief period, an attractive power in that your fundamental principle. You have conquered by it more in seventy-five years than Rome by arms in centuries. [*Good! Good!*] Your principles will conquer the world. By the glorious example of your freedom, welfare, and security, mankind is about to become conscious of its aim. The lesson you give to humanity will not be lost. The respect for State rights in the Federal Government of America, and in its several States, will become an instructive example for universal toleration, forbearance, and justice to the future States and Republics of Europe. Upon this basis will be got rid of the mischievous question of language-nationalities, raised by cunning despotism in Europe to murder liberty. Smaller States will find security in the principle of federative union, while they will conserve their national freedom by the principle of sovereign self-government; and while larger States, abdicating the principle of centralization, will cease to be a bloody field to sanguinary usurpation and a tool to ambition of wicked men, municipal institutions will insure the development of local particular elements; freedom, formerly an abstract political theory, will become the household benefit to municipalities; and out of the welfare and contentment of all parts will flow happiness, peace, and security for the whole. [*Applause.*]...

Yours is a happy country, gentlemen. You had more than fair play. You had active operative aid from Europe in your struggle for independence, which, once achieved, you so wisely used as to become a prodigy of freedom and welfare and a book of life to nations.

But we in Europe—we, unhappily, have no such fair play. With us, against every palpitation of liberty all despots are united in a common league; and you may be sure that despots will never yield to the moral influence of your great example. They hate the very existence of this example. It is the sorrow of their thoughts, and the incubus of their dreams. To stop its moral influence abroad, and to check its spreading development at home, is what they wish, instead of yielding to its influence.... But one single word even here I may be permitted to say—only such a word as may secure me from being misunderstood. I came to the noble-minded people of the United States to claim its generous operative sympathy for the impending struggle of oppressed freedom on the European continent; and I freely interpreted the hopes and wishes which those oppressed nations entertain; but, as to your great Republic, as a State, as a Power on earth, I stand before the statesmen, senators, and legislators of that Republic only to ascertain from their wisdom and experience what is their judgment upon a question of national law and international right. I hoped, and now hope, that they will, by the foreboding events on the other great continent, feel induced to pronounce in time their vote about that law and those rights. And I hoped, and hope, that, pronouncing their vote, it will be in favor of broad principles of international justice, consonant with their republican institutions and their democratic life. That is all. I know, and Europe knows, the immense weight of such a pronunciation from such a place. But *never* had I the impious wish to try to entangle this great Republic into difficulties inconsistent with its own welfare, its own security, its own interest. I rather repeatedly, earnestly declared that a war on this account by your country is utterly impossible, and a mere phantom. I always declared that the United States, remaining masters of their action under *every* circumstance, will act as they judge consistent with their supreme duties to themselves. But I said, and say, that such a declaration of just principles would insure to the nations of Europe

"fair play" in their struggle for freedom and independence, because the declaration of such a Power as your Republic is will be respected even where it should be not liked; and Europe's oppressed nations will feel cheered in resolution and doubled in strength to maintain the decision of their American brethren in their own behalf, with their own lives. There is an immense power in the idea to be right, when this idea is sanctioned by a nation like yours. [*Applause.*] And when the foreboding future will become present, there is an immense field for private benevolence and sympathy upon the basis of the broad principles of international justice pronounced in the sanctuary of your people's collective majesty.... Your generosity is a loud protestation of republican principles against despotism. I firmly trust to those principles; and, relying upon this very fact of your generosity, I may be permitted to say that that respectable organ of the free press was mistaken which announced that I considered my coming hither to be a failure.

I confidently trust that the nations of Europe have a future. I am aware that this future is contradicted by bayonets of absolutism; but I know that bayonets may support, but afford no chair to sit upon. I trust to the future of my native land, because I know that it is worthy to have it, and that it is necessary to the destinies of humanity. I trust to the principles of republicanism; and, whatever be my personal fate, so much I know, that my country will conserve to you and your glorious land an everlasting gratitude. [*Here the whole audience rose and cheered vociferously.*]

QUESTIONS

1. How does Kossuth characterize the impact of the United States on the rest of the world?
2. What kind of support does he want the United States to give the Hungarian independence movement?
3. How does Kossuth characterize the kind of democracy that he wants to bring to Europe?

CHAPTER 12

RELIGION AND REFORM, 1820–1850

12.1. MARGARET FULLER, "UNDAUNTED ROME," EXCERPT FROM A LETTER TO HER BROTHER, K. F. FULLER (1849)

Margaret Fuller emerged in the 1840s as a leading voice in American literary criticism and journalism. She wrote for both the *New York Tribune* and independently on women's rights and other reform efforts of the day. In 1846, the *Tribune* sent her to Europe to cover the revolutionary movements there, particularly the movement to create a unified Italian republic.

Rome, May 6, 1849.

I write you from barricaded Rome. The "Mother of Nations" is now at bay against them all. Rome was suffering before. The misfortunes of other regions of Italy, the defeat at Novara, preconcerted in hope to strike the last blow at Italian independence, the surrender and painful condition of Genoa, the money-difficulties,—insuperable unless the government could secure confidence abroad as well as at home,—prevented her people from finding that foothold for which they were ready.

The vacillations of France agitated them; still they could not seriously believe she would ever act the part she has. We must say France, because, though many honorable men have washed their hands of all share in the perfidy, the Assembly voted funds to sustain the expedition to Civita Vecchia; and the nation, the army, have remained quiescent. No one was, no one could be, deceived as to the scope of this expedition. It was intended to restore the Pope to the temporal sovereignty, from which the people, by the use of suffrage, had deposed him. No doubt the French, in case of success, proposed to temper the triumph of Austria and Naples, and stipulate for conditions that might soothe the Romans and make their act less odious. They were probably deceived, also, by the representations of Gaëta, and believed that a large party, which had been intimidated by the republicans, would declare in favor of the Pope when they found themselves likely

Source: Arthur B. Fuller, ed., *At Home and Abroad; Or, Things and Thoughts in America and Europe,* rev. ed. (New York: Tribune Association, 1869), 433–36.

to be sustained. But this last pretext can in noway avail them. They landed at Civita Vecchia, and no one declared for the Pope. They marched on Rome. Placards were affixed within the walls by hands unknown, calling upon the Papal party to rise within the town. Not a soul stirred. The French had no excuse left for pretending to believe that the present government was not entirely acceptable to the people. Notwithstanding, they assail the gates; they fire upon St. Peter's, and their balls pierce the Vatican. They were repulsed, as they deserved, retired in quick and shameful defeat, as surely the brave French soldiery could not, if they had not been demoralized by the sense of what an infamous course they were pursuing.

France, eager to destroy the last hope of Italian emancipation,—France, the alguazil of Austria, the soldiers of republican France, firing upon republican Rome! If there be angel as well as demon powers that interfere in the affairs of men, those bullets could scarcely fail to be turned back against their own breasts. Yet Roman blood has flowed also; I saw how it stained the walls of the Vatican Gardens on the 30th of April—the first anniversary of the appearance of Pius IX.'s too famous encyclic letter. Shall he, shall any Pope, ever again walk peacefully in these gardens? It seems impossible! The temporal sovereignty of the Popes is virtually destroyed by their shameless, merciless measures taken to restore it. The spiritual dominion ultimately falls, too, into irrevocable ruin. What may be the issue at this moment, we cannot guess. The French have retired to Civita Vecchia, but whether to reëmbark or to await reinforcements, we know not. The Neapolitan force has halted within a few miles of the walls; it is not large, and they are undoubtedly surprised at the discomfiture of the French. Perhaps they wait for the Austrians, but we do not yet hear that these have entered the Romagna. Meanwhile, Rome is strongly barricaded, and, though she cannot stand always against a world in arms, she means at least to do so as long as possible. Mazzini is at her head; she has now a guide "who understands his faith," and all there is of a noble spirit will show itself. We all feel very sad, because the idea of bombs, barbarously thrown in, and street-fights in Rome, is peculiarly dreadful. Apart from all the blood and anguish inevitable at such times, the glories of Art may perish, and mankind be forever despoiled of the most beautiful inheritance. Yet I would defend Rome to the last moment. She must not be false to the higher hope that has dawned upon her. She must not fall back again into servility and corruption.

And no one is willing. The interference of the French has roused the weakest to resistance. "From the Austrians, from the Neapolitans," they cried, "we expected this; but from the French—it is too infamous; it cannot be borne;" and they all ran to arms and fought nobly.

The Americans here are not in a pleasant situation. Mr. Cass, the Chargé of the United States, stays here without recognizing the government. Of course, he holds no position at the present moment that can enable him to act for us. Beside, it gives us pain that our country, whose policy it justly is to avoid armed interference with the affairs of Europe, should not use a moral influence. Rome has, as we did, thrown off a government no longer tolerable; she has made use of the suffrage to form another; she stands on the same basis as ourselves. Mr. Rush did us great honor by his ready recognition of a principle as represented by the French Provisional Government; had Mr. Cass been empowered to do the same, our country would have acted nobly, and all that is most truly American in America would have spoken to sustain the sickened hopes of European democracy. But of this more when I write next. Who knows what I may have to tell another week?

QUESTIONS

1. What does Fuller's position as a war correspondent (the first ever employed in this capacity) suggest about the relationship between events in Europe and the United States?
2. According to Fuller, why are other nations interfering in the effort to create an Italian republic?
3. What role did America play in this effort?

12.2. CHARLES G. FINNEY, EXCERPTS FROM "WHAT A REVIVAL OF RELIGION IS" (1835)

Charles Finney was one of the leading ministers of the Second Great Awakening, a religious revival movement that occurred during the 1820s and 1830s. Originally a Presbyterian, Finney preached a widely accessible evangelical Christian message intended to create converts and energize believers to improve their own behavior and their society.

TEXT.—O Lord, revive thy work in the midst of the years, in the midst of the years make known; in wrath remember mercy. —HAB. iii. 2.

Religion is the work of man. It is something for man to do. It consists in obeying God with and from the heart. It is man's duty. It is true, God induces him to do it. He influences him by his Spirit, because of his great wickedness and reluctance to obey. If it were not necessary for God to influence men—if men were disposed to obey God, there would be no occasion to pray, "O Lord, revive thy work." The ground of necessity for such a prayer is, that men are wholly indisposed to obey; and unless God interpose the influence of his Spirit, not a man on earth will ever obey the commands of God.

A "Revival of Religion" presupposes a declension. Almost all the religion in the world has been produced by revivals. God has found it necessary to take advantage of the excitability there is in mankind, to produce powerful excitements among them, before he can lead them to obey. Men are so spiritually sluggish, there are so many things to lead their minds off from religion, and to oppose the influence of the Gospel, that it is necessary to raise an excitement among them, till the tide rises so high as to sweep away the opposing obstacles. They must be so excited that they will break over these counteracting influences, before they will obey God. Not that excited feeling is religion, for it is not; but it is excited desire, appetite and feeling that prevents religion. The will is, in a sense, enslaved by the carnal and worldly desires. Hence it is necessary to awaken men to a sense of guilt and danger, and thus produce an excitement of counter feeling and desire which will break the power of carnal and worldly desire and leave the will free to obey God.... There is so little principle in the church, so little firmness and stability of purpose, that unless the religious feelings are awakened and kept excited, counter worldly feeling and excitement will prevail, and men will not obey God. They have so little knowledge, and their principles are so weak, that unless they are excited, they will go back from the path of duty, and do nothing to promote the glory of God. The state of the world is still such, and probably will be till the millennium is fully come, that religion must be mainly promoted by means of revivals. How long and how often has the experiment been tried, to bring the church to act steadily for God, without these periodical excitements. Many good men have supposed, and still suppose, that the best way to promote religion, is to go along uniformly, and gather in the ungodly gradually, and without excitement. But however sound such reasoning may appear in the abstract, facts demonstrate its futility. If the church were far enough advanced in knowledge, and had stability of principle enough to keep awake, such a course would do; but the church is so little enlightened, and there are so many counteracting causes, that she will not go steadily to work without a special interest being awakened. As the millennium advances, it is probable

Source: Lectures on the Revivals of Religion Delivered by the Rev. Charles G. Finney, rev. ed. (Oberlin, OH: E. J. Goodrich, 1868). Also see http://www.gospeltruth.net/1868Lect_on_Rev_of_Rel/68revlec01.htm.

that these periodical excitements will be unknown. Then the church will be enlightened, and the counteracting causes removed, and the entire church will be in a state of habitual and steady obedience to God. The entire church will stand and take the infant mind, and cultivate it for God. Children will be trained up in the way they should go, and there will be no such torrents of worldliness, and fashion, and covetousness, to bear away the piety of the church, as soon as the excitement of a revival is withdrawn. . . .

Backslidden Christians will be brought to repentance. A revival is nothing else than a new beginning of obedience to God. Just as in the case of a converted sinner, the first step is a deep repentance, a breaking down of heart, a getting down into the dust before God, with deep humility, and forsaking of sin. . . .

Christians will have their faith renewed. While they are in their backslidden state they are blind to the state of sinners. Their hearts are as hard as marble. The truths of the Bible only appear like a dream. They admit it to be all true; their conscience and their judgment assent to it; but their faith does not see it standing out in bold relief, in all the burning realities of eternity. But when they enter into a revival, they no longer see men as trees walking, but they see things in that strong light which will renew the love of God in their hearts. This will lead them to labor zealously to bring others to him. They will feel grieved that others do not love God, when they love him so much. And they will set themselves feelingly to persuade their neighbors to give him their hearts. So their love to men will be renewed. They will be filled with a tender and burning love for souls. They will have a longing desire for the salvation of the whole world. They will be in an agony for individuals whom they want to have saved—their friends, relations, enemies. They will not only be urging them to give their hearts to God, but they will carry them to God in the arms of faith, and with strong crying and tears beseech God to have mercy on them, and save their souls from endless burnings. . . .

FINALLY. —I have a proposal to make to you who are here present. I have not commenced this course of Lectures on Revivals to get up a curious theory of my own on the subject. I would not spend my time and strength merely to give you instructions, to gratify your curiosity, and furnish you something to talk about. I have no idea of preaching about revivals. It is not my design to preach so as to have you able to say at the close, "We understand all about revivals now," while you do nothing. But I wish to ask you a question. What do you hear lectures on revivals for? Do you mean that whenever you are convinced what your duty is in promoting a revival, you will go to work and practise it?

Will you follow the instructions I shall give you from the word of God, and put them in practise in your own lives? Will you bring them to bear upon your families, your acquaintance, neighbors, and through the city? Or will you spend the winter in learning about revivals, and do nothing for them? I want you, as fast as you learn any thing on the subject of revivals, to put it in practice, and go to work and see if you cannot promote a revival among sinners here. If you will not do this, I wish you to let me know at the beginning, so that I need not waste my strength. You ought to decide now whether you will do this or not. You know that we call sinners to decide on the spot whether they will obey the Gospel. And we have no more authority to let you take time to deliberate whether you will obey God, than we have to let sinners do so. We call on you to unite now in a solemn pledge to God, that you will do your duty as fast as you learn what it is, and to pray that He will pour out his Spirit upon this church and upon all the city this winter.

QUESTIONS

1. What is Finney's critique of the established Christian churches?
2. What does Finney ask of his listeners?
3. How might people converted in this manner engage with public problems?

12.3. FREDERICK DOUGLASS, EXCERPTS FROM "WHAT TO THE SLAVE IS THE FOURTH OF JULY?" (JULY 5, 1852)

By 1852, Frederick Douglass was the most well-known black abolitionist in the United States. Having freed himself from slavery in 1838, Douglass built his reputation as a spellbinding speaker and a prodigious writer against slavery. He wrote for a variety of newspapers and eventually published his own out of Rochester, New York.

Fellow-citizens, pardon me, allow me to ask, why am I called upon to speak here to-day? What have I, or those I represent, to do with your national independence? Are the great principles of political freedom and of natural justice, embodied in that Declaration of Independence, extended to us? and am I, therefore, called upon to bring our humble offering to the national altar, and to confess the benefits and express devout gratitude for the blessings resulting from your independence to us?

Would to God, both for your sakes and ours, that an affirmative answer could be truthfully returned to these questions! Then would my task be light, and my burden easy and delightful. For who is there so cold, that a nation's sympathy could not warm him? Who so obdurate and dead to the claims of gratitude, that would not thankfully acknowledge such priceless benefits? Who so stolid and selfish, that would not give his voice to swell the hallelujahs of a nation's jubilee, when the chains of servitude had been torn from his limbs? I am not that man. In a case like that, the dumb might eloquently speak, and the "lame man leap as an hart."

But, such is not the state of the case. I say it with a sad sense of the disparity between us. I am not included within the pale of this glorious anniversary! Your high independence only reveals the immeasurable distance between us. The blessings in which you, this day, rejoice, are not enjoyed in common. The rich inheritance of justice, liberty, prosperity and independence, bequeathed by your fathers, is shared by you, not by me. The sunlight that brought life and healing to you, has brought stripes and death to me. This Fourth [of] July is yours, not mine. You may rejoice, I must mourn. To drag a man in fetters into the grand illuminated temple of liberty, and call upon him to join you in joyous anthems, were inhuman mockery and sacrilegious irony. Do you mean, citizens, to mock me, by asking me to speak to-day? If so, there is a parallel to your conduct. And let me warn you that it is dangerous to copy the example of a nation whose crimes, lowering up to heaven, were thrown down by the breath of the Almighty, burying that nation in irrecoverable ruin! I can to-day take up the plaintive lament of a peeled and woe-smitten people!

"By the rivers of Babylon, there we sat down. Yea! we wept when we remembered Zion. We hanged our harps upon the willows in the midst thereof. For there, they that carried us away captive, required of us a song; and they who wasted us required of us mirth, saying, Sing us one of the songs of Zion. How can we sing the Lord's song in a strange land? If I forget thee, O Jerusalem, let my right hand forget her cunning. If I do not remember thee, let my tongue cleave to the roof of my mouth."

Source: Oration, Delivered in Corinthian Hall, Rochester, by Frederick Douglass, July 5th, 1852 (Rochester, NY: Lee, Mann, & Co., 1852). Also see http://teachingamericanhistory.org/library/index.asp?document=162.

Fellow-citizens; above your national, tumultuous joy, I hear the mournful wail of millions! whose chains, heavy and grievous yesterday, are, to-day, rendered more intolerable by the jubilee shouts that reach them. If I do forget, if I do not faithfully remember those bleeding children of sorrow this day, "may my right hand forget her cunning, and may my tongue cleave to the roof of my mouth!" To forget them, to pass lightly over their wrongs, and to chime in with the popular theme, would be treason most scandalous and shocking, and would make me a reproach before God and the world. My subject, then fellow-citizens, is AMERICAN SLAVERY. I shall see, this day, and its popular characteristics, from the slave's point of view. Standing, there, identified with the American bondman, making his wrongs mine, I do not hesitate to declare, with all my soul, that the character and conduct of this nation never looked blacker to me than on this 4th of July! Whether we turn to the declarations of the past, or to the professions of the present, the conduct of the nation seems equally hideous and revolting. America is false to the past, false to the present, and solemnly binds herself to be false to the future. Standing with God and the crushed and bleeding slave on this occasion, I will, in the name of humanity which is outraged, in the name of liberty which is fettered, in the name of the constitution and the Bible, which are disregarded and trampled upon, dare to call in question and to denounce, with all the emphasis I can command, everything that serves to perpetuate slavery—the great sin and shame of America! "I will not equivocate; I will not excuse;" I will use the severest language I can command; and yet not one word shall escape me that any man, whose judgment is not blinded by prejudice, or who is not at heart a slaveholder, shall not confess to be right and just.... Would you have me argue that man is entitled to liberty? that he is the rightful owner of his own body? You have already declared it. Must I argue the wrongfulness of slavery? Is that a question for Republicans? Is it to be settled by the rules of logic and argumentation, as a matter beset with great difficulty, involving a doubtful application of the principle of justice, hard to be understood? How should I look to-day, in the presence of Americans, dividing, and subdividing a discourse, to show that men have a natural right to freedom? speaking of it relatively, and positively, nega-

tively, and affirmatively. To do so, would be to make myself ridiculous, and to offer an insult to your understanding. There is not a man beneath the canopy of heaven that does not know that slavery is wrong for him.... What, to the American slave, is your 4th of July? I answer: a day that reveals to him, more than all other days in the year, the gross injustice and cruelty to which he is the constant victim. To him, your celebration is a sham; your boasted liberty, an unholy license; your national greatness, swelling vanity; your sounds of rejoicing are empty and heartless; your denunciations of tyrants, brass fronted impudence; your shouts of liberty and equality, hollow mockery; your prayers and hymns, your sermons and thanksgivings, with all your religious parade, and solemnity, are, to him, mere bombast, fraud, deception, impiety, and hypocrisy—a thin veil to cover up crimes which would disgrace a nation of savages. There is not a nation on the earth guilty of practices, more shocking and bloody, than are the people of these United States, at this very hour.... Behold the practical operation of this internal slave-trade, the American slave-trade, sustained by American politics and American religion. Here you will see men and women reared like swine for the market. You know what is a swine-drover? I will show you a man-drover. They inhabit all our Southern States. They perambulate the country, and crowd the highways of the nation, with droves of human stock. You will see one of these human flesh-jobbers, armed with pistol, whip and bowie-knife, driving a company of a hundred men, women, and children, from the Potomac to the slave market at New Orleans. These wretched people are to be sold singly, or in lots, to suit purchasers. They are food for the cotton-field, and the deadly sugar-mill. Mark the sad procession, as it moves wearily along, and the inhuman wretch who drives them. Hear his savage yells and his blood-chilling oaths, as he hurries on his affrighted captives! There, see the old man, with locks thinned and gray. Cast one glance, if you please, upon that young mother, whose shoulders are bare to the scorching sun, her briny tears falling on the brow of the babe in her arms. See, too, that girl of thirteen, weeping, yes! weeping, as she thinks of the mother from whom she has been torn! The drove moves tardily. Heat and sorrow have nearly consumed their strength; suddenly you hear a quick snap, like the discharge of a rifle; the fetters clank, and the chain rattles simultaneously; your ears are saluted with a scream, that seems to have torn its way to the center of your soul! The crack you heard, was the sound of the slave-whip; the scream you heard, was from the woman you saw with the babe. Her speed had faltered under the weight of her child and her chains! that gash on her shoulder tells her to move on. Follow the drove to New Orleans. Attend the auction; see men examined like horses; see the forms of women rudely and brutally exposed to the shocking gaze of American slave-buyers. See this drove sold and separated forever; and never forget the deep, sad sobs that arose from that scattered multitude. Tell me citizens, WHERE, under the sun, you can witness a spectacle more fiendish and shocking. Yet this is but a glance at the American slave-trade, as it exists, at this moment, in the ruling part of the United States.

I was born amid such sights and scenes. To me the American slave-trade is a terrible reality. When a child, my soul was often pierced with a sense of its horrors. I lived on Philpot Street, Fell's Point, Baltimore, and have watched from the wharves, the slave ships in the Basin, anchored from the shore, with their cargoes of human flesh, waiting for favorable winds to waft them down the Chesapeake. There was, at that time, a grand slave mart kept at the head of Pratt Street, by Austin Woldfolk. His agents were sent into every town and county in Maryland, announcing their arrival, through the papers, and on flaming "hand-bills," headed CASH FOR NEGROES. These men were generally well dressed men, and very captivating in their manners. Ever ready to drink, to treat, and to gamble. The fate of many a slave has depended upon the turn of a single card; and many a child has been snatched from the arms of its mother by bargains arranged in a state of brutal drunkenness.... But a still more inhuman, disgraceful, and scandalous state of things remains to be presented.

By an act of the American Congress, not yet two years old, slavery has been nationalized in its most horrible and revolting form. By that act, Mason & Dixon's line has been obliterated; New York has become as Virginia; and the power to hold, hunt, and sell men, women, and children as slaves remains no longer a mere state institution, but is now an institution of the whole United States. The power is co-extensive with the Star-Spangled Banner and American Christianity.

Where these go, may also go the merciless slave-hunter. Where these are, man is not sacred. He is a bird for the sportsman's gun. By that most foul and fiendish of all human decrees, the liberty and person of every man are put in peril. Your broad republican domain is hunting ground for men. Not for thieves and robbers, enemies of society, merely, but for men guilty of no crime. Your lawmakers have commanded all good citizens to engage in this hellish sport. Your President, your Secretary of State, your lords, nobles, and ecclesiastics, enforce, as a duty you owe to your free and glorious country, and to your God, that you do this accursed thing. Not fewer than forty Americans have, within the past two years, been hunted down and, without a moment's warning, hurried away in chains, and consigned to slavery and excruciating torture. Some of these have had wives and children, dependent on them for bread; but of this, no account was made. The right of the hunter to his prey stands superior to the right of marriage, and to all rights in this republic, the rights of God included! For black men there are neither law, justice, humanity, nor religion. The Fugitive Slave Law makes MERCY TO THEM, A CRIME; and bribes the judge who tries them. An American JUDGE GETS TEN DOLLARS FOR EVERY VICTIM HE CONSIGNS to slavery, and five, when he fails to do so. The oath of any two villains is sufficient, under this hell-black enactment, to send the most pious and exemplary black man into the remorseless jaws of slavery! His own testimony is nothing. He can bring no witnesses for himself. The minister of American justice is bound by the law to hear but one side; and that side, is the side of the oppressor. Let this damning fact be perpetually told. Let it be thundered around the world, that, in tyrant-killing, king-hating, people-loving, democratic, Christian America, the seats of justice are filled with judges, who hold their offices under an open and palpable bribe, and are bound, in deciding in the case of a man's liberty, [to] hear only his accusers!

In glaring violation of justice, in shameless disregard of the forms of administering law, in cunning arrangement to entrap the defenseless, and in diabolical intent, this Fugitive Slave Law stands alone in the annals of tyrannical legislation. I doubt if there be another nation on the globe, having the brass and the baseness to put such a law on the statute-book. If any man in this assembly thinks differently from me in this matter, and feels able to disprove my statements, I will gladly confront him at any suitable time and place he may select....

THE CHURCH RESPONSIBLE

But the church of this country is not only indifferent to the wrongs of the slave, it actually takes sides with the oppressors. It has made itself the bulwark of American slavery, and the shield of American slave-hunters. Many of its most eloquent Divines, who stand as the very lights of the church, have shamelessly given the sanction of religion and the Bible to the whole slave system. They have taught that man may, properly, be a slave; that the relation of master and slave is ordained of God; that to send back an escaped bondman to his master is clearly the duty of all the followers of the Lord Jesus Christ; and this horrible blasphemy is palmed off upon the world for Christianity.

For my part, I would say, welcome infidelity! welcome atheism! welcome anything! in preference to the gospel, as preached by those Divines! They convert the very name of religion into an engine of tyranny, and barbarous cruelty, and serve to confirm more infidels, in this age, than all the infidel writings of Thomas Paine, Voltaire, and Bolingbroke, put together, have done! These ministers make religion a cold and flinty-hearted thing, having neither principles of right action, nor bowels of compassion. They strip the love of God of its beauty, and leave the throng of religion a huge, horrible, repulsive form. It is a religion for oppressors, tyrants, man-stealers, and thugs. It is not that "pure and undefiled religion" which is from above, and which is "first pure, then peaceable, easy to be entreated, full of mercy and good fruits, without partiality, and without hypocrisy." But a religion which favors the rich against the poor; which exalts the proud above the humble; which divides mankind into two classes, tyrants and slaves; which says to the man in chains, stay there; and to the oppressor, oppress on; it is a religion which may be professed and enjoyed by all the robbers and enslavers of mankind; it makes God a respecter of persons, denies his fatherhood of the race, and tramples in the dust the great truth of the brotherhood of man. All this we affirm to be true of the popular church, and the popular worship of our land and nation—a religion, a church, and a worship which, on the authority of inspired wisdom, we pronounce to be an abomination in the sight of God. In the language of Isaiah, the American church might be well addressed, "Bring no more vain ablations; incense is an abomination unto me: the new moons and Sabbaths, the calling of assemblies, I cannot away with; it is iniquity even the solemn meeting. Your new moons and your appointed feasts my soul hateth. They are a trouble to me; I am weary to bear them; and when ye spread forth your hands I will hide mine eyes from you. Yea! when ye make many prayers, I will not hear. YOUR HANDS ARE FULL OF BLOOD; cease to do evil, learn to do well; seek judgment; relieve the oppressed; judge for the fatherless; plead for the widow."

The American church is guilty, when viewed in connection with what it is doing to uphold slavery; but it is superlatively guilty when viewed in connection with its ability to abolish slavery. The sin of which it is guilty is one of omission as well as of commission. Albert Barnes but uttered what the common sense of every man at all observant of the actual state of the case will receive as truth, when he declared that "There is no power out of the church that could sustain slavery an hour, if it were not sustained in it."...

THE CONSTITUTION

...Fellow-citizens! there is no matter in respect to which, the people of the North have allowed themselves to be so ruinously imposed upon, as that of the pro-slavery character of the Constitution. In that instrument I hold there is neither warrant, license, nor sanction of the hateful thing; but, interpreted as it ought to be interpreted, the Constitution is a GLORIOUS LIBERTY DOCUMENT. Read its preamble, consider its purposes. Is slavery among them? Is it at the gateway? or is it in the temple? It is neither. While I do not intend to argue this question on the present occasion, let me ask, if it be not somewhat singular that, if the Constitution were intended to be, by its framers and adopters, a slave-holding instrument, why neither slavery, slaveholding, nor slave can anywhere be found in it. What would be thought of an instrument, drawn up, legally drawn up, for the purpose of entitling the city of Rochester to a track of land, in which no mention of land was made? Now, there are certain rules of interpretation, for the proper understanding of all legal instruments. These rules are well established.

They are plain, common-sense rules, such as you and I, and all of us, can understand and apply, without having passed years in the study of law. I scout the idea that the question of the constitutionality or unconstitutionality of slavery is not a question for the people. I hold that every American citizen has a fight to form an opinion of the constitution, and to propagate that opinion, and to use all honorable means to make his opinion the prevailing one....

Allow me to say, in conclusion, notwithstanding the dark picture I have this day presented of the state of the nation, I do not despair of this country. There are forces in operation, which must inevitably work the downfall of slavery. "The arm of the Lord is not shortened," and the doom of slavery is certain. I, therefore, leave off where I began, with hope. While drawing encouragement from the Declaration of Independence, the great principles it contains, and the genius of American Institutions, my spirit is also cheered by the obvious tendencies of the age. Nations do not now stand in the same relation to each other that they did ages ago. No nation can now shut itself up from the surrounding world, and trot round in the same old path of its fathers without interference. The time was when such could be done. Long established customs of hurtful character could formerly fence themselves in, and do their evil work with social impunity. Knowledge was then confined and enjoyed by the privileged few, and the multitude walked on in mental darkness. But a change has now come over the affairs of mankind.

Walled cities and empires have become unfashionable. The arm of commerce has borne away the gates of the strong city. Intelligence is penetrating the darkest corners of the globe. It makes its pathway over and under the sea, as well as on the earth. Wind, steam, and lightning are its chartered agents. Oceans no longer divide, but link nations together. From Boston to London is now a holiday excursion. Space is comparatively annihilated. Thoughts expressed on one side of the Atlantic are, distinctly heard on the other. The far off and almost fabulous Pacific rolls in grandeur at our feet. The Celestial Empire, the mystery of ages, is being solved. The fiat of the Almighty, "Let there be Light," has not yet spent its force. No abuse, no outrage whether in taste, sport or avarice, can now hide itself from the all-pervading light. The iron shoe, and crippled foot of China must be seen, in contrast with nature. Africa must rise and put on her yet unwoven garment. "Ethiopia shall stretch out her hand unto God."

QUESTIONS

1. What kind of critique of slavery does Douglass offer?
2. What role did the federal government play in protecting slavery in the 19th century?
3. What role did religious institutions play in supporting it?
4. What does Douglass foresee as the future of slavery in the United States?

12.4. ELIZABETH CADY STANTON, "DECLARATION OF SENTIMENTS" (1848)

This document was primarily written by Elizabeth Cady Stanton, a leading activist for the full citizenship of women. Passed at the Seneca Falls Convention in 1848, Stanton modeled her document after the Declaration of Independence.

Source: Elizabeth Cady Stanton, Susan B. Anthony, and Matilda Joslyn Gage, eds., *History of Woman Suffrage* (Rochester, NY: Charles Mann, 1887), 70–71.

When, in the course of human events, it becomes necessary for one portion of the family of man to assume among the people of the earth a position different from that which they have hitherto occupied, but one to which the laws of nature and of nature's God entitle them, a decent respect to the opinions of mankind requires that they should declare the causes that impel them to such a course.

We hold these truths to be self-evident: that all men and women are created equal; that they are endowed by their Creator with certain inalienable rights; that among these are life, liberty, and the pursuit of happiness; that to secure these rights governments are instituted, deriving their just powers from the consent of the governed. Whenever any form of government becomes destructive of these ends, it is the right of those who suffer from it to refuse allegiance to it, and to insist upon the institution of a new government, laying its foundation on such principles, and organizing its powers in such form, as to them shall seem most likely to effect their safety and happiness. Prudence, indeed, will dictate that governments long established should not be changed for light and transient causes; and accordingly all experience hath shown that mankind are more disposed to suffer, while evils are sufferable, than to right themselves by abolishing the forms to which they were accustomed. But when a long train of abuses and usurpations, pursuing invariably the same object evinces a design to reduce them under absolute despotism, it is their duty to throw off such government, and to provide new guards for their future security. Such has been the patient sufferance of the women under this government, and such is now the necessity which constrains them to demand the equal station to which they are entitled.

The history of mankind is a history of repeated injuries and usurpations on the part of man toward woman, having in direct object the establishment of an absolute tyranny over her. To prove this, let facts be submitted to a candid world.

He has never permitted her to exercise her inalienable right to the elective franchise.

He has compelled her to submit to laws, in the formation of which she had no voice.

He has withheld from her rights which are given to the most ignorant and degraded men—both natives and foreigners.

Having deprived her of this first right of a citizen, the elective franchise, thereby leaving her without representation in the halls of legislation, he has oppressed her on all sides.

He has made her, if married, in the eye of the law, civilly dead.

He has taken from her all right in property, even to the wages she earns.

He has made her, morally, an irresponsible being, as she can commit many crimes with impunity, provided they be done in the presence of her husband. In the covenant of marriage, she is compelled to promise obedience to her husband, he becoming, to all intents and purposes, her master—the law giving him power to deprive her of her liberty, and to administer chastisement.

He has so framed the laws of divorce, as to what shall be the proper causes, and in case of separation, to whom the guardianship of the children shall be given, as to be wholly regardless of the happiness of women—the law, in all cases, going upon a false supposition of the supremacy of man, and giving all power into his hands.

After depriving her of all rights as a married woman, if single, and the owner of property, he has taxed her to support a government which recognizes her only when her property can be made profitable to it.

He has monopolized nearly all the profitable employments, and from those she is permitted to follow, she receives but a scanty remuneration. He closes against her all the avenues to wealth and distinction which he considers most honorable to himself. As a teacher of theology, medicine, or law, she is not known.

He has denied her the facilities for obtaining a thorough education, all colleges being closed against her.

He allows her in Church, as well as State, but a subordinate position, claiming Apostolic authority for her exclusion from the ministry, and, with some exceptions, from any public participation in the affairs of the Church.

He has created a false public sentiment by giving to the world a different code of morals for men and women, by which moral delinquencies which exclude women from society, are not only tolerated, but deemed of little account in man.

He has usurped the prerogative of Jehovah himself, claiming it as his right to assign for her a sphere of action, when that belongs to her conscience and to her God.

He has endeavored, in every way that he could, to destroy her confidence in her own powers, to lessen her self-respect, and to make her willing to lead a dependent and abject life.

Now, in view of this entire disfranchisement of one-half the people of this country, their social and religious degradation—in view of the unjust laws above mentioned, and because women do feel themselves aggrieved, oppressed, and fraudulently deprived of their most sacred rights, we insist that they have immediate admission to all the rights and privileges which belong to them as citizens of the United States.

In entering upon the great work before us, we anticipate no small amount of misconception, misrepresentation, and ridicule; but we shall use every instrumentality within our power to effect our object. We shall employ agents, circulate tracts, petition the State and National legislatures, and endeavor to enlist the pulpit and the press in our behalf. We hope this Convention will be followed by a series of Conventions embracing every part of the country.

QUESTIONS

1. What are the chief criticisms that this document makes regarding the treatment of women in 1840s America?
2. What is the effect of Stanton's decision to copy the language of the Declaration of Independence?
3. How would Americans in the 1840s have interpreted this comparison?

12.5. DAVID WALKER, PREAMBLE OF *APPEAL TO THE COLOURED CITIZENS OF THE WORLD* (1830)

David Walker, a free African American from North Carolina, drafted a vigorous critique of slavery and a call for its destruction in this 1829 pamphlet. The document circulated widely around the United States, despite the efforts of Southern whites to suppress it.

My dearly beloved Brethren and Fellow Citizens. Having travelled over a considerable portion of these United States, and having, in the course of my travels, taken the most accurate observations of things as they exist—the result of my observations has warranted the full and unshaken conviction, that we, (coloured people of these United States,) are the most degraded, wretched, and abject set of beings that ever lived since the world began; and I pray God that none like us ever may live again until time shall be no more. They tell us of the Israelites in Egypt, the Helots in Sparta, and of the Roman Slaves, which last were made up from almost every nation under heaven, whose sufferings under those ancient and heathen nations, were, in comparison with ours, under this enlightened and Christian nation, no more than a cypher—or, in other words, those heathen nations of antiquity, had but little more among them than the name and form of

Source: Walker's Appeal, in Four Articles; Together with a Preamble, to the Coloured Citizens of the World, but in Particular, and Very Expressly, to Those Citizens of the United States of America, Written in Boston, State of Massachusetts, September 28, 1829. Third and Last Edition, with Additional Notes, Corrections, &c. (Boston: David Walker, 1830). Also see http://docsouth.unc.edu/nc/walker/walker.html.

slavery; while wretchedness and endless miseries were reserved, apparently in a phial, to be poured out upon our fathers, ourselves and our children, by Christian Americans!...

I am fully aware, in making this appeal to my much afflicted and suffering brethren, that I shall not only be assailed by those whose greatest earthly desires are, to keep us in abject ignorance and wretchedness, and who are of the firm conviction that Heaven has designed us and our children to be slaves and beasts of burden to them and their children. I say, I do not only expect to be held up to the public as an ignorant, impudent and restless disturber of the public peace, by such avaricious creatures, as well as a mover of insubordination—and perhaps put in prison or to death, for giving a superficial exposition of our miseries, and exposing tyrants. But I am persuaded, that many of my brethren, particularly those who are ignorantly in league with slaveholders or tyrants, who acquire their daily bread by the blood and sweat of their more ignorant brethren—and not a few of those too, who are too ignorant to see an inch beyond their noses, will rise up and call me cursed—Yea, the jealous ones among us will perhaps use more abject subtlety, by affirming that this work is not worth perusing, that we are well situated, and there is no use in trying to better our condition, for we cannot. I will ask one question here.—Can our condition be any worse?—Can it be more mean and abject? If there are any changes, will they not be for the better though they may appear for the worst at first? Can they get us any lower? Where can they get us? They are afraid to treat us worse, for they know well, the day they do it they are gone. But against all accusations which may or can be preferred against me, I appeal to Heaven for my motive in writing—who knows what my object is, if possible, to awaken in the breasts of my afflicted, degraded and slumbering brethren, a spirit of inquiry and investigation respecting our miseries and wretchedness in this Republican Land of Liberty!!!!!!...I will not here speak of the destructions which the Lord brought upon Egypt, in consequence of the oppression and consequent groans of the oppressed—of the hundreds and thousands of Egyptians whom God hurled into the Red Sea for afflicting his people in their land—of the Lord's suffering people in Sparta or Lacedaemon, the land of the truly famous Lycurgus—nor have I time to comment upon the cause which produced the fierceness with which Sylla usurped the title, and absolutely acted as dictator of the Roman people—the conspiracy of Cataline—the conspiracy against, and murder of Caesar in the Senate house—the spirit with which Marc Antony made himself master of the commonwealth—his associating Octavius and Lipidus with himself in power—their dividing the provinces of Rome among themselves—their attack and defeat, on the plains of Phillipi—of the last defenders of their liberty, (Brutus and Cassius)—the tyranny of Tiberius, and from him to the final overthrow of Constantinople by the Turkish Sultan, Mahomed II. A.D. 1453. I say, I shall not take up time to speak of the causes which produced so much wretchedness and massacre among those heathen nations, for I am aware that you know too well, that God is just, as well as merciful!—I shall call your attention a few moments to that Christian nation, the Spaniards—while I shall leave almost unnoticed, that avaricious and cruel people, the Portuguese, among whom all true hearted Christians and lovers of Jesus Christ, must evidently see the judgments of God displayed. To show the judgments of God upon the Spaniards, I shall occupy but a little time, leaving a plenty of room for the candid and unprejudiced to reflect.

All persons who are acquainted with history, and particularly the Bible, who are not blinded by the God of this world, and are not actuated solely by avarice—who are able to lay aside prejudice long enough to view candidly and impartially, things as they were, are, and probably will be—who are willing to admit that God made man to serve Him alone, and that man should have no other Lord or Lords but Himself—that God Almighty is the sole proprietor or master of the WHOLE human family, and will not on any consideration admit of a colleague, being unwilling to divide his glory with another—and who can dispense with prejudice long enough to admit that we are men, notwithstanding our improminent noses and woolly heads, and believe that we feel for our fathers, mothers, wives and children, as well as the whites do for theirs.—I say, all who are permitted to see and believe these things, can easily recognize the judgments of God among the Spaniards. Though others may lay the cause of the fierceness with which they cut each other's throats, to some other circumstance, yet they who believe that God is a God of justice, will believe that SLAVERY is the principal cause.

QUESTIONS

1. Why does Walker situate the experience of U.S. slaves in the context of the classical societies of biblical Egypt, Greece, and Rome?

2. What would have been the effect of the broad global comparisons that Walker advances in the penultimate paragraph?

3. How does Walker use religion to advance his argument?

12.6. VISUAL DOCUMENT: WOODCUT, "A HORRID MASSACRE" (1831)

In 1831, an enslaved man, Nat Turner, led a slave revolt in Southampton County, Virginia. Turner used his experience as a preacher to the county's slaves to create a network of lieutenants and plan the attack. His group killed 56 white people but could not seize the county armory before the local militia counterattacked and dispersed them. Turner was later captured and executed. The woodcut shown here circulated widely in Virginia newspapers.

Source: F&A Archive/The Art Archive at Art Resource, NYImage.

QUESTIONS

1. How does the author of this woodcut represent blacks and whites as individuals?
2. How does the difference in weapons suggest attitudes about the positions of black and white men in the society?
3. How does the bottom sequence present the organization and intent of the two sides in the struggle?

12.7. WALT WHITMAN, "ONE'S-SELF I SING" (1872)

The rise of an authentic American literature accelerated in the 1840s and 1850s as figures such as Nathaniel Hawthorne, Emily Dickinson, Herman Melville, and Walt Whitman wrote some of their most famous works. Whitman was a pioneer in the use of free verse and in his attention to the lived experience of citizens from all walks of his life. His frank discussions of sexuality and the body alienated and energized equal numbers of readers.

One's-Self I sing—a simple separate Person;
Yet utter the word Democratic, the word
   En-Masse.

Of Physiology from top to toe I sing;
Not physiognomy alone, nor brain alone, is worthy for the muse—I say the Form complete is
   worthier far;
The Female equally with the Male I sing.

Of Life immense in passion, pulse, and power,
Cheerful—for freest action form'd under the laws
   divine,
The Modern Man I sing.

QUESTIONS

1. How does Whitman present the idea of individualism?
2. What kind of person is the "modern" American, according to Whitman?
3. Is this poem an argument for gender equality?

Source: Walt Whitman, *Leaves of Grass* (Philadelphia: David McKay, 1900). Also see http://www.whitmanarchive.org/published/ LG/1871/poems/2.

12.8. VISUAL DOCUMENT: THE ORIGINAL AND ONLY COLORED MINSTREL TROUPE

In the 1840s, minstrelsy emerged as one of the most popular forms of theater and music in America. Especially popular in New York City, minstrelsy relied on exaggerated or stereotyped notions of black dress, movement, and speech and was used to lampoon black Americans.

QUESTIONS

1. What kinds of racial attitudes do these images convey?
2. What impression does the clothing of the figures convey?
3. How does it matter that these objects were intended as toys or collectibles for the home?

Source: Robert C. Toll, *Blacking Up: The Minstrel Show in Nineteenth-Century America* (New York: Oxford University Press, 1974).

CHAPTER 13

A HOUSE DIVIDING, 1844–1860

13.1. NAPOLEON JACKSON TECUMSEH DANA, EXCERPT FROM A LETTER TO SUSAN DANA (OCTOBER 5, 1846)

The Mexican War begun by President Polk brought American soldiers into Mexico and into close contact with Hispanic Catholics for the first time. Dana, a West Point graduate and first lieutenant in the U.S. Army, wrote regularly to his wife with his observations about the places and people he encountered. When Winfield Scott's army captured Monterrey in September 1846, Dana's unit was one of those that remained behind temporarily as an occupying force.

October 5. I am on guard today, my dearest wife, and in what time I am unemployed by my duties I will pick up snatches and employ them in talking to you.

First, let me tell you how I am living just now. The day after the articles of capitulation were signed, General Worth's division went into quarters in the city. The Fifth and Seventh Regiments took possession of two large, fine houses belonging to rich people who had probably gone into the country to wait till the fighting was over. But all the officers of our regiment lived in one very large room. It was fully capacious enough but was not so very agreeable, living all together. There

was a library there, two cupboards filled with china, decanters, and so forth, a lady's workbox, some artificial flowers made of hair, and a good many things which showed that wealthy people [lived] there. The yard was filled with oranges and limes. In the evening some three or four of us got out a decanter, china bowls, tumbler, sugar dish, and so forth, and made some fine punch, for which we were much obliged to the hospitable owners of the house....

Out of my room a door opened on a small porch. In my room I found a table, several straw-bottomed chairs, a wardrobe, and cot, and I was quite comfortable, but I was destined to another move. My company

Source: Robert H. Ferrell, ed., *Monterrey Is Ours! The Mexican War Letters of Lieutenant Dana, 1845–1847* (Lexington: University Press of Kentucky, 1990), 140–42.

was not comfortably quartered, and the council chamber of this state (Nuevo Leon) was taken for it. It is a very large and handsome room with large pictures in it, tables, chairs, and so forth. Under this were two very nice rooms, quite private, and in cold weather could be far more comfortable than the room I had. Little and myself were told that we might take these rooms.

They were owned and occupied by one of the aristocracy of the country, one Don Manuel Somebody. He was a very rich bachelor. He temporized with me for two days, promising to move, when at last I got out of patience, thinking there was but little chance of his going, and I took a wagon and six men to his house, told him to show me his baggage and I would load it for him and have it carried wherever he should designate. All he said was "Mil gracias," for he knew he had to go then, and I moved over....

As I sit in my room now and hear our wagons rattle by on the paved streets (which, by the way, are much better paved than many of our cities), I can imagine myself in New Orleans or New York again. Were it not for the old-style fabrication of the Mexican house and the great, great void in my heart owing to the absence of my beloved one, the delusion would sometimes be almost complete. How happily, I have thought, how more than happily could we live, my dearest one, even in this little room so far from our friends and our native land. God grant that we may 'ere long meet somewhere, better away out here than be separated longer by a cruel and almost useless war.

All the best houses belong to the wealthiest citizens of the place [and] are taken for the uses of the army. Some are filled with mirrors and [illegible]. Occupied or nor, if one is wanted, the alcalde is called upon to have it vacated immediately. General Worth, General Butler, General Smith, all have fine houses. Arista had just finished for himself here a perfect palace. The grounds in rear are most beautiful, such as you may have seen in pictures of Italian gardens in older times, filled with vases, images, streams, baths, oranges, lemons, limes, flowers, and so forth. This we have made a hospital of. I suppose we have in use at least a hundred private houses in the city.

Our division alone is in the city. The other two are still at the camp at Walnut Springs. Some of the Texan volunteers are quartered in the city. They have committed some dreadful outrages since the capitulation. In one night they killed seven Mexicans because one of their comrades had been killed in a row. This afternoon an old Mexican soldier, a lancer who had been left behind to wait on a cavalry officer, was following this officer, both mounted and in uniform, on their road to Saltillo, when one of these lawless scoundrels shot the harmless old fellow dead in the street. General Worth is searching high and low for the offender. It is one of the most barbarous, cold-blooded murders I have ever heard of. The man who would do such a thing is a second Cain. It will tend to excite the Mexican soldiery to acts of cruelty when they can get a chance. They will understand though the difference between troops of the line, as they call us, and volunteers....

So you had a dispute with your uncle about my looking at the naked girls at Camargo. Everybody looked at them, dearest one, and no one could go to the river without seeing them. If men were in swimming, the women would not mind it but would come right in too. They think nothing of such things, but I would look at them as I would look at so many wild beasts, orangutans, for they had no more beauty. And as to kissing them, one look was almost enough sometimes to turn one's stomach. These are only the lower classes who are so public. They are quite dark and most excellently ugly. Did you tell your uncle, dear Sue, that your legs, titties, and so forth were the only ones I liked to look at closely? I would get a spyglass for them but not for others. He is teasing you, but it is something new for you to talk to gentlemen about such things. Weren't you ashamed? Tell your uncle from me that I do not want your young and guileless heart to be all undeceived in relation to this wicked world.

QUESTIONS

1. How does Dana describe the encounters between Americans and the people whose houses they occupy?
2. What problems did the Americans encounter in occupying the city?
3. How do Dana's comments on Mexican women reveal a gendered attitude toward racial difference?

13.2. VISUAL DOCUMENT: CARL NEBEL, *GENL. SCOTT'S ENTRANCE INTO MEXICO CITY* (1847)

Scott's army landed on Mexico's eastern coast in early 1847 and defeated the Mexican army in a series of engagements. On September 14, 1847, he occupied Mexico City, effectively ending the war. Carl Nebel, a German artist, created this painting in 1851 for inclusion in a book about the war by a journalist who had accompanied U.S. troops on some of their campaigns.

QUESTIONS

1. Based on Nebel's portrait, what kind of city is Mexico City?
2. What does the representation of cavalry suggest about the U.S. military and its presence in Mexico?
3. What are the figures in the left foreground intended to signal about the Mexicans encountered by the army?

Source: The Art Archive/National History Museum Mexico City/Gianni Dagli Orti.

13.3. VISUAL DOCUMENT: GEORGE CATLIN, *COMANCHE FEATS OF HORSEMANSHIP* (1834)

Born in Pennsylvania, Catlin became the most well-known and well-regarded artist of Indian life in the United States. He traveled extensively in the West during the 1830s and completed many portraits of chiefs and members of western tribes. Although Catlin clearly posed his subjects to create his artwork, he also considered his work a chronicle of American Indian people and their material life.

QUESTIONS

1. What does this painting convey about Comanche martial skill?

2. How does the artist's representation of Comanche bodies reflect attitudes about differences between Indian and European men?

Source: Smithsonian Institution, Washington, DC, USA/The Bridgeman Art Library.

13.4. CONSTITUTION OF THE STATE COUNCIL OF THE AMERICAN PARTY OF MASSACHUSETTS (AUGUST 7, 1855)

In the early 1850s, a grassroots political movement aimed at restricting the rights and role of immigrants in the United States developed into a political party. Called the "American Party" in some places (and, informally, the "Know-Nothings," because members sometimes pledged to deny knowledge of the group), their nativist platform drew native-born white Protestant voters away from the Whig Party. Although they passed few of the legislative changes for which they advocated, the American Party contributed to the realignment of the American electorate in the decade before the Civil War.

We, whose names are here annexed, desirous of supporting and protecting the rights of American Citizens against all Foreign Influence and every form of Oppression, either of the bodies or the souls of men; in view of the imminent peril of Freedom, both from internal and external foes, do hereby pledge ourselves to be governed by the following DECLARATION OF PRINCIPLES AND CONSTITUTION.

DECLARATION OF PRINCIPLES

1. An essential modification of the naturalization laws, so that the immigrant shall not be permitted to exercise the elective franchise until he shall have acquired a knowledge of our language, our laws, and institutions, by a residence in this country of at least twenty-one years.

2. Stringent penalties against the fraudulent transfer of naturalization papers, and such a description of the peculiarities of the person applying for naturalization as shall render such transfer impossible.

3. Opposition to all attempts to establish foreign military or political organizations to perpetuate old national prejudices; but encouragement of such a policy as shall tend to assimilate the foreign population, in sentiment and feeling, with the mass of American citizens.

4. Efficient laws to prevent the deportation of criminals and paupers, by foreign authorities, to our shores; but a hospitable reception to the persecuted and oppressed of every clime.

5. The witholding of grave diplomatic and political trusts from persons of foreign birth.

6. The right to worship God according to the dictates of one's conscience to be preserved inviolate. Resistance to any politico-ecclesiastical hierarchy, which through its agents, be they pope, bishops, or priests, attempts to invade this right, or acquire political power. Hence, we rebuke all attempts to appropriate the public funds to the establishment of sectarian schools, all attempts to exclude the Bible, as a text-book, therefrom, and all attempts to wrest from the laity and give to the priesthood the control of church property. We also rebuke, in indignant terms, such sentiments as these put forth by the representatives of the Papal Power. That "Protestantism has no rights in the presence of Catholicism," that "Religious liberty is only to be endured until the opposite can be established with safety to the Catholic world," and that "the Catholics of America are bound to abide by the interpretation put upon the Constitution of the United States by the Pope of Rome."

7. That the Bible, as the source and fountain of all true and rational liberty should be made the basis

Source: Massachusetts Historical Society, http://www.masshist.org/database/327use-onview-id.

of all popular education, and should be open to, and in the hands of, every man, woman, and child. And the man or men who may attempt, directly or indirectly, to shut it out of our schools or to keep it from the hands and hearts of our people, or any portion of them, should be deemed guilty of a crime against society, and of a treason against liberty itself.

Whereas, The aggressive policy which has been uniformly pursued by the slave power from the commencement of our national existence down to the abrogation of the Missouri compact, evinces a determination to "crush out" the *spirit* as well as the *forms* of liberty from among us, and to subject the free States to a relentless despotism; and, *whereas*, the success of the Southern delegates to the National Council, recently held in Philadelphia, in making abject and uncomplaining submission to pro-slavery legislation a fundamental article in the creed of the National American Party—renders it imperative upon us to express on views upon the great question of the country and the age: Therefore, we declare,

First, That the action of the legislative, executive, and judicial departments of the government ought to be controlled by the principle taught by the framers and purest interpreters of the Constitution—that "freedom is national and slavery sectional."

Second, That repose for the country and stability to the Union must be sought by relieving the General Government, so far as its jurisdiction extends, of all connection with and accountability for American slavery.

Third, That the independence and sovereignty of the State, in its Legislation and Judiciary, should be maintained inviolate.

Fourth, That the great barrier to slavery, ruthlessly broken down by the repeal of the Missouri prohibition, ought to be speedily restored; and that, in any event, no State, erected from any part of the territory covered by that compromise, ought ever to be admitted to the Union as a slave State.

Fifth, That the right of actual settlers in the Territories to the free and undisturbed exercise of their elective franchise granted to them by the laws under which they are organized, should be promptly protected by the national executive whenever violated or threatened.

QUESTIONS

1. What motivated the American Party's concern about the place of immigrants in American life?
2. How does the Party reconcile a desire to "worship God according to the dictates of one's own conscience" (Sec. 6) with a requirement that the "Bible…should be made the basis of all popular education" (Sec. 7)?
3. What is the Party's position on slavery, and why is this position explained here?

13.5. GOVERNOR JAMES HENRY HAMMOND, EXCERPTS FROM A LETTER TO THOMAS CLARKSON (1845)

Hammond served as governor and senator for South Carolina in the 1840s and 1850s. He emerged as one of the most vigorous defenders of slavery and the Southern social order. The document here, a response to the English abolitionist Thomas Clarkson's critique of Southern slavery, circulated widely in the United States and Britain.

Source: *Gov. Hammond's Letters on Southern Slavery: Addressed to Thomas Clarkson, the English Abolitionist* (Charleston: Walker and Burke, 1845).

Let us... turn to American slavery, to which you have now directed your attention, and against which a crusade has been preached as enthusiastic and ferocious as that of Peter the Hermit—destined, I believe, to be about as successful. And here let me say, there is not a vast difference between the two, though you may not acknowledge it. The wisdom of ages has concurred in the justice and expediency of establishing rights by prescriptive use, however tortious in their origin they may have been. You would deem a man insane whose keen sense of equity would lead him to denounce your right to the lands you hold, and which perhaps you inherited from a long line of ancestry, because your title was derived from a Saxon or Norman conqueror, and your lands were originally wrested by violence from the vanquished Britons. And so would the New England Abolitionist regard any one who would insist that he should restore his farm to the descendants of the slaughtered Red men, to whom, God has as clearly given it, as he gave life and freedom to the kidnapped African. That time does not consecrate wrong, is a fallacy which all history exposes; and which the best and wisest men of all ages and professions of religious faith, have practically denied. The means, therefore, whatever they may have been, by which the African race now in this country, have been reduced to slavery, cannot affect us, since they are our property, as your land is yours, by inheritance or purchase and prescriptive right. You will say that man cannot hold *property in man*. The answer is, that he can, and *actually does* hold property in his fellow all the world over, in a variety of forms, and *has always done so*. I will show presently his authority for doing it.

If you were to ask me whether I was an advocate of slavery in the abstract, I should probably answer, that I am not, according to my understanding of the question. I do not like to deal in abstractions; it seldom leads to any useful ends. There are few universal truths. I do not now remember any single moral truth universally acknowledged. We have no assurance that it is given to our finite understanding to comprehend abstract moral truth. Apart from Revelation and the Inspired writings, what ideas should we have even of God, Salvation and Immortality? Let the Heathen answer. Justice itself is impalpable as an abstraction, and abstract liberty the merest phantasy that ever amused the imagination. This world was made for man, and man for the world as it is. Ourselves, our relations with one another, and with all matter, are real, not ideal. I might say that I am no more in favor of slavery in the abstract, than I am of pover[t]y, disease, deformity, idiocy or any other inequality in the condition of the human family; that I love perfection, and think I should enjoy a Millenium such as God has promised. But what would it amount to? A pledge that I would join you to set about eradicating those apparently inevitable evils of our nature, in equalizing the condition of all mankind, consummating the perfection of our race, and introducing the Millenium? By no means. To effect these things belongs exclusively to a higher power, and would be well for us to leave the Almighty to perfect His own works and fulfil His own covenants. Especially, as the history of all the past shows how entirely futile all human efforts have proved, when made for the purpose of aiding Him in carrying out even His revealed designs, and how invarially he has accomplished them by unconscious instruments, and in the face of human expectation. Nay more, that every attempt which has been made by fallible man to extort from the world obedience to his "abstract" notions of right and wrong, has been invariably attended with calamities, dire and extended, just in proportion to the breadth and vigor of the movement. On slavery in the abstract then, it would not be amiss to have as little as possible to say. Let us contemplate it as it is. And thus contemplating it, the first question we have to ask ourselves is, whether it is contrary to the Will of God, as revealed to us in His holy scriptures—the only certain means given us to ascertain His will. If it is, then slavery is a sin; and I admit at once that every man is bound to set his face against it, and to emancipate his slaves, should he hold any....

I think, then, I may safely conclude, and I firmly believe, that American slavery is not only not a sin, but especially commanded by God through Moses, and approved by Christ through his apostles. And here I might close its defence; for what God ordained and Christ sanctifies, should surely command the respect and toleration of man. But I fear there has grown up in our time a Transcendental Religion which is throwing even Transcendental Philosophy into the shade; a religion too pure and elevated for the Bible; which seeks to erect among men a higher standard of morals than the Almighty has revealed or our Saviour preached, and which is probably destined to do more to impede the extension of God's Kingdom on earth than all the Infidels who have ever lived. Error is error. It is as dangerous to deviate to the right hand as to the left. And when men professing to be holy men, and who are by numbers so regarded, declare those things to be sinful which our Creator has expressly authorized and instituted, they do more to destroy his authority among mankind than the most wicked can affect by proclaiming that to be innocent which He has forbidden. To this self-righteous and self-exalted class belong all the Abolitionists whose writings I have read. With them it is no end of the argument to prove your propositions by the test of the Bible, interpreted according to its plain and palpable meaning, and as understood by all mankind for three thousand years before their time. They are more ingenious in construing and interpolating to accommodate it to their new-fangled and etherial code of morals, than ever were Voltaire or Hume in picking it to pieces to free the world from what they considered a delusion. When the Abolitionists proclaim "man-stealing" to be a sin, and show me that it is so written down by God, I admit them to be right, and shudder at the idea of such a crime. But when I show them that to hold "bond-men forever" is ordained by God, *they deny the Bible, and set up in its place a Law of their own making.* I must then cease to reason with them on this branch of the question. Our religion differs as widely as our manners. The Great Judge in our day of final account must decide between us....I indorse without reserve, the much abused sentiment of Gov. M'Duffie, that "slavery is the corner stone of our republican edifice;" while I repudiate, as ridiculously absurd, that much lauded but no where accredited dogma, of Mr. Jefferson, that "all men are born equal." No Society has ever yet existed, and I have already incidentally quoted the highest authority to show that none ever will exist, without a natural variety of classes. The most marked of these must in a country like ours, be the rich and the poor, the educated and the ignorant. It will scarcely be disputed that the very poor have less leisure to prepare themselves for the proper discharge of public duties than the rich; and that the ignorant are wholly unfit for them at all. In all countries save ours, these two classes, or the poor rather, who are presumed to be necessarily ignorant, are by law expressly excluded from all participation in the management of public affairs. In a republican [*sic*] Government this cannot be done. Universal suffrage, though not essential in theory, seems to be in fact, a necessary appendage to a republican system. Where universal suffrage obtains, it is obvious that the Government is in the hands of a numerical majority: and it is hardly necessary to say, that in every part of the world more than half the people are ignorant and poor. Though no one can look upon poverty as a crime, and we do not generally here regard it as any objection to a man in his individual capacity, still it must be admitted that it is a wretched and insecure government which is administered by its most ignorant citizens, and those who have the least at stake under it. Though intelligence and wealth have great influence here as everywhere, in keeping in check reckless and unenlightened numbers, yet it is evident to close observers, if not to all, that these are rapidly usurping all power in the non-slave-holding States, and threaten a fearful crisis in Republican Institutious [*sic*] there at no remote period. In the slave-holding States, however, nearly one half of the whole population, and those the poorest and most ignorant, have no political influence whatever, because they are slaves. Of the other half, a large proportion are both educated and independent in their circumstances, while those who unfortunately are not so, being still elevated far above the mass, are higher toned and more deeply interested in preserving a stable and well ordered government, than the same class in any other country. Hence, slavery is truly the "corner stone" and foundation of every well designed and durable "Republican edifice."...I have yet to reply to the main ground on which you and your coadjutors rely for the overthrow of our system of slavery. Failing in all your attempts to prove that it is sinful in its nature, immoral in its effects, a political evil, and profitless to those who maintain it, you appeal to the sympathies of mankind, and attempt to arouse the world against us by the most shocking charges of tyranny and cruelty. You begin by a vehement denunciation of "the irresponsible power of one man over his fellowmen." The question of the responsibility of power is a vast one. It is the great political question of modern times. Whole nations divide off upon it and establish different fundamental systems of government. That "responsibility," which to one set of millions seems amply sufficient to check the government, to the support of which they devote their lives and fortunes, appears to another set of millions a mere mockery of restraint. And accordingly as the opinions of these millions differ, they honor each other with the epithets of "Serfs" or "Anarchists." It is ridiculous to introduce such an idea as this into the discussion of a mere Domestic Institution. But since you have introduced it, I deny that the power of the slaveholder in America is "irresponsible." He is responsible to God. He is responsible to the world—a responsibility which Abolitionists do not intend to allow him to evade— and in acknowledgment of which I write you this letter. He is responsible to the community in which he lives, and to the laws under which he enjoys his civil rights. Those laws do not permit him to kill, to maim, or to punish beyond certain limits, or to overtask or to refuse to feed and clothe his slave. In short, they forbid him to be tyrannical or cruel. If any of those laws have grown obsolete, it is because they are so seldom violated that they are forgotten. You have disinterred one of them from a compilation by some Judge STROUD, of Philapelphia [*sic*], to stigmatize its inadequate penalties for killing, maiming, &c. Your objects appears to be—you can have no other—to produce the impression that it must be often violated on account of its insufficiency. You say as much, and that it marks our estimate of the slave. You forget to state that this law was enacted by *Englishmen*, and only indicates *their* opinion of the reparation due for these offences. Ours is proved by the fact, though perhaps unknown to Judge STROUD or yourself, that we have essentially altered this law; and the murder of a slave has for many years been punishable with death in this State. And so it is, I believe, in most or all the slave States. You seem well aware, however, that laws have been recently passed in all these States making it penal to teach slaves to read. Do you know what occasioned their passage, and renders their stringent enforcement necessary. I can tell you: it was the abolition agitation. If the slave is not allowed to read his Bible, the sin rests upon the Abolitionists; for they stand prepared to furnish him with a key to it, which would make it, not a book of hope and love and peace, but of despair, hatred and blood; which would convert the reader, not into a Christian, but a Demon. To preserve him from such a horrid destiny, it is a sacred duty which we owe to slaves, not less than to ourselves, to interpose the most decisive means. If the Catholics deem it wrong to trust the Bible to the hands of ignorance, shall we be excommunicated because we will not give and with it the corrupt and fatal commentaries of the Abolitionists, to our slaves? Allow our slaves to read your pamphlets, stimulating them to cut our throats! Can you believe us to be such unspeakable fools.... Is timely preparation and gradual emancipation suggested to avert these horrible consequences? I thought your experience in the West Indies had at least done so much as to explode that idea. If it failed there, much more would it fail here, where the two races, approximating to equality in numbers, are daily and hourly in the closest contact. Give room for but a single spark of real jealousy to be kindled between them, and the explosion would be instantaneous and universal. It is the most fatal of all fallacies to suppose that these two races can exist together, after any length of time or any process of preparation, on terms at all approaching to equality. Of this, both of them are finally and fixedly convinced. They differ essentially, in all the leading traits that characterise the varieties of the human species, and color draws an indellible and insuperable line of separation between them. Every scheme founded upon the idea that they can remain together on the same soil, beyond the briefest period, in any other relation than precisely that which now subsists between them, is not only preposterous, but fraught with deepest danger. If there was no alternative but to try the "experiment" here, reason and humanity dictate that the suffering of "gradualism" should be saved, and the catastrophe of "immediate abolition," enacted as rapidly as possible. Are you impatient for the performance to commence? Do you long to gloat over the scenes I have suggested, but could not hold the pen to portray? In your long life many such have passed under your review. You know that *they* are not "*impossible*." Can they be to your taste? Do you believe that in laboring to bring them about the Abolitionists are doing the will of God? No! God is not there. It is the work of Satan. The Arch-fiend, under specious guise, has found his way into your souls, and with false appeals to philanthropy, and foul insinuations to ambition, instigates them to rush head-long to the accomplishment of his diabolical designs.

QUESTIONS

1. How does Hammond distinguish between slavery in the abstract and slavery in practice?

2. Compare his argument regarding the Bible's defense of slavery to David Walker's argument from Chapter 12. How do they differ?

3. What is Hammond's political argument for slavery, and why does he believe that slavery is necessary in order for democracy to function?

13.6. REPUBLICAN PARTY PLATFORM (1856)

The Republican Party emerged from the collapse of the Whig Party in the mid-1850s. It combined some of the Whig's economic development policies (and, in some cases, parts of the American Party's nativism platform) with a significant opposition to the expansion of slavery in the western territories. 1856 was the first year that the party ran a presidential candidate, and although he lost, Republican congressional candidates won seats all across the North.

This Convention of Delegates, assembled in pursuance of a call addressed to the people of the United States, without regard to past political differences or divisions, who are opposed to the repeal of the Missouri Compromise; to the policy of the present Administration; to the extension [of] Slavery into Free Territory; in favor of the admission of Kansas as a Free State; of restoring the action of the Federal Government to the principles of Washington and Jefferson; and for the purpose of presenting candidates for the offices of President and Vice-President, do... Resolved: That, with our Republican fathers, we hold it to be a self-evident truth, that all men are endowed with the inalienable right to life, liberty, and the pursuit of happiness, and that the primary object and ulterior design of our Federal Government were to secure these rights to all persons under its exclusive jurisdiction; that, as our Republican fathers, when they had abolished Slavery in all our National Territory, ordained that no person shall be deprived of life, liberty, or property,

without due process of law, it becomes our duty to maintain this provision of the Constitution against all attempts to violate it for the purpose of establishing Slavery in the Territories of the United States by positive legislation, prohibiting its existence or extension therein. That we deny the authority of Congress, of a Territorial Legislation, of any individual, or association of individuals, to give legal existence to Slavery in any Territory of the United States, while the present Constitution shall be maintained.

Resolved: That the Constitution confers upon Congress sovereign powers over the Territories of the United States for their government; and that in the exercise of this power, it is both the right and the imperative duty of Congress to prohibit in the Territories those twin relics of barbarism—Polygamy, and Slavery.

Resolved: That while the Constitution of the United States was ordained and established by the people, in order to "form a more perfect union, establish justice,

Source: http://www.ushistory.org/gop/convention_1856republicanplatform.htm.

insure domestic tranquility, provide for the common defense, promote the general welfare, and secure the blessings of liberty," and contain ample provision for the protection of the life, liberty, and property of every citizen, the dearest Constitutional rights of the people of Kansas have been fraudulently and violently taken from them.

Their Territory has been invaded by an armed force;

Spurious and pretended legislative, judicial, and executive officers have been set over them, by whose usurped authority, sustained by the military power of the government, tyrannical and unconstitutional laws have been enacted and enforced;

The right of the people to keep and bear arms has been infringed.

Test oaths of an extraordinary and entangling nature have been imposed as a condition of exercising the right of suffrage and holding office.

The right of an accused person to a speedy and public trial by an impartial jury has been denied;

The right of the people to be secure in their persons, houses, papers, and effects, against unreasonable searches and seizures, has been violated;

They have been deprived of life, liberty, and property without due process of law;

That the freedom of speech and of the press has been abridged;

The right to choose their representatives has been made of no effect;

Murders, robberies, and arsons have been instigated and encouraged, and the offenders have been allowed to go unpunished;

That all these things have been done with the knowledge, sanction, and procurement of the present National Administration; and that for this high crime against the Constitution, the Union, and humanity, we arraign that Administration, the President, his advisers, agents, supporters, apologists, and accessories, either before or after the fact, before the country and before the world; and that it is our fixed purpose to bring the actual perpetrators of these atrocious outrages and their accomplices to a sure and condign punishment thereafter.

Resolved, That Kansas should be immediately admitted as a state of this Union, with her present Free Constitution, as at once the most effectual way of securing to her citizens the enjoyment of the rights and privileges to which they are entitled, and of ending the civil strife now raging in her territory.... Resolved, That a railroad to the Pacific Ocean by the most central and practicable route is imperatively demanded by the interests of the whole country, and that the Federal Government ought to render immediate and efficient aid in its construction, and as an auxiliary thereto, to the immediate construction of an emigrant road on the line of the railroad.

Resolved, That appropriations by Congress for the improvement of rivers and harbors, of a national character, required for the accommodation and security of our existing commerce, are authorized by the Constitution, and justified by the obligation of the Government to protect the lives and property of its citizens.

Resolved, That we invite the affiliation and cooperation of the men of all parties, however differing from us in other respects, in support of the principles herein declared; and believing that the spirit of our institutions as well as the Constitution of our country, guarantees liberty of conscience and equality of rights among citizens, we oppose all legislation impairing their security.

QUESTIONS

1. How do the Republicans root their opposition to slavery in the Constitution?
2. How does this argument differ from that of more traditional abolitionists such as Douglass (Document 12.3)?
3. Why was the condition of Kansas, where few slaves lived, so important to the Republican Party?

13.7. VICTOR HUGO, EXCERPTS FROM A LETTER TO THE *LONDON NEWS* REGARDING JOHN BROWN (DECEMBER 2, 1859)

In 1859, John Brown, a white abolitionist, attacked the U.S. armory at Harpers Ferry, Virginia, in a failed slave revolt. Brown was executed for attempting to incite an insurrection. Victor Hugo was one of the most well-known French writers of the 19th century. He worked in a variety of forms and gained fame for his poetry, novels, and plays. Hugo evolved into an ardent republican and championed democratic movements around the world.

To the Editor of the London News:

Sir: When our thoughts dwell upon the United States of America, a majestic form rises before the eye of imagination. It is a Washington!

Look, then, to what is taking place in that country of Washington at this present moment.

In the Southern States of the Union there are slaves; and this circumstance is regarded with indignation, as the most monstrous of inconsistencies, by the pure and logical conscience of the Northern States. A white man, a free man, John Brown, sought to deliver these negro slaves from bondage. Assuredly, if insurrection is ever a sacred duty, it must be when it is directed against Slavery. John Brown endeavored to commence the work of emancipation by the liberation of slaves in Virginia. Pious, austere, animated with the old Puritan spirit, inspired by the spirit of the Gospel, he sounded to these men, these oppressed brothers, the rallying cry of Freedom. The slaves, enervated by servitude, made no response to the appeal. Slavery afflicts the soul with weakness. Brown, though deserted, still fought at the head of a handful of heroic men; he was riddled with balls; his two young sons, sacred martyrs, fell dead at his side, and he himself was taken. This is what they call the affair at Harper's Ferry.

John Brown has been tried, with four of his comrades, Stephens, Coppic, Gree and Copeland.

What has been the character of his trial? Let us sum it up in a few words:—

John Brown, upon a wretched pallet, with six half gaping wounds, a gun-shot wound in his arm, another in his loins, and two in his head, scarcely conscious of surrounding sounds, bathing his mattress in blood, and with the ghastly presence [of] his two dead sons ever beside him; his four fellow-sufferers wounded, dragging themselves along by his side; Stephens bleeding from saber wounds; justice in a hurry, and overleaping all obstacles; an attorney, Hunter, who wishes to proceed hastily, and a judge, Parker, who suffers him to have his way; the hearing cut short, almost every application for delay refused, forged and mutilated documents produced, the witnesses for the defence kidnapped, every obstacle thrown in the way of the prisoner's counsel, two cannon loaded with canister stationed in the Court, orders given to the jailers to shoot the prisoners if they sought to escape, forty minutes of deliberation, and three men sentenced to die! I declare on my honor that all this took place, not in Turkey, but in America!

Such things cannot be done with impunity in the face of the civilized world. The universal conscience of humanity is an ever-watchful eye. Let the judges of Charlestown, and Hunter and Parker, and the

Source: http://en.wikisource.org/wiki/Victor_Hugo%27s_letter_to_the_London_News_regarding_John_Brown.

slaveholding jurors, and the whole population of Virginia, ponder it well: they are watched! They are not alone in the world. At this moment, America attracts the eyes of the whole of Europe.

John Brown, condemned to die....The more one loves, the more one admires, the more one venerates that Republic, the more heart-sick one feels at the contemplation of such a catastrophe. A single State ought not to have the power to dishonor all the rest, and in this case there is an obvious justification for a federal intervention. Otherwise, by hesitating to interfere when it might prevent a crime, the Union becomes a participator in its guilt. No matter how intense may be the indignation of the generous Northern States, the Southern States force them to share the opprobrium of this murder. All of us, no matter who we may be, who are bound together as compatriots by the common tie of a democratic creed, feel ourselves in some measure compromised. If the scaffold should be erected on the 16th of December, the incorruptible voice of history would thenceforward testify that the august Confederation of the New World, had added to all its rites of holy brotherhood a brotherhood of blood, and the fasces of that splendid Republic would be bound together with the running noose that hung from the gibbet of Brown!

This is a bond that kills.

When we reflect on what Brown, the liberator, the champion of Christ, has striven to effect, and when we remember that he is about to die, slaughtered by the American Republic, that crime assumes an importance co-extensive with that of the nation which commits it—and when we say to ourselves that this nation is one of the glories of the human race; that, like France, like England, like Germany, she is one of the great agents of civilization; that she sometimes even leaves Europe in the rear by the sublime audacity of some of her progressive movements; that she is the Queen of an entire world, and that her brow is irradiated with a glorious halo of freedom, we declare our conviction that John Brown will not die; for we recoil

horror-struck from the idea of so great a crime committed by so great a people.

Viewed in a political light, the murder of Brown would be an irreparable fault. It would penetrate the Union with a gaping fissure which would lead in the end to its entire disruption. It is possible that the execution of Brown might establish slavery on a firm basis in Virginia, but it is certain that it would shake to its centre the entire fabric of American democracy. You preserve your infamy, but you sacrifice your glory. Viewed in a moral light, it seems to me that a portion of the enlightenment of humanity would be eclipsed, that even the ideas of justice and injustice would be obscured on the day which should witness the assassination of Emancipation by Liberty.

As for myself, though I am but a mere atom, yet being, as I am, in common with all other men, inspired with the conscience of humanity, I fall on my knees, weeping before the great starry banner of the New World; and with clasped hands, and with profound and filial respect, I implore the illustrious American Republic, sister of the French Republic, to see to the safety of the universal moral law, to save John Brown, to demolish the threatening scaffold of the 16th of December, and not to suffer that beneath its eyes, and I add, with a shudder, almost by its fault, a crime should be perpetrated surpassing the first fratricide in iniquity.

For—yes, let America know it, and ponder on it well—there is something more terrible than Cain slaying Abel: It is Washington slaying Spartacus!

Victor Hugo
Hautville House, Dec. 2d, 1859.

QUESTIONS

1. How does Hugo characterize the actions of John Brown?

2. How might Americans have responded to Hugo's engagement with the event?

3. What role does he envision for Europe in the fight against American slavery?

13.8. VISUAL DOCUMENT: VICTOR HUGO, *THE HANGING OF JOHN BROWN* (1860)

This image appeared as the frontispiece of a pamphlet that Hugo published in 1860.

QUESTIONS

1. What does this image convey about Hugo's conception of John Brown?
2. Why is Brown represented alone, without the presence of the guards and executioner who were present?
3. What is the significance of the light that fills the upper left corner of the image?

Source: Virginia Historical Society, Richmond, Virginia, USA/The Bridgeman Art Library.

13.9. STEPHEN F. HALE, EXCERPTS FROM A LETTER TO B. MAGOFFIN (DECEMBER 27, 1860)

An Alabamian, Stephen Hale served in the U.S. Army and accepted a commission in the Confederate Army during the Civil War. In the winter of 1860–1861, Hale served as one of several "commissioners" sent by Deep South states into the Upper South to convince those states to secede. Like the other commissioners, Hale addressed a variety of public and private audiences while in Kentucky.

RANKFORT, December 27, 1860.

His Excellency B. MAGOFFIN,
Governor of the Commonwealth of Kentucky:

I have the honor of placing in your hands herewith a commission from the Governor of the State of Alabama, accrediting me as a commissioner from that State to the sovereign State of Kentucky, to consult in reference to the momentous issues now pending between the Northern and Southern States of this confederacy. Although each State, as a sovereign political community, must finally determine these grave issues for itself, yet the identity of interests, sympathy, and institutions, prevailing alike in all of the slaveholding States, in the opinion of Alabama renders it proper that there should be a frank and friendly consultation by each one with her sister Southern States touching their common grievances and the measures necessary to be adopted to protect the interest, honor, and safety of their citizens. I come, then, in a spirit of fraternity, as the commissioner on the part of the State of Alabama, to confer with the authorities of this Commonwealth in reference to the infraction of our constitutional rights, wrongs done and threatened to be done, as well as the mode and measure of redress proper to be adopted by the sovereign States aggrieved to preserve their sovereignty, vindicate their rights, and protect their citizens. In order to a clear understanding of the appropriate remedy, it may be proper to consider the rights and duties, both of the State and citizen, under the Federal compact, as well as the wrongs done and threatened. I therefore submit for the consideration of Your Excellency the following propositions, which I hope will command your assent and approval....3. The Federal Government results from a compact entered into between separate, sovereign, and independent States, called the Constitution of the United States, and amendments thereto, by which these sovereign States delegated certain specific powers to be used by that Government for the common defense and general welfare of all the States and their citizens; and when these powers are abused, or used for the destruction of the rights of any State or its citizens, each State has an equal right to judge for itself as well of the violations and infractions of that instrument as of the mode and measure of redress; and if the interest or safety of her citizens demands it, may resume the powers she had delegated without let or hindrance from the Federal Government or any other power on earth.

4. Each State is bound in good faith to observe and keep on her part all the stipulations and covenants inserted for the benefit of other States in the constitutional compact (the only bond of union by which the several States are bound together), and when persistently violated by one party to the prejudice of her sister States, ceases to be obligatory on the States so aggrieved, and they may rightfully declare the

Source: United States War Department, *The War of Rebellion: A Compilation of the Official Records of the Union and Confederate Armies*, series 4, vol. 1 (Washington, DC: Government Printing Office, 1880–1901), 4–11.

compact broken, the union thereby formed dissolved, and stand upon their original rights as sovereign and independent political communities; and further, that each citizen owes his primary allegiance to the State in which he resides, and hence it is the imperative duty of the State to protect him in the enjoyment of all his constitutional rights, and see to it that they are not denied or withheld from him with impunity by any other State or government....At the time of the adoption of the Federal Constitution African slavery existed in twelve of the thirteen States. Slaves are recognized both as property and as a basis of political power by the Federal compact, and special provisions are made by that instrument for their protection as property. Under the influences of climate and other causes, slavery has been banished from the Northern States; the slaves themselves have been sent to the Southern States and there sold, and their price gone into the pockets of their former owners at the North. And in the meantime African slavery has not only become one of the fixed domestic institutions of the Southern States, but forms an important element of their political power, and constitutes the most valuable species of their property, worth, according to recent estimates, not less than $4,000,000,000; forming, in fact, the basis upon which rests the prosperity and wealth of most of these States, and supplying the commerce of the world with its richest freights, and furnishing the manufactories of two continents with the raw material, and their operatives with bread. It is upon this gigantic interest, this peculiar institution of the South, that the Northern States and their people have been waging an unrelenting and fanatical war for the last quarter of a century; an institution with which is bound up not only the wealth and prosperity of the Southern people, but their very existence as a political community. This war has been waged in every way that human ingenuity, urged on by fanaticism, could suggest. They attack us through their literature, in their schools, from the hustings, in their legislative halls, through the public press, and even their courts of justice forget the purity of their judicial ermine to strike down the rights of the Southern slave-holder and override every barrier which the Constitution has erected for his protection; and the sacred desk is desecrated to this unholy crusade against our lives, our property,

and the constitutional rights guaranteed to us by the compact of our fathers. During all this time the Southern States have freely conceded to the Northern States and the people of those States every right secured to them by the Constitution, and an equal interest in the common territories of the Government; protected the lives and property of their citizens of every kind, when brought within Southern jurisdiction; enforced through their courts, when necessary, every law of Congress passed for the protection of Northern property, and submitted ever since the foundation of the Government, with scarcely a murmur, to the protection of their shipping, manufacturing, and commercial interests, by odious bounties, discriminating tariffs, and unjust navigation laws, passed by the Federal Government to the prejudice and injury of their own citizens....The same fell spirit, like an unchained demon, has for years swept over the plains of Kansas, leaving death, desolation, and ruin in its track. Nor is this the mere ebullition of a few half-crazy fanatics, as is abundantly apparent from the sympathy manifested all over the.North, where, in many places, the tragic death of John Brown, the leader of the raid upon Virginia, who died upon the gallows a condemned felon, is celebrated with public honors, and his name canonized as a martyr to liberty; and many, even of the more conservative papers of the Black Republican school, were accustomed to speak of his murderous attack upon the lives of the unsuspecting citizens of Virginia in a half-sneering and half-apologetic tone. And what has the Federal Government done in the meantime to protect slave property upon the common territories of the Union? Whilst a whole squadron of the American Navy is maintained on the coast of Africa at an enormous expense to enforce the execution of the laws against the slave-trade (and properly, too), and the whole Navy is kept afloat to protect the lives and property of American citizens upon the high seas, not a law has been passed by Congress or an arm raised by the Federal Government to protect the slave property of citizens from Southern States upon the soil of Kansas, the common territory and common property of the citizens of all the States, purchased alike by their common treasure, and held by the Federal Government, as declared by the Supreme Court of the United States, as the trustee for all their citizens; but, upon the contrary, a territorial government, created by Congress and supported out of the common treasury, under the influence and control of emigrant-aid societies and abolition emissaries, is permitted to pass laws excluding and destroying all that species of property within her limits, thus ignoring on the part of the Federal Government one of the fundamental principles of all good governments—the duty to protect the property of the citizen—and wholly refusing to maintain the equal rights of the States and the citizens of the States upon their common territories.

As the last and crowning act of insult and outrage upon the people of the South, the citizens of the Northern States, by overwhelming majorities, on the 6th day of November last, elected Abraham Lincoln and Hannibal Hamlin President and Vice-President of the United States. Whilst it may be admitted that the mere election of any man to the Presidency is not *per se* a sufficient cause for a dissolution of the Union, yet when the issues upon and circumstances under which he was elected are properly appreciated and understood, the question arises whether a due regard to the interest, honor, and safety of their citizens, in view of this and all the other antecedent wrongs and outrages, do not render it the imperative duty of the Southern States to resume the powers they have delegated to the Federal Government and interpose their sovereignty for the protection of their citizens....If the policy of the Republicans is carried out according to the programme indicated by the leaders of the party, and the South submits, degradation and ruin must overwhelm alike all classes of citizens in the Southern States. The slave-holder and non-slave-holder must ultimately share the same fate; all be degraded to a position of equality with free negroes, stand side by side with them at the polls, and fraternize in all the social relations of life, or else there will be an eternal war of races, desolating the land with blood, and utterly wasting and destroying all the resources of the country. Who can look upon such a picture without a shudder? What Southern man, be he slave-holder or non-slave-holder, can without indignation and horror contemplate the triumph of negro equality, and see his own sons and daughters in the not distant future associating with free negroes upon terms of political and social equality, and the white man stripped by the heaven-daring hand of fanaticism of that title to superiority over the black race which God himself has bestowed? In the Northern States, where free negroes are so few as to form no appreciable part of the community, in spite of all the legislation for their protection, they still remain a degraded caste, excluded by the ban of society from social association with all but the lowest and most degraded of the white race. But in the South, where in many places the African race largely predominates, and as a consequence the two races would be continually pressing together, amalgamation or the extermination of the one or the other would be inevitable. Can Southern men submit to such degradation and ruin? God forbid that they should....Will the South give up the institution of slavery and consent that her citizens be stripped of their property, her civilization destroyed, the whole land laid waste by fire and sword? It is impossible. She cannot; she will not. Then why attempt longer to hold together hostile States under the stipulations of a violated Constitution? It is impossible. Disunion is inevitable. Why, then, wait longer for the consummation of a result that must come? Why waste further time in expostulations and appeals to Northern States and their citizens, only to be met, as we have been for years past, by renewed insults and repeated injuries? Will the South be better prepared to meet the emergency when the North shall be strengthened by the admission of the new Territories of Kansas, Nebraska, Washington, Jefferson, Nevada, Idaho, Chippewa, and Arizona as non-slave-holding States, as we are warned from high sources will be done within the next four years, under the administration of Mr. Lincoln? Can the true men at the North ever make a more powerful or successful rally for the preservation of our rights and the Constitution than they did in the last Presidential contest? There is nothing to inspire a hope that they can.

Shall we wait until our enemies shall possess themselves of all the powers of the Government; until abolition judges are on the Supreme Court bench, abolition collectors at every port, and abolition postmasters in every town; secret mail agents traversing the whole land, and a subsidized press established in our midst to demoralize our people? Will we be stronger then or better prepared to meet the struggle, if a struggle must come? No, verily. When that time shall come, well may our adversaries laugh at our folly and deride our impotence. The deliberate judgment of Alabama, as indicated by the joint resolutions of her General Assembly, approved February 24, 1860, is that prudence, patriotism, and loyalty to all the great principles of civil liberty, incorporated in our Constitution and consecrated by the memories of the past, demand that all the Southern States should now resume their delegated powers, maintain the rights, interests, and honor of their citizens, and vindicate their own sovereignty. And she most earnestly but respectfully invites her sister sovereign State, Kentucky, who so gallantly vindicated the sovereignty of the States in 1798, to the consideration of these grave and vital questions, hoping she may concur with the State of Alabama in the conclusions to which she has been driven by the impending dangers that now surround the Southern States.

QUESTIONS

1. What is Hale's critique of Northern actions against slavery?
2. What future does he predict under a Republican presidential administration?
3. Why does Hale believe that all the slaveholding states should secede and found a new government?

CHAPTER 14

THE CIVIL WAR, 1860–1865

14.1. CHIEF JUSTICE ROGER TANEY, EXCERPTS FROM *EX PARTE MERRYMAN* (1861)

At the start of the Civil War, Lincoln issued a proclamation of martial law and suspended the right to habeas corpus in parts of eastern Maryland, where secessionist sentiment ran high. John Merryman, a pro-Southern newspaper editor, encouraged Maryland's secession in his paper. He was arrested by military authorities and detained without charges in a military jail.

Arrest of John Merryman and Proceedings Thereon.

The case, then, is simply this: A military officer residing in Pennsylvania issues an order to arrest a citizen of Maryland, upon vague and indefinite charges, without any proof, so far as appears. Under this order his house is entered in the night; he is seized as a prisoner, and conveyed to Fort McHenry, and there kept in close confinement. And when a *habeas corpus* is served on the commanding officer, requiring him to produce the prisoner before a Justice of the Supreme Court, in order that he may examine into the legality of the imprisonment, the answer of the officer is that he is authorized by the President to suspend the writ of *habeas corpus* at his discretion, and, in the exercise of that discretion, suspends it in this case, and on that ground refuses obedience to the writ.

As the case comes before me, therefore, I understand that the President not only claims the right to suspend the writ of *habeas corpus* himself, at his discretion, but to delegate that discretionary power to a military officer, and to leave it to him to determine whether he will or will not obey judicial process that may be served upon him....I can see no ground whatever for supposing that the President, in any emergency or in any state of things, can authorize the suspension of the privilege of the writ of *habeas corpus*, or arrest a citizen, except in aid of the judicial power. He certainly does not faithfully execute the laws if he takes upon himself legislative power by suspending the writ of *habeas corpus*—and the judicial power, also, by arresting and imprisoning a person without due process of law. Nor can any argument be drawn from the nature of sovereignty, or the necessities of

Source: Ex Parte Merryman, 17 F. Cas. 144 (C.C.D. Md. 1861) (No. 9487), http://teachingamericanhistory.org/library/index. asp?document=442.

government for self-defense, in times of tumult and danger. The Government of the United States is one of delegated and limited powers. It derives it existence and authority altogether from the Constitution, and neither of its branches—executive, legislative or judicial—can exercise any of the powers of government beyond those specified and granted. For the tenth article of the amendments to the Constitution, in express terms, provides that "the powers not delegated to the United States by the Constitution, nor prohibited by it to the States, are reserved to the States, respectively, or to the people." ...The Constitution provides, as I have before said, that "no person shall be deprived of life, liberty, or property, without due process of law." It declares that "the right of the people to be secure in their persons, houses, papers, and effects against unreasonable searches and seizures shall not be violated, and no warrant shall issue but upon probable cause, supported by oath or affirmation, and particularly describing the place to be searched and the persons or things to be seized." It provides that the party accused shall be entitled to a speedy trial in a court of justice.

And these great and fundamental laws, which Congress itself could not suspend, have been disregarded and suspended, like the writ of *habeas corpus*, by a military order, supported by force of arms. Such is the case now before me; and I can only say that if the authority which the Constitution has confided to the judiciary department and judicial officers may thus upon any pretext or under any circumstances be usurped by the military power at its discretion, the people of the United States are no longer living under a Government of laws, but every citizen holds life, liberty, and property at the will and pleasure of the army officer in whose military district he may happen to be found.

In such a case my duty was too plain to be mistaken. I have exercised all the power which the Constitution and laws confer on me, but that power has been resisted by a force too strong for me to overcome. It is possible that the officer who has incurred this grave responsibility may have misunderstood his instructions, and exceeded the authority intended to be given him. I shall, therefore, order all the proceedings in this case, with my opinion, to be filed and recorded in the Circuit Court of the United States for the District of Maryland, and direct the clerk to transmit a copy, under seal, to the President of the United States. It will then remain for that high officer, in fulfilment of his constitutional obligation to "take care that the laws be faithfully executed," to determine what measures he will take to cause the civil process of the United States to be respected and enforced.

R. B. Taney,
Chief Justice of the Supreme Court of the United States

QUESTIONS

1. What is Taney's argument rejecting the right of the president to suspend habeas corpus?
2. What conclusions does he draw about the state of American democracy from Lincoln's actions?
3. What would Southerners have made of Taney's opinion?

14.2. KARL MARX, LETTER TO FREDERICK ENGELS (SEPTEMBER 10, 1862)

Together, Karl Marx and Frederick Engels helped shape the advent of socialism in Europe in the 1840s and 1850s. During the Civil War, Marx traveled to the United States as a journalist for the Viennese newspaper *Die Presse*. He also contributed pieces to the *New York Daily Tribune*. His letter here was written at a point when the Union had suffered serious military defeats in the eastern theater—the region on which foreign observers focused.

London, 10 September

Dear Engels,

...As to the Yankees, I am firmly of the opinion, now as before, that the North will win in the end; true, the Civil War may pass through all kinds of episodes, perhaps even ceasefires, and be long-drawn-out. The South would or could conclude peace only on condition that it gained possession of the border slave states. In that case, California would also fall to it, the North-West would follow suit and the entire Federation, with the exception, perhaps, of the New England states, would again form one country, this time under the acknowledged supremacy of the slaveholders. It would be the reconstruction of the United States on the basis demanded by the South. But that is impossible and won't happen.

The North, for its part, can conclude peace only if the Confederacy is restricted to the old slave states, and then only to those bounded by the Mississippi River and the Atlantic. In which case the Confederacy would soon come to a happy end. In the intervening period, ceasefires, etc., on the basis of a status quo could at most occasion pauses in the course of the war.

The way in which the North is waging the war is none other than might be expected of a *bourgeois* republic, where humbug has reigned supreme for so long. The South, an oligarchy, is better suited to the purpose, especially an oligarchy where all productive labour devolves on the niggers and where the 4 million 'white trash' are *flibustiers* by calling. For all that, I'm prepared to bet my life on it that these fellows will come off worst, 'Stonewall. Jackson' notwithstanding. It is, of course, possible that some sort of revolution will occur beforehand in the North itself.

QUESTIONS

1. What was the likelihood of the fractured "federation" outcome that Marx predicts could be one result of the war?
2. Why does he refer to the South as an "oligarchy"?
3. Would Northerners have agreed with his assessment of the war?

Source: http://www.marxists.org/archive/marx/works/1862/letters/62_09_10.htm.

14.3. HENRY TURNER, "REMINISCENCES OF EMANCIPATION DAY" (JANUARY 1, 1863)

Born a free black in South Carolina, Henry Turner became a prominent minister and eventually a bishop of the African Methodist Episcopal church. He ministered to a large congregation in Washington, DC, and served as a chaplain for a U.S. Colored Troops regiment during the war. The Emancipation Proclamation went into effect on January 1, 1863.

On the first day of January, 1863, odd and unique conditions attended every mass-meeting, and the papers of the following day were not able to give them in anything like detail. Long before sunset Israel Church and its yard were crowded with people. The writer was vociferously cheered in every direction he went because in a sermon I tried to deliver I had said that Richmond, the headquarters of the Southern Confederacy, would never fall till black men led the army against this great slave-mart, nor did it fall and succumb to the general government till black men went in first. This was only a popular prediction, and delivered under a general excitement, but strange to say, it was fully realized.

Seeing such a multitude of people in and around my church, I hurriedly went up to the office of the first paper in which the proclamation of freedom could be printed, known as the "Evening Star," and squeezed myself through the dense crowd that was waiting for the paper. The first sheet run off with the proclamation in it was grabbed for by three of us, but some active young man got possession of it and fled. The next sheet was grabbed for by several, and was torn into tatters. The third sheet from the press was grabbed for by several, but I succeeded in procuring so much of it as contained the proclamation, and off I went for life and death. Down Pennsylvania Ave. I ran as for my life, and when the people saw me coming with the paper in my hand they raised a shouting cheer that was almost deaf-

ening. As many as could get around me lifted me to a great platform, and I started to read the proclamation. I had run the best end of a mile, I was out of breath, and could not read. Mr. Hinton, to whom I handed the paper, read it with great force and clearness. While he was reading every kind of demonstration and gesticulation was going on. Men squealed, women fainted, dogs barked, white and colored people shook hands, songs were sung, and by this time cannons began to fire at the navy-yard, and follow in the wake of the roar that had for some time been going on behind the White House. Every face had a smile, and even the dumb animals seemed to realize that some extraordinary event had taken place. Great processions of colored and white men marched to and fro and passed in front of the White House and congratulated President Lincoln on his proclamation. The President came to the window and made responsive bows, and thousands told him, if he would come out of that palace, they would hug him to death. Mr. Lincoln, however, kept at a safe distance from the multitude, who were frenzied to distraction over his proclamation.

I do not know the extent that the excitement in Russia led to, when the humane Emperor proclaimed the freedom of twenty-two million serfs, I think in 1862, but the jubilation that attended the proclamation of freedom by His Excellency Abraham Lincoln, I am sure has never been surpassed, if it has ever been equaled. Nor do I believe it will ever be duplicated again. Rumor said

---

Source: Edwin S. Redkey, ed., *Respect Black: The Writings and Speeches of Henry McNeal Turner* (New York: Arno Press, 1971), 1–4.

that in several instances the very thought of being set at liberty and having no more auction blocks, no more Negro-traders, no more forced parting of man and wife, no more separation of parents and children, no more horrors of slavery, was so elative and heart gladdening that scores of colored people literally fell dead with joy. It was indeed a time of times, and a half time, nothing like it will ever be seen again in this life. Our entrance into Heaven itself will only form a counterpart.

QUESTIONS

1. Turner had prophesied the role of black Union troops as a vanguard for the North. How would Southerners have responded to this call?
2. What benefits of emancipation does Turner emphasize?
3. What political impact would Turner's optimism have had on the course of the war in 1863?

14.4. CORPORAL WILBUR FISK, EXCERPTS FROM LETTERS TO THE *GREEN MOUNTAIN FREEMAN* (MAY 20, 1862, AND APRIL 7, 1864)

Wilbur Fisk, born and raised in Vermont, enlisted in Company E of the 2nd Vermont Volunteers in 1861. Over the course of the war, Fisk wrote over 100 letters to the Montpelier *Green Mountain Free-man*, his community's newspaper. The first letter below was written in the midst of the failed Union effort to seize Richmond. The second was written at a later point in the war, when the North was experiencing more success.

May 20, 1862

The inevitable negro question would of course be the subject of the most animated conversation of anything we could bring up, for that inexhaustible subject claims preeminence in camp as well as court, and there are almost as many opinions expressed in regard to it in a tent's company as there are in Congress. The boys think it *their* duty to put down rebellion and nothing more, and they view the abolition of slavery in the present time as saddling so much additional labor upon them before the present great work is accomplished. Negro prejudice is as strong here as anywhere and most of the boys would think it a humiliating compromise to the dignity of their work to have it declared that the object of their services was to free the repulsive creatures from slavery, and raise the negro to an equality with themselves. I verily believe if such a declaration was made to-day a majority would be inclined to lay down their arms and quit the service in disgust. The most cordial reception by far that we have received since we left the free states, was tendered us by this sable species of human property. As we were passing by the premises of one of the more wealthy farmers on our way here, a group of negroes, a score or more composed of men, women and children of all ages, climbed upon the fence by the roadside and greeted us in in their earnest simple way "God bress you," "I's glad to see you," "I's glad you's come," "God bress you," and many similar exclamations as

Source: Emil and Ruth Rosenblatt, eds., *Hard Marching Every Day: The Civil War Letters of Private Wilbur Fisk, 1861–1865* (Lawrence: University Press of Kansas, 1983).

they bowed, and courtesied, and waved their hands to us, attesting their childish glee at seeing so many Union soldiers. They were dirty and ragged and probably as a perfectly natural result were ignorant and degraded, but they seemed to understand, as nearly all the negroes here do, that somehow all this commotion has a connection with them and will bring about their freedom in the end. They seem conscious of being at the the bottom of all this trouble, and all the deceptions their masters could invent have failed to rob them of this knowledge....

April 7, 1864

Great confidence is felt in the plans that General Grant will adopt, and the means that he will have to use in crushing the last vestige of this Heaven accursed rebellion. Having authority that extends from the Atlantic to the Mississippi from Mobile to Washington, we may reasonably expect a concert of action in the coming campaigns that will ensure us success and victory. God grant that we may not be disappointed.

Success and victory! whose heart does not beat quicker at the thought? What consequences will have been achieved when this great rebellion shall have been forever humbled. It is not merely that this terrible war may be ended, and we safely at liberty again, that we hope to conquer our enemies and be once more at peace, but that the great principles of a free government, whose worth no mind short of Infinite Wisdom can estimate, and which even after the world has stood so long is still considered an experiment, may not be overthrown, and the progress of civilization and freedom may not be rolled back for ages, or receive a blow from which they may never recover. We are anxious of course to get out of this war, for we long most earnestly to return to the almost sacred hills and valleys of old Vermont, but we are not so anxious for this, as we are that the faith of the world in the intelligence and virtue of the common people, and their ability to govern themselves and maintain national unity without being rent asunder by internal strife and discord—a faith that despots the world over profess to sneer at, and hold to be a delusion, and which stimulates the noblest energies of the masses of mankind—that this may be maintained, increased and perpetuated. If these principles succeed, Slavery must fall, and fall forever. The two are so antagonistical that, even

if both are right, or neither of them, men embracing each could not possibly live together in peace, unless we are to suppose that God has given them a larger spirit of forbearance than is vouchsafed to humanity in general. There never was a real unity between them, and there never can be. Slavery is a relic of the darkest ages, and the poorest government on earth is better in principle than that. If we are going to have a free government at all, let us have it all free, or else we had better give up the name. Slavery has fostered an aristocracy of the rankest kind, and this aristocracy is the bitterest foe that a really free government can have. Slavery and despotism have challenged war with us, and by it she must abide. Slavery was jealous of the comelier strength that Freedom possessed; and maliciously envied her irresistible march onward to a higher destiny. Slavery drew the sword, and would have stabbed Freedom to the heart, had not God denied her the strength. She could not bear that her more righteous neighbor should be prospered, while she herself was accursed, and in her foolish madness she has tried to rend the Union in twain. With that institution it is success or death. Compromise with Slavery, and restore the Union with Slavery in it still! As well might Jehovah compromise with Satan and give him back part of Heaven.

There never before was a rebellion like this one. Generally a rebellion has been the outbreak of the people against the tyranny of a few. Their cause has usually been the cause of liberty, and more or less just. Knit together by the idea of freeing themselves from an odious despotism, and armed with justice, and backed by numbers, they have often succeeded, and history has applauded their bravery. In this war it has been different. The people have not rebelled against the few, but the few have rebelled against the people. Our government is the people's, and against this government the proud slaveholder has rebelled. With Slavery for a corner stone they hope to rob our government of her honor, and erect within our borders a rival government, which every attribute of the Almighty must detest. Can they succeed? Is the glory of our nation to be destroyed forever? Is the great experiment which our forefathers have made, and which has been our pride and boast so long, to be a failure after all? If the North will do her duty, we answer, Never! And the North *will* do her duty. She knows what it is, and she does not fear it. Never in a war before did the rank and file feel a more resolute earnestness for a just cause, and a more invincible determination to succeed, than in this war; and what the rank and file are determined to do everybody knows will surely be done. We mean to be thorough about it too. We are not going to destroy the military power of the dragon Confederacy and not destroy its fangs also. We have as a nation yielded to their rapacious demands times enough. We have cringed before Slavery as long as we will.

"Far better die in such a strife,
Than still to Slavery's claims concede,
Than crouch beneath her frown for life,
Far better in the field to bleed:
To live thus wage a life-long shame,
To die is victory and fame."

I almost lose my temper sometimes (what little I have got) when I hear men that really ought to know better, call this war a mere crusade to free the negroes, "a nigger war" and nothing more. But even if I was fighting to free the negroes simply, I don't know why I should be acting from a motive that I need be ashamed of. I verily believe that He who when He was on the earth healed foul leprosy, gave sight to the blind beggars, and preached the gospel to the poor,

would not be ashamed to act from such a motive. And if he would not, why should I? Fighting to free the "niggers!" Why yes, my dear fellow, we are doing just that and a great deal more. But, sir, I am going to tell you, you would not speak of that so contemptuously, if you had not all your life long fed your soul upon motives so small, so mean, and so selfish, that the sublimer motives of sacrificing blood and treasure to elevate a degraded and downtrodden race, is entirely beyond your comprehension. Should such an event, however, rather help than hinder the success of this war, we trust that you will acquiesce in the result, and when the future of this country shall have become by this means more glorious than the past has ever been, we shall hope that you will find that your own liberty and happiness has not been at all infringed upon by giving the same liberty and happiness to a few ignorant and despised sons of Africa.

QUESTIONS

1. How does Fisk characterize the attitudes of his fellow soldiers toward blacks and slavery?
2. How does he explain the relationship between slavery and democracy?
3. Why is Fisk fighting the war?

14.5. KATE STONE, EXCERPTS FROM JOURNAL (APRIL 21, 1863)

Kate Stone's mother owned a large cotton plantation 30 miles northwest of Vicksburg, Mississippi, the main target of the Union army in 1862 and 1863 because of its commanding position on the Mississippi River. "Brokenburn," the Stone plantation, encompassed 1,260 acres and was tended by 150 slaves, making it one of the largest estates in both the region and the United States. Rather than greet the Union forces at their home, Kate and her family fled south, eventually settling as refugees in east Texas.

Source: John Q. Anderson, ed., *Brokenburn: The Journal of Kate Stone, 1861–1865* (Baton Rouge: Louisiana State University Press, 1995), 190–93.

Friday we came down to Delhi in an immense dugout, a trip of six hours. All seven of us, Mamma, Aunt Laura, Sister, Beverly, I, and the two boys, with an assorted cargo of corn, bacon, hams, Negroes, their baggage, dogs and cats, two or three men, and our scant baggage. It was a dreadful trip. We were very crowded, the hot sun beaming on us as we were creeping down the bayou, hungry and tired. There was a very strong reflection from the water, and one of our poor Negroes was sick, groaning most of the way, and could not be made comfortable. We were glad enough to get out at the railroad bridge and walk the mile to reach Delhi.

The scene there beggars description: such crowds of Negroes of all ages and sizes, wagons, mules, horses, dogs, baggage, and furniture of every description, very little of it packed. It was just thrown in promiscuous heaps—pianos, tables, chairs, rosewood sofas, wardrobes, parlor sets, with pots, kettles, stoves, beds and bedding, bowls and pitchers, and everything of the kind just thrown pell-mell here and there, with soldiers, drunk and sober, combing over it all, shouting and laughing. While thronging everywhere were refugees—men, women, and children—everybody and everything trying to get on the cars, all fleeing from the Yankees or worse still, the Negroes.

All have lost heavily, some with princely estates and hundreds of Negroes, escaping with ten or twenty of their hands and only the clothes they have on. Others brought out clothes and household effects but no Negroes, and still others sacrificed everything to run their Negroes to a place of safety.

Everybody was animated and excited. All had their own tales to tell of the Yankee insolence and oppression and their hairbreadth escapes. All were eager to tell their own stories of hardship and contrivance, and everybody sympathized with everybody else. All were willing to lend a helping hand and to give advice to anybody on any subject. Nearly everybody took his trials cheerfully, making a joke of them, and nearly all are bound for Texas. Nobody "crying over spilled milk." Not a tear all day, though one knows there were heavy hearts bravely borne.

We got off from Delhi about sunset and reached Monroe after twelve. Nearly all remained on the cars until daylight, as it was impossible to get accommodations in town. It was amusing to watch the people wake up in the morning, wash their faces, smooth at their hair, and go to eating breakfast as leisurely and with as much *sang-froid* as though in their breakfast rooms at home. Everyone traveling on the cars now carries his own provisions, as you can get nothing if you do not, and no room if you get off.

We and the Lowry family were the last to leave the cars. Jimmy arranged his affairs, and about eleven when we were all thoroughly worn out we set off in a four-horse stage. We drove through Monroe, which seems to be a beautiful little town, but I was suffering with fever too much to like anything. The road up the Ouachita was lovely. It is a clear bright stream with forest shaded banks. The hard dry road was appreciated after the mud and water of the last months. The profusion of catalpa trees, all in full bloom, lining the streets of Monroe was indescribably fair in the early morning light. The deep green leaves seemed heaped with pyramids of snow. We never thought the catalpa could be so pretty.

We crossed the river at Trenton on a flat and came out two miles in the hills to this place, Mr. Deane's, but we hope to be here only a few days. The woods around here are beautiful with quantities of wild flowers and fruits. I have been sick in bed until today.

Yesterday Mamma and Jimmy went back to Delhi to get a party of soldiers to go back home with Jimmy and bring out the Negroes left there. All our and Aunt Laura's house servants, the most valuable we own, were left. She returned today, having succeeded in getting the soldiers, and the party with Jimmy as guide will leave this morning. We shall be very anxious until Jimmy returns as it is a most hazardous undertaking. Mamma did not realize the great danger until her return on the train. Some of the gentlemen were speaking of its hardihood, and fear if those of the party are captured they may be hanged as spies. She is very much alarmed.

We hear that the Negroes are still on the place, but the furniture and all movables have been carried out to camp by the Yankees. The Negroes quarreled over the division of our clothes. I have barely a change and the others have but little more. Our beds are all in the quarters. Webster, our most trusted servant, claims the plantation as his own and is renowned as the greatest villain in the country.

If we succeed in getting the Negroes we may say farewell to the buildings as no doubt they will be burned, but that may happen at any time. Mrs. Barr's and Maj. Haywood's homes have gone up in smoke.

QUESTIONS

1. How does Stone describe the experience of being a refugee?
2. How did white Southerners perceive the Union army's intentions?
3. What happened to slavery as the Union army advanced into the South?

14.6. SPOTSWOOD RICE, LETTERS WRITTEN FROM HOSPITAL (SEPTEMBER 3, 1864)

Spotswood Rice, an enslaved man, worked as a tobacco roller before the Civil War. During the war, he enlisted in the 67th U.S. Colored Infantry. When he wrote the following letters, the first to his children and the second to his daughter's owner, Rice was confined to the hospital with chronic rheumatism.

[Benton Barracks Hospital, St. Louis, Mo., September 3, 1864]

My Children   I take my pen in hand to rite you A few lines to let you know that I have not forgot you and that I want to see you as bad as ever   now my Dear Children I want you to be contented with whatever may be your lots   be assured that I will have you if it cost me my life   on the 28th of the mounth. 8 hundred White and 8 hundred blacke solders expects to start up the rivore to Glasgow and above there thats to be jeneraled by a jeneral that will give me both of you   when they Come I expect to be with, them and expect to get you both in return.   Dont be uneasy my children   I expect to have you.   If Diggs dont give you up this Government will and I feel confident that I will get you   Your Miss Kaitty said that I tried to steal

you   But I'll let her know that god never intended for man to steal his own flesh and blood.   If I had no confidence in God I could have confidence in her   But as it is If I ever had any Confidence in her I have none now and never expect to have   And I want her to remember if she meets me with ten thousand soldiers she [will?] meet her enemy   I once [thought] that I had some respect for them but now my respects is worn out and have no sympathy for Slaveholders.   And as for her cristianantty I expect the Devil has Such in hell   You tell her from me that She is the frist Christian that I ever hard say that aman could Steal his own child especially out of human bondage

You can tell her that She can hold to you as long as she can   I never would expect to ask her again to let you come to me because I know that the devil has got her hot set against that that is write   now my Dear

Source: Ira Berlin, Joseph P. Reidy, and Leslie S. Rowland, eds., *Freedom: A Documentary History of Emancipation, 1861–1867, Series II: The Black Military Experience* (Cambridge: Cambridge University Press, 1982), 689.

children I am a going to close my letter to you   Give my love to all enquiring friends   tell them all that we are well and want to see them very much and Corra and Mary receive the greater part of it you sefves   and dont think hard of us not sending you any thing   I you father have a plenty for you when I see you   Spott & Noah sends their love to both of you   Oh! My Dear children how I do want to see you

HL   [Spotswood Rice]

[Benton Barracks Hospital, St. Louis, Mo.,
September 3, 1864]

I received a leteter from Cariline telling me that you say I tried to steal to plunder my child away from you   now I want you to understand that mary is my Child and she is a God given rite of my own and you may hold on to hear as long as you can but I want you to remembor this one thing that the longor you keep my Child from me the longor you will have to burn in hell and the qwicer youll get their   for we are now makeing up a bout one thoughsand blacke troops to Come up tharough and wont to come through Glasgow and when we come wo be to Copperhood rabbels and to the Slaveholding rebbels for we dont expect to leave them there root neor branch   but we thinke how ever that we that have Children in the hands of you devels we will trie your [vertues?] the day that we enter Glasgow   I want you to understand kittey diggs that where ever you and I meets we are enmays to each orthere   I offered once to pay you forty dollers for my own Child but I am glad now that you did not accept it   Just hold on now as long as you can and the worse it will be for you you never in you life befor I came down hear did you give Children any thing not eny thing whatever not even a dollers worth of expencs   now you call my children your pro[per]ty   not so with me   my Children is my own and I expect to get them and when I get ready to come after mary I will have bout a powrer and autherity to bring hear away and to exacute vengencens on them that holds my Child   you will then know how to talke to me   I will assure that and you will know how to talk rite too   I want you now to just hold on to hear if you want to   iff your conchosence tells that's the road go that road and what it will brig you to kittey diggs   I have no fears about getting mary out of your hands   this whole Government gives chear to me and you cannot helps your self

ALS   Spotswood Rice

QUESTIONS

1. How does Christianity inform Rice's commentary on slavery?

2. How would "Miss Kaitty" have responded to the reversal of power to which Rice refers when he says that he will come to her with ten thousand soldiers?

3. What does Rice's letter tell us about slave families and the relationship between parents and children?

14.7. GENERAL WILLIAM T. SHERMAN, LETTER TO MAYOR JAMES M. CALHOUN AND ATLANTA CITY COUNCIL REPRESENTATIVES E. E. RAWSON AND S. C. WELLS (SEPTEMBER 12, 1864)

William Sherman emerged as a leading Union military commander in 1863. He worked closely with Ulysses S. Grant in the West, and when Grant came east to manage the overall Union war effort, he directed Sherman to move his army through the center of the South. After Sherman's army surrounded Atlanta and defeated the opposing Confederates, he ordered the evacuation of the remaining civilian inhabitants, which the City Council opposed.

Headquarters Military Division of the Mississippi,
In the field, Atlanta, Georgia, September 12, 1864.

Gentleman: I have your letter of the 11th, in the nature of a petition to revoke my orders removing all the inhabitants from Atlanta. I have read it carefully, and give full credit to your statements of distress that will be occasioned, and yet shall not revoke my orders, because they were not designed to meet the humanities of the cause, but to prepare for the future struggles in which millions of good people outside of Atlanta have a deep interest. We must have *peace*, not only at Atlanta, but in all America. To secure this, we must stop the war that now desolates our once happy and favored country. To stop war, we must defeat the rebel armies which are arrayed against the laws and Constitution that all must respect and obey. To defeat those armies, we must prepare the way to reach them in their recesses, provided with the arms and instruments which enable us to accomplish our purpose. Now, I know the vindictive nature of our enemy, that we may have many years of military operations from this quarter; and, therefore, deem it wise and prudent to prepare in time. The use of Atlanta for warlike purposes in inconsistent with its character as a home for families. There will be no manufacturers, commerce, or agriculture here, for the maintenance of families, and sooner or later want will compel the inhabitants to go. Why not *go now*, when all the arrangements are completed for the transfer, instead of waiting till the plunging shot of contending armies will renew the scenes of the past month? Of course, I do not apprehend any such things at this moment, but you do not suppose this army will be here until the war is over. I cannot discuss this subject with you fairly, because I cannot impart to you what we propose to do, but I assert that our military plans make it necessary for the inhabitants to go away, and I can only renew my offer of services to make their exodus in any direction as easy and comfortable as possible.

You cannot qualify war in harsher terms than I will. War is cruelty, and you cannot refine it; and those who brought war into our country deserve all the curses and maledictions a people can pour out. I know I had no hand in making this war, and I know I will make more sacrifices today than any of you to secure peace. But you cannot have peace and a division of our country. If the United States submits to a division now, it will not stop, but will go on until we reap the fate of Mexico, which is eternal war. The United States

Source: Memoirs of General William T. Sherman (New York: Appleton, 1889), 851–55.

does and must assert its authority, wherever it once had power; for, if it relaxes one bit to pressure, it is gone, and I believe that such is the national feeling. This feeling assumes various shapes, but always comes back to that of Union. Once admit the Union, once more acknowledge the authority of the national Government, and, instead of devoting your houses and streets and roads to the dread uses of war, I and this army become at once your protectors and supporters, shielding you from danger, let it come from what quarter it may. I know that a few individuals cannot resist a torrent of error and passion, such as swept the South into rebellion, but you can point out, so that we may know those who desire a government, and those who insist on war and its desolation.

You might as well appeal against the thunderstorm as against these terrible hardships of war. They are inevitable, and the only way the people of Atlanta can hope once more to live in peace and quiet at home, is to stop the war, which can only be done by admitting that it began in error and is perpetuated in pride.

We don't want your Negroes, or your horses, or your lands, or any thing you have, but we do want and will have a just obedience to the laws of the United States. That we will have, and if it involved the destruction of your improvements, we cannot help it.

You have heretofore read public sentiment in your newspapers, that live by falsehood and excitement; and the quicker you seek for truth in other quarters, the better. I repeat then that, [by] the original compact of government, the United States had certain rights in Georgia, which have never been relinquished and never will be; that the South began the war by seizing forts, arsenals, mints, custom-houses, etc., etc., long before Mr. Lincoln was installed, and before the South had one jot or title of provocation. I myself have seen in Missouri, Kentucky, Tennessee, and Mississippi,

hundreds and thousands of women and children fleeing from your armies and desperadoes, hungry and with bleeding feet. In Memphis, Vicksburg, and Mississippi, we fed thousands and thousands of the families of rebel soldiers left on our hands, and whom we could not see starve. Now that war comes to you, you feel very different. You deprecate its horrors, but did not feel them when you sent car-loads of soldiers and ammunition, and moulded shells and shot, to carry war into Kentucky and Tennessee, to desolate the homes of hundreds and thousands of good people who only asked to live in peace at their old homes, and under the Government of their inheritance. But these comparisons are idle. I want peace, and believe it can only be reached through union and war, and I will ever conduct war with a view to perfect an [and] early success.

But, my dear sirs, when peace does come, you may call on me for any thing. Then will I share with you the last cracker, and watch with you to shield your homes and families against danger from every quarter.

Now you must go, and take with you the old and feeble, feed and nurse them, and build for them, in more quiet places, proper habitations to shield them against the weather until the mad passions of men cool down, and allow the Union and peace once more to settle over your old homes in Atlanta. Yours in haste,

W.T. Sherman, Major-General commanding

QUESTIONS

1. How does Sherman explain the cause of the Civil War?
2. What responsibility does he assume for the hardships suffered by Southern civilians?
3. How does Sherman view the relationship between civilians and their own army in war?

14.8. VISUAL DOCUMENT: ANDREW J. RUSSELL, *RUINS IN RICHMOND* (APRIL 1865)

After a long siege, the Union Army forced the Confederates to abandon their capital in early April 1865. Before leaving the city, Confederates set fire to material they did want the Union to seize. The fire ran out of control and consumed much of the downtown business district. Andrew Russell worked with the U.S. Military Railroad Construction Corps during the conflict.

QUESTIONS

1. What image of war does this photo offer?
2. How would Southerners and Northerners have explained the reasons that the war produced this level of destruction?
3. What lessons does the photo suggest regarding the costs of war?

Source: Library of Congress Prints and Photographs Division.

14.9. VISUAL DOCUMENT: *ALBANY EVENING JOURNAL*, "GENERAL LEE AND HIS ARMY HAVE SURRENDERED" (APRIL 10, 1865)

After abandoning Richmond, Robert E. Lee's army retreated west until Grant's troops cut them off at Appomattox Courthouse, a small village about 100 miles west of the city. Although one major Confederate army remained in the field (in North Carolina), many Northerners interpreted Lee's defeat as the end of the war.

QUESTIONS

1. How does the newspaper explain the purpose and accomplishments of the war?
2. What is the relationship between emancipation and reunion in the announcement?
3. What does the word "treason" suggest about how Confederates might be treated after the war?

Source: Courtesy University of Virginia Periodicals Collections.

CHAPTER 15

RECONSTRUCTING AMERICA, 1865–1877

15.1. JOURDON ANDERSON, LETTER TO P. H. ANDERSON (AUGUST 7, 1865)

Jourdon Anderson was one of the many ex-slaves who made their way north out of Tennessee and Kentucky into southern Ohio after the Civil War. The confused state of the labor market in the South led some masters to try to recruit former slaves back to their property to work as paid laborers.

Dayton, Ohio, August 7, 1865

To My Old Master, Colonel P. H. Anderson, Big Spring, Tennessee

Sir: I got your letter and was glad to find you had not forgotten Jourdon, and that you wanted me to come back and live with you again, promising to do better for me than anybody else can. I have often felt uneasy about you. I thought the Yankees would have hung you long before this for harboring Rebs they found at your house. I suppose they never heard about your going to Col. Martin's to kill the Union soldier that was left by his company in their stable. Although you shot at me twice before I left you, I did not want to hear of your being hurt, and am glad you are still living. It would do me good to go back to the dear old home again and see Miss Mary and Miss Martha and

Allen, Esther, Green, and Lee. Give my love to them all, and tell them I hope we will meet in the better world, if not in this. I would have gone back to see you all when I was working in the Nashville Hospital, but one of the neighbors told me Henry intended to shoot me if he ever got a chance.

I want to know particularly what the good chance is you propose to give me. I am doing tolerably well here; I get $25 a month, with victuals and clothing; have a comfortable home for Mandy,—the folks here call her Mrs. Anderson),—and the children—Milly, Jane and Grundy—go to school and are learning well; the teacher says Grundy has a head for a preacher. They go to Sunday-School, and Mandy and me attend church regularly. We are kindly treated; sometimes we overhear others saying, "Them colored people were slaves" down in Tennessee. The children feel hurt when

Source: Lydia Maria Child, *The Freedmen's Book* (Boston: Tickenor and Fields, 1865), 265–67. Also see http://historymatters. gmu.edu/d/6369/.

they hear such remarks, but I tell them it was no disgrace in Tennessee to belong to Col. Anderson. Many darkies would have been proud, as I used to be, to call you master. Now, if you will write and say what wages you will give me, I will be better able to decide whether it would be to my advantage to move back again.

As to my freedom, which you say I can have, there is nothing to be gained on that score, as I got my free papers in 1864 from the Provost-Marshal-General of the Department of Nashville. Mandy says she would be afraid to go back without some proof that you are sincerely disposed to treat us justly and kindly; and we have concluded to test your sincerity by asking you to send us our wages for the time we served you. This will make us forget and forgive old scores, and rely on your justice and friendship in the future. I served you faithfully for thirty-two years and Mandy twenty years. At twenty-five dollars a month for me, and two dollars a week for Mandy, our earnings would amount to eleven thousand six hundred and eighty dollars. Add to this the interest for the time our wages has been kept back and deduct what you paid for our clothing and three doctor's visits to me, and pulling a tooth for Mandy, and the balance will show what we are in justice entitled to. Please send the money by Adams Express, in care of V. Winters, Esq., Dayton, Ohio. If you fail to pay us for faithful labors in the past we can have little faith in your promises in the future. We trust the good Maker has opened your eyes to the wrongs which you and your fathers have done to me and my fathers, in making us toil for you for generations without recompense. Here I draw my wages every Saturday night, but in Tennessee there was never any payday for the Negroes any more than for the horses and cows. Surely there will be a day of reckoning for those who defraud the laborer of his hire.

In answering this letter please state if there would be any safety for my Milly and Jane, who are now grown up and both good-looking girls. You know how it was with Matilda and Catherine. I would rather stay here and starve, and die if it comes to that, than have my girls brought to shame by the violence and wickedness of their young masters. You will also please state if there has been any schools opened for the colored children in your neighborhood, the great desire of my life now is to give my children an education, and have them form virtuous habits.

P.S. —Say howdy to George Carter, and thank him for taking the pistol from you when you were shooting at me.

From your old servant,
Jourdon Anderson

QUESTIONS

1. What do Anderson's comments reveal about the economic knowledge of former slaves?
2. What are the attributes of freedom that Anderson identifies as most important?
3. Explain the new power dynamic between Anderson and his former master. How would each of the participants have understood it?

15.2. CONGRESSMAN THADDEUS STEVENS, EXCERPTS FROM A SPEECH DELIVERED IN LANCASTER COUNTY (SEPTEMBER 6, 1865)

Thaddeus Stevens served as one of the leading radical Republicans in Congress during the Civil War and Reconstruction. A Pennsylvania native, Stevens used sarcasm, wit, and a strong command of House rules to advance his policies. Stevens supported a "hard" Reconstruction of the South that would erase the gross inequalities in wealth created by slavery, but his plans for land redistribution were not supported by more moderate members of his party.

Fellow Citizens:

In compliance with your request, I have come to give my views of the present condition of the Rebel States—of the proper mode of reorganizing the Government, and the future prospects of the Republic. During the whole progress of the war, I never for a moment felt doubt or despondency. I knew that the loyal North would conquer the Rebel despots who sought to destroy freedom. But since that traitorous confederation has been subdued, and we have entered upon the work of "reconstruction" or "restoration," I cannot deny that my heart has become sad at the gloomy prospects before us.

Four years of bloody and expensive war, waged against the United States by eleven States, under a government called the "Confederate States of America," to which they acknowledged allegiance, have overthrown all governments within those States which could be acknowledged as legitimate by the Union. The armies of the Confederate States having been conquered and subdued, and their territory possessed by the United States, it becomes necessary to establish governments therein, which shall be republican in form and principles, and form a more "perfect Union" with the parent Government. It is desirable that such a course should be pursued as to exclude from those governments every

vestige of human bondage, and render the same forever impossible in this nation; and to take care that no principles of self-destruction shall be incorporated therein. In effecting this, it is to be hoped that no provision of the Constitution will be infringed, and no principle of the law of nations disregarded. Especially must we take care that in rebuking this unjust and treasonable war, the authorities of the Union shall indulge in no acts of usurpation which may tend to impair the stability and permanency of the nation. Within these limitations, we hold it to be the duty of the Government to inflict condign punishment on the rebel belligerents, and so weaken their hands that they can never again endanger the Union; and so reform their municipal institutions as to make them republican in spirit as well as in name....Upon the character of the belligerent, and the justice of the war, and the manner of conducting it, depends our right to take the lives, liberty and property of the belligerent. This war had its origin in treason without one spark of justice. It was prosecuted before notice of it, by robbing our forts and armories, and our navy-yards; by stealing our money from the mints and depositories, and by surrendering our forts and navies by perjurers who had sworn to support the Constitution. In its progress our prisoners, by the authority of their government, were slaughtered in cold blood.

Source: Beverly Wilson Palmer and Holly Byers Ochoa, eds., *Selected Papers of Thaddeus Stevens, Volume 2: April 1865–August 1868* (Pittsburgh: University of Pittsburgh Press, 1998), 12–25.

Ask Fort Pillow and Fort Wagner. Sixty thousand of our prisoners have been deliberately starved to death because they would not enlist in the rebel armies. The graves at Andersonville have each an accusing tongue. The purpose and avowed object of the enemy "to found an empire whose corner-stone should be slavery," rendered its perpetuity or revival dangerous to human liberty.

Surely, these things are sufficient to justify the exercise of the extreme rights of war—"to execute, to imprison, to confiscate." How many captive enemies it would be proper to execute, as an example to nations, I leave others to judge. I am not fond of sanguinary punishments, but surely some victims must propitiate the manes of our starved, murdered, slaughtered martyrs. A court-martial could do justice according to law.

But we propose to confiscate all the estate of every rebel belligerent whose estate was worth $10,000, or whose land exceeded two hundred acres in quantity. Policy if not justice would require that the poor, the ignorant, and the coerced should be forgiven. They followed the example and teachings of their wealthy and intelligent neighbors. The rebellion would never have originated with them. Fortunately those who would thus escape form a large majority of the people, though possessing but a small portion of the wealth. The proportion of those exempt compared with the punished would be I believe about nine tenths.

There are about six millions of freedmen in the South. The number of acres of land is 465,000,000. Of this, those who own above two hundred acres each number about 70,000 persons, holding, in the aggregate, (together with the States,) about 394,000,000 acres, leaving for all the others below 200 each, about 71,000,000 of acres. By thus forfeiting the estates of the leading rebels, the government would have 394,000,000 of acres, beside their town property, and yet nine-tenths of the people would remain untouched. Divide this land into convenient farms. Give, if you please, forty acres to each adult male freedman. Suppose there are one million of them. That would require 40,000,000 of acres, which, deducted from 394,000,000, leaves three hundred and fifty-four millions of acres for sale. Divide it into suitable farms, and sell it to the highest bidders. I think it, including town property, would average at least ten dollars per

acre. That would produce $3,540,000,000—three billions five hundred and forty millions of dollars.

Let that be applied as follows to wit:

1. Invest $300,000,000 in six per cent government bonds, and add the interest semi-annually to the pensions of those who have become entitled by this villainous war.
2. Appropriate $200,000,000 to pay the damages done to loyal men, North and South, by the rebellion.
3. Pay the residue, being $3,040,000,000 towards the payment of the National debt.

What loyal man can object to this? Look around you, and every where behold your neighbors, some with an arm, some with a leg, some with an eye, carried away by rebel bullets. Others horribly mutilated in every form. And yet numerous others wearing the weeds which mark the death of those on whom they leaned for support. Contemplate these monuments of rebel perfidy, and of patriotic suffering, and then say if too much is asked for our valiant soldiers.... The whole fabric of southern society *must* be changed, and never can it be done if this opportunity is lost. Without this, this Government can never be, as it never has been, a true republic. Heretofore, it had more the features of aristocracy than of democracy. The Southern States have been despotisms, not governments of the people. It is impossible that any practical equality of rights can exist where a few thousand men monopolize the whole landed property. The larger the number of small proprietors the more safe and stable the government. As the landed interest must govern, the more it is subdivided and held by independent owners, the better. What would be the condition of the State of New York if it were not for her independent yeomanry? She would be overwhelmed and demoralized by the Jews, Milesians and vagabonds of licentious cities. How can republican institution, free schools, free churches, free social intercourse, exist in a mingled community of nabobs and serfs; of the owners of twenty thousand acre manors with lordly palaces, and the occupants of narrow huts inhabited by "low white trash?" If the South is ever to be made a safe republic, let her lands be cultivated by the toil of the owners or the free labor of intelligent citizens. This must be done even though it drive her nobility into exile. If they go, all the better. It will be hard to persuade the owner of ten thousand acres of land, who drives a coach and four, that he is not degraded by sitting at the same table, or in the same pew, with the embrowned and hard-handed farmer who has himself cultivated his own thriving homestead of 150 acres. This subdivision of the lands will yield ten bales of cotton to one that is made now, and he who produced it will own it and *feel himself a man.*

It is far easier and more beneficial to exile 70,000 proud, bloated and defiant rebels, than to expatriate four millions of laborers, native to the soil and loyal to the Government.... Let us forget all parties and build on the broad platform of "reconstructing" the government out of the conquered territory converted into new and free States, and admitted into the Union by the sovereign power of Congress, with another plank— "THE PROPERTY OF THE REBELS SHALL PAY OUR NATIONAL DEBT, *and indemnify freed-men and*

loyal sufferers—and that under no circumstances will we suffer the National debt to be repudiated, or the interest scaled below the contract rates; nor permit any part of the rebel debt to be assumed by the nation."

Let all who approve of these principles rally with us. Let all others go with Copperheads and rebels. Those will be the opposing parties. Young men, this duty devolves on you. Would to God, if only for that, that I were still in the prime of life, that I might aid you to fight through this last and greatest battle of freedom!

QUESTIONS

1. On what basis does Stevens draw his authority for advocating a full Reconstruction of the South?
2. How does he propose to reorganize the land holdings of the South?
3. What kind of effect does he anticipate this policy will have on the region?

15.3. VISUAL DOCUMENT: THOMAS NAST, *ANDREW JOHNSON'S RECONSTRUCTION* IN *HARPER'S WEEKLY* (SEPTEMBER 1, 1866)

During the summer of 1866, Memphis and New Orleans experienced horrible race riots, in which whites murdered dozens of blacks indiscriminately. Many Northerners felt that Johnson's lenient policies fomented a recalcitrant and unapologetic white South. Thomas Nast drew political cartoons for *Harper's Weekly*, the most widely read periodical in the country. He was an early critic of Johnson and a strong proponent for a Reconstruction that treated African Americans fairly.

QUESTIONS

1. What is Nast's critique of Johnson's Reconstruction policy?
2. What do the images around the margins of the cartoon portray as Johnson's responsibility for the riots?
3. Why does Nast portray the lone black individual as a wounded Union soldier?

Source: Ben and Beatrice Goldstein Foundation Collection/Library of Congress.

15.4. JOSÉ INÁCIO BARROS COBRA, EXCERPTS FROM "SLAVE PROPERTY IS AS SACRED AS ANY OTHER" (JULY 21, 1871)

After the emancipation of slaves in the United States, Brazilian and Cuban slaveholders began to consider ways to manage the end of slavery in their own countries (the last remaining slave nations in the western hemisphere). In Brazil, the parliament considered "Free Birth" legislation, which would have freed the newborns of enslaved women as a way to gradually transition to free labor. Even this modest proposal generated criticism from slaveholders, who worked to delay the process. Barros Cobra was a member of the Brazilian parliament who delivered the speech below opposing free-birth legislation.

Gentlemen, it is true that in this country there exists a point of view that demands a solution to the great problem of slavery. The existence of this opinion is undeniable in the abstract, in principle; fortunately there is not one Brazilian who wishes the permanent preservation of slavery in the Empire; in this sense there is unanimous agreement: the cause of abolition is definitely decided upon.

To the honor of the Brazilian Empire, we do not need to overcome the difficulties, prejudices, and animosities against which the legislators of France and the United States had to struggle; the natural generosity of the Brazilian character, the religious spirit and the principles of morality and civilization decided the theoretical question a long time ago.... When we attempt to solve this great question, we should not be motivated by abstractions, philosophical concepts, or sentimental inspirations, but rather by the high and venerable interests that are associated with it and that constitute the foundations of Brazilian society [*hear! hear!*]; much may be said, much may be desired in this regard, but a study and practical knowledge of our circumstances and of what can reasonably be done are what should guide us, in order that we may go forward securely. [*Hear! Hear!*] Gentlemen, I reflected very serenely about how we might most conveniently solve this important problem, which demands full attention and challenges the deepest meditation. I considered it with total calm, far from my legislative responsibilities, and with my mind uncluttered by other concerns. Momentarily the idea of freeing the womb seemed an acceptable method (to this chamber I confess the feelings of my inner conscience); however, further thought convinced me that this idea, which at first glance is so appealing, is the most dangerous way to go in this country. [*Hear! Hear!*]

History, that great preceptress of experience, shows us that almost all the nations that tried to abolish slavery gradually did not achieve this, but were instead forced to rush headlong and disastrously toward total abolition; this was the experience of England, France, and Portugal herself. A contrary example, such as that of the United States, may be mentioned; but none of those states had a tenth of the slave population which we have, and so cannot constitute an argument in favor of the government's bill.[1] The illustrious special committee asked in their report: "What reasons do we have to fear that in our country things will go differently

Source: Robert Conrad, *Children of God's Fire: A Documentary History of Black Slavery in Brazil* (University Park: Pennsylvania State University Press, 1984), 436–46.

1   This contention is false. In 1860, Georgia had a slave population of 462,000, which was more than any Brazilian province recorded during that country's entire history.

from the way they did in countries where, after experiencing the same exaggerated fears, the same transformations were brought about?"

But those countries did not find themselves in circumstances identical to ours; they did not possess the number of slaves that we unfortunately possess, nor was agriculture almost the sole basis of their private and public wealth; nor like us did they have a free population spread out over an immense territory and, in terrifying contrast, a slave population concentrated in the main production centers. These different circumstances call for different ways to cure the evil. [*Hear! Hear!*]...Brazil's circumstances in this regard are very special, and we must not lose sight of them....The slave born of a slave woman, who belongs to her master in virtue of principles sanctified in civil legislation, represents capital and is an instrument of labor; however, it is understood that the value of the slave is precisely dependent upon the services that he can perform [*hear! hear!*]; nobody would want an unused slave for the mere joy of possessing him. The capital here is represented by the instrument of labor, whose value is in direct proportion to the greater or lesser usefulness which as such he can render; in just the same way that the price of a slave is more or less, depending upon his capacity and fitness for work.

This being the case, which seems to me undeniable, it is entirely obvious that the intention here is to indemnify the masters with the identical thing that belongs to them by law, and which they cannot be deprived of without receiving full compensation. There is, however, a single difference: they are granted the use of the individual for thirteen years, a usufruct which, according to law, would otherwise belong to them for as long as the slave might live. It seems to me, therefore, that the right to property, sanctified and

guaranteed by the Constitution of the Empire, which cannot be taken from the citizen of Brazil without prior indemnification, is in this case confiscated without any indemnification whatsoever, or with a false indemnification, which amounts to the same thing....

It is known that, thanks to the generous and humane character of the Brazilians, slavery among us is so mild that the condition of our slaves is greatly preferable to that of the working classes of some European countries; on the largest agricultural establishments, order and subordination are maintained entirely by means of a prudent system of constant and severe discipline, in which careful preventive measures ordinarily make repression unnecessary. Once the proposed law is enforced, that system cannot be maintained, and it will be seriously and dangerously undermined by the simultaneous existence in those establishments of slave parents and free children, not as an exceptional or accidental situation, but as a regular and permanent reality, and by the unavoidable meddling of the authorities responsible for enforcement of the law. This situation will awaken in those who remain slaves a dangerous impatience and a terrible hopelessness which must shatter all ties of subordination and respect for their masters....

QUESTIONS

1. What lessons does the speaker draw from the American experience?
2. Can you identify any other influences of U.S. emancipation on the discussion here?
3. How does the speaker's treatment of slavery compare to the opinions of U.S. authorities on the subject, such as that of James Henry Hammond, presented in Chapter 13?

15.5. GEORGES CLEMENCEAU, NOTES ON JOHNSON AND RECONSTRUCTION (SEPTEMBER 10, 1867)

By late 1867, Andrew Johnson, a wartime Republican who ascended to the presidency after Lincoln's assassination, had alienated himself from congressional Republicans because of his conservative approach to Reconstruction. Johnson turned to Northern Democrats and Southerners for support (even though many Southerners remained disenfranchised following the war). Georges Clemenceau, a French physician and journalist, covered Washington politics for a French newspaper. He served as prime minister of France during the last year of World War I and helped draft the Treaty of Versailles.

September 10, 1867. The war between the President and Congress goes on, complicated from time to time by some unexpected turn. Contrary to all that has happened, is happening, and will happen in certain countries, the legislative power here has the upper hand. That is the peculiarity of the situation, or rather of this government. Congress may, when it pleases, take the President by the ear and lead him down from his high seat, and he can do nothing about it except to struggle and shout. But that is an extreme measure, and the radicals are limiting themselves, for the present, to binding Andrew Johnson firmly with good brand-new laws. At each session they add a shackle to his bonds, tighten the bit in a different place, file a claw or draw a tooth, and then when he is well bound up, fastened, and caught in an inextricable net of laws and decrees, more or less contradicting each other, they tie him to the stake of the Constitution and take a good look at him, feeling quite sure he cannot move this time.

But then Seward, the Dalila of the piece, rises up and shouts: "Johnson, here come the radicals with old Stevens at their head; they are proud of having subjected you and are coming to enjoy the sight of you in chains." And Samson summons all his strength, and bursts his cords and bonds with a mighty effort,

and the Philistines (I mean the radicals) flee in disorder to the Capitol to set to work making new laws stronger than the old, which will break in their turn at the first test. This has been going on now for two years, and though in the course of things it is inevitable that Samson will be beaten, one must admit that he has put up a game fight. Even a sceptic, if this word has any meaning in America, would be interested in the struggle....A new amnesty has been proclaimed for the former rebels in the South, and we shall soon see the struggle begin on a new point, that is, the interpretation to be given this proclamation of amnesty and the conclusions to be drawn from it. This is the second proclamation of amnesty which Mr. Johnson has issued. Though it still insists on the obligation to swear the oath of allegiance to the Constitution and the Union, it is infinitely more liberal in its terms than the first proclamation. Instead of the fourteen classes of exceptions defined in the proclamation of amnesty of May 29, 1865, the proclamation of September 8, 1867, defines only three. None are excluded from the benefits of amnesty except the military and civil heads of the Confederate government, those who treated Federal prisoners contrary to the laws of warfare, and those who took part in the conspiracy which

Source: Fernand Baldensperger, ed., *American Reconstruction, 1865–1870, and the Impeachment of Andrew Johnson* (New York: Dial Press, 1928), 102–07.

ended in the assassination of Lincoln. The *Tribune* estimated that the first proclamation left about one hundred thousand citizens out of the amnesty, and that this one leaves out one or two thousand. There is no harm done so far, but the question will be what are the exact rights conferred by the amnesty, in other words, whether the President has the power to reinstate the former rebels in their rights and to make voters of them. The President and the Democrats say *Yes*, Congress and the Republicans say *No*....The Indians in the West have arrayed themselves against the whites, for the thousandth time. Massacres are being carried on by both sides, with brutal ferocity. The whites hunt down and drive the Indians as they formerly did the negroes in the South, and the Indians, in return, when they take prisoners, send them back to their relatives in pieces, without regard for age or sex. It is sad to be obliged to state that the first and real offenders are nearly always the white men.

QUESTIONS

1. How does Clemenceau characterize the relationship between the president and Congress?
2. How would Johnson's more liberal amnesty rules affect the landscape of postwar politics?
3. What connections exist between the Indian wars of the West and the Civil War?

15.6. SECRETARY OF WAR, LETTER ON "FREEDMEN'S AFFAIRS IN KENTUCKY AND TENNESSEE" (1868)

Founded in 1866, the Ku Klux Klan was a terrorist organization devoted to driving black people out of positions of public authority in the South. Its members operated in secret and used all manner of threats and violence to break the political alliances between blacks and whites in the Republican Party and the social institutions built by black Southerners in the postwar years.

Notice has been sent to Mrs. L. A. Baldwin, teacher of freedmen's school No. 1, Bowling Green, Kentucky, with post office dated April 27, 1868, of which the following is a copy:

Mrs. L. A. Baldwin, teacher colored school, Bonding Green, Kentucky:

KU KLUX KLANS!
BLOOD! POISON! POWDER! TORCH!
Leave in five days, or hell's your portion!
Rally, rally, watch your chance,
First blood, first premium K. K. K.

If ball, or torch, or poison fails,
The house beneath you shall be blown to hell, or move you.

K. K. K.

QUESTIONS

1. Why would the KKK attack teachers?
2. What threat did education pose to the social order?
3. How would the anonymous nature of the threat delivered to Mrs. L. A. Baldwin affect the social fabric of the Kentucky community in which she lived?

Source: Secretary of War, House Executive Document No. 329, 40th Cong., 2nd sess., 19.

15.7. U.S. SENATE, REPORTS ON "OUTRAGES COMMITTED BY DISLOYAL PERSONS" (1870)

Republican officials in the South collected evidence of Ku Klux Klan atrocities, which led to widely publicized congressional hearings in 1871. Public pressure in the North encouraged Congress to pass a series of laws that empowered the federal government and the newly created Department of Justice to crack down on conspiracies such as the KKK. A raft of prosecutions and some convictions broke up the formal organizations, but many of the members reorganized under new names and continued their campaigns of terror until Southern Republicans were driven from office.

Roxboro, Person County, North Carolina,
October 7, 1870.

Dear Sir: The first victim to Ku-Klux violence was Mr. S. L. Wiles; lived four miles south of Roxboro; an industrious and, in his dealings with persons, strictly honest man. The alleged charge against him was that he was living in adultery with a colored woman. (Can't say as to the truth of the charge.) The woman's name is Harriet Bran, who also, with Wiles, was cruelly whipped, and both of them driven from the farm he had rented for the year. The next and only other instance I can call to mind was against Wm. B. Hudgens; the supposed cause was that he was living on land the title of which is in dispute. The party not in possession had ordered him to leave the premises, threatening at the same time if he failed to do so within a certain time he would be Ku-Kluxed off. He failed to leave as ordered, and was afterwards cruelly and most terribly beaten by disguised men, (26 in number,) and forced to leave the premises he had leased for two years.

Hudgens has always voted the democratic ticket; Wiles the republican. I don't think politics had anything to do with either case.

Most respectfully, & c.

P. S.—I had liked to have forgotten to mention the case of a Mr. Thomas, United States detective, who visited Roxboro on business pertaining to his duty, and, during the night, had a coffin placed at his door, with the following inscription tacked on it, to wit: "You and all other damned radicals had better leave these parts or else you will fill this furniture."

A true copy of original letter on file in executive department
of North Carolina.
J. B. NEATHERY,
Private Secretary.

Lincolnton, North Carolina,
October 17, 1870.

Dear Sir: According to your request we send you the below list of names of persons that have been maltreated in Lincoln County:

| Harriet Quickel | Black | Whipped and shot. |
| Sam Ward, wife, and daughter | do | Whipped. |

Source: "Message of the President of the United States, Communicating, in Compliance with the Resolution of the Senate of the 16 of December, 1870, Information in Relation to Outrages Committed by Disloyal Persons in North Carolina, and Other Southern States," Senate Executive Document No. 16, 41st Cong., 3rd sess., 10–11.

Rufus Friday and Wife	do	Whipped.
James Falls	do	Whipped.
Charles Sumner	do	Whipped and robbed of $15.
John Connely	do	Whipped and shot.
William Magbee	do	Robbed in the woods of all his money.
Reuben Litton	do	Whipped and shot.
Jerry Wood	do	Whipped and drove from home; life threatened if he returned.
J. Barringer	do	Whipped and drove from home; life threatened if he returned.
Rufus Bindhardt	do	Whipped and shot dangerously.
E. Wilfong	do	Whipped and shot dangerously.
Peter Hoover	do	Whipped.
Lawson Friday	do	Whipped and shot.
S. Motz	do	Whipped.
John Miller	White	Whipped and shot.
Adeline Fisher	do	Whipped.
Mary Fisher	do	Whipped.
Sally Fisher	do	Whipped.
J. McMellen	do	Whipped.
Jeff Herndon	Black	House robbed of two guns.

There are a number of other cases, but we cannot get their names.

The colored man, Wilfong, was shot in the back and is mutilated for life.

For the sake of my family please not mention my name in this matter.

Asheboro, North Carolina, October 28, 1870.

Dear Sir: Yours of the 30th ultimo is to hand. I am sorry to have to inform you that Randolph County is almost entirely governed by the Ku-Klux. I supposed before the election that there were a good many in the county, but I had no idea that they were half so well organized; but I am proud to say that my township gave a large republican majority. The Ku-Klux have not committed many gross outrages in this county, like they have in some others. Their object seemed to be to decoy as many as possible into the organization by making them believe it was not a very bad thing. They paraded through several neighborhoods just before the election, in order to terrify the most timid republicans, and by their threats, &c., make them stay away from the election. They knew very well who was easily scared. They have not been so bold since the militia was called out. If the republicans had not (some of them, both white and colored) been so easily intimidated and staid at home, we could easily have carried Randolph. It is very hard to know whom to put confidence in. I know a great many men who laid out during the war, who were whipped, kicked, and handcuffed by the rebels during the war, who are now among the Ku-Klux, and voted for the men that abused them so badly. I don't know that any person in this county has been murdered by the Ku-Klux. I only know of two that have been whipped; one was a colored boy, I think, by the name of Cheek, who was taken to Franklinsville last spring, in the night, and tied up and whipped in the village. James Brookshire, a colored man, was whipped at his own house last spring, and his gun taken away, and he forced to leave the neighborhood. One school-house was burned in 1869; it belonged to the colored people. A great many, both white and colored, were visited by the Ku-Klux, and severe threats made against them if they voted the republican ticket.

Respectfully, yours,
JOEL ASHEWORTH.

QUESTIONS

1. Why would the KKK target an interracial couple?
2. What do these letters suggest about the Klan's social policies apart from their political objectives?
3. How would the Klan's institutionalization of violence in the postwar South reshape the political order?

15.8. VISUAL DOCUMENT: THOMAS NAST, TILDEN-HAYES CARTOON IN *HARPER'S WEEKLY* (MARCH 17, 1877)

Republicans and Democrats disputed the returns of several states in the presidential election of 1876. After a long, tense winter, an agreement was reached to count the electoral votes of Louisiana, Florida, and South Carolina for the Republican candidate, Rutherford B. Hayes, but give control of the state governments to the Democrats. Historians generally regard the election as marking the end of Reconstruction, because the three states listed above were the last states to shift back to Democratic regimes.

Mrs. U. S.—"Thanks, Mr. TILDEN. I have promised to dance this set with Mr. HAYES."

QUESTIONS

1. How does Nast's representation of the two candidates signal his preference?

2. Why does the cartoon avoid the controversy that surrounded the election?

3. Does the cartoon "naturalize" Hayes's victory?

Source: The Granger Collection, NYC.